MW01232822

# RISING THRU EVERY FALL

# Rising thru every Fall

## The Journey of a Notre Dame Football Player Overcoming Injuries, Changes, & Doubts

MATT SHELTON

Publisher's Cataloging-in-Publication Data

Names: Shelton, Matt, 1982- author.
Title: Rising thru every fall : the journey of a Notre Dame football player overcoming injuries, changes & doubts / Matt Shelton ; [photos by] Michael & Susan Bennett, Lighthouse Imaging ; [back cover photo courtesy of] University of Notre Dame Archives.
Description: Monterey, TN : Rising thru every Fall, 2024.
Identifiers: LCCN 2024903316 (print) | ISBN 979-8-9893133-0-3 (paperback) | ISBN 979-8-9893133-1-0 (hardcover) | ISBN 979-8-9893133-2-7 (ebook) | ISBN 979-8-9893133-3-4 (audiobook)
Subjects: LCSH: Football players--United States--Biography. | University of Notre Dame--Football--History. | Sports--History. | Football--history. | Conduct of life. | BISAC: BIOGRAPHY & AUTOBIOGRAPHY / Sports. | SPORTS & RECREATION / Football. | BODY, MIND & SPIRIT / Inspiration & Personal Growth. | BIOGRAPHY & AUTOBIOGRAPHY / Memoirs.
Classification: LCC GV939.S54 A3 2024 (print) | LCC GV939.S54 (ebook) | DDC 796.332092--dc23.

Library of Congress Control Number: 2024903316
ISBN: 979-8-9893133-0-3 (Paperback)
ISBN: 979-8-9893133-1-0 (Hardcover)
ISBN: 979-8-9893133-2-7 (eBook)
ISBN: 979-8-9893133-3-4 (audiobook)

Content Editor: Matt Shelton
Editor: Taylor Lanier
Book Cover Design: Michelle Szajko
Photos by (Front Cover and all Interior Notre Dame Pictures):
    Michael & Susan Bennett Lighthouse Imaging, c/o Michelle Szajko
Back Cover Photo: University of Notre Dame Archives

ATTENTION: For information about special discounts for bulk purchases, please contact us via email with the subject line "Bulk Order" — and for speaking engagements or book signings, please use the subject line "Engagements" — Thank you! Email: RisingThruEveryFall@gmail.com.

Website: www.RisingThruEveryFall.com
Social Media / Instagram / Facebook: RisingThruEveryFall

# DEDICATION

*To my Family and Friends, thank you for the support, the memories, and the laughs. My journey would not be the same without you. You are all appreciated and loved.*

# Contents

# Foreword & A Note

## Dr. David Bruton Jr., PT, DPT

**THE FOREWORD:** As I sit down with you to embark on the journey that is the remarkable narrative encapsulated within the pages of "Rising Thru Every Fall: The Journey of a Notre Dame Football Player Overcoming Injuries, Changes, and Doubts," I am overcome with a sense of profound gratitude and humility. To be entrusted with contributing to Matt Shelton's story in this foreword, a tale of resilience, fortitude, and unwavering determination, is a privilege beyond measure.

My name is David Bruton Jr., and my story, too, is testament to the transformative power of athletic pursuit and the enduring bonds forged through shared triumphs and tribulations. With eight years of professional football experience, including the honor of being part of the Denver Broncos' historic Super Bowl 50 victory, I have traversed the highs and lows of the gridiron, emerging not only as a seasoned athlete but as a compassionate advocate for the healing journey that follows.

Before my NFL days, however, my journey began on the fields of the University of Notre Dame, where fate intertwined my path with that of Matt Shelton. Under the watchful guidance of mentors, like head high school football coach Tim Lewis and my father David Bruton Sr., I navigated the labyrinthine landscape of collegiate football, ultimately finding myself immersed in the storied traditions of the Fighting Irish. It was here, amidst the echoes of legends past and the promise of future glories, that I forged lifelong friendships and honed the skills that would carry me to the pinnacle of professional sports.

But beyond the accolades and triumphs lies a deeper, more resonant truth — a truth that Matt Shelton's journey embodies with unwavering clarity. It is a truth that speaks to the essence of the human spirit, to our innate capacity for resilience in the face of adversity, and to the transformative power of perseverance in pursuit of our dreams.

As I transitioned from the gridiron to the realm of physical therapy, I found myself drawn to the intersection of athleticism and healing — a nexus where the pain of injury intersects with the promise of recovery, and where the indomitable human spirit finds solace in the promise of renewal. Through my work with patients grappling with the aftermath of injury, I have borne witness to the profound impact of athletic pursuits on the human psyche — the unrelenting pressure to return to form, the existential questioning of identity in the wake of physical limitations, and the enduring hope that springs forth from the depths of despair.

In addition to my endeavors in sports and healthcare, I am also the founder of Bruton's Books, a charitable organization dedicated to childhood literacy with a focus on K-3rd grade. Our mission is to address accessibility and provide books, iPads, and supplemental programs to combat the literacy problem in the Denver Public School System. It is a cause close to my heart, one that speaks to the importance of education and the transformative power of literacy in shaping young minds and building brighter futures.

Sports, with its myriad challenges and triumphs, serves as a crucible for personal growth and development. It teaches invaluable life lessons, instilling in athletes the resilience to overcome adversity, the discipline to adhere to timelines, the importance of teamwork, the ability to thrive under pressure, and the cultivation of social skills essential for success in all aspects of life. While the risk of injury looms as a constant threat, the lessons and skills gained through sports are guaranteed — a testament to the enduring power of athletic pursuit to shape character and fortify the human spirit.

In "Rising Thru Every Fall," we embark on a journey of self-discovery, guided by Matt Shelton's unyielding resolve and unwavering courage. From the depths of injury-induced despair to the dizzying heights of triumphant return, Matt's story serves as a beacon of hope — a testament to the resilience that resides within each of us, waiting to be awakened in times of greatest need.

Through the lens of Matt's experiences, we confront the specter of doubt and uncertainty, grappling with the existential questions that accompany life's most formidable challenges. We bear witness to the evolution of rehabilitation, particularly in the context of ACL injuries, and the profound impact of such injuries on the psyche of athletes at every level of competition.

As we journey through the pages of "Rising Thru Every Fall," I invite you to join me in celebrating the triumphs, commiserating in the setbacks, and ultimately, embracing the resilience that defines us all. For in Matt's story, we discover not just a tale of athletic prowess, but a testament to the indomitable human spirit — a spirit that knows no bounds and refuses to be broken, even in the face of seemingly insurmountable odds.

**Note to the Reader:** In the journey of life, the destination is often revered, celebrated, and anticipated. Yet, it's the path we tread, the winding roads and unexpected turns, that truly define our experience. Each step forward is marked by a myriad of emotions, challenges, and revelations. It's a journey of self-discovery, resilience, and transformation.

Throughout this voyage, we encounter moments of triumph and moments of defeat. We face obstacles that seem insurmountable and setbacks that test our resolve. But it's in these moments of struggle that we find our strength, our determination, and our capacity to overcome.

The journey is not a linear progression but a web woven with threads of perseverance, courage, and growth. It's in the midst of uncertainty and doubt that we uncover our true potential and embrace the beauty of the process.

So, to you, the reader, embarking on your own journey, remember that it is not solely about the destination but the profound lessons learned along the way. Embrace the challenges, cherish the victories, and above all, revel in the growth that comes from every step taken. For it is in the journey itself that life's true beauty resides.

Within these pages lies a testament to the beauty of the journey. It's a narrative that celebrates resilience, embraces vulnerability, and honors the transformative power of growth. Through the highs and lows, we navigate the complexity of life, discovering new strengths, confronting our fears, and emerging, not unscathed, but enriched by the voyage.

With deepest gratitude,
Dr. David Bruton Jr., PT, DPT

Notre Dame Alumni 2008,
Super Bowl 50 Champion & Three-Year Captain with the Denver Broncos,
Founder of Between the Line Physical Therapy & Bruton's Books.

# FOUNDATIONAL FACTS

THE FOUNDATION, THE FRAMEWORK of this book was written my senior year in 2005 while frequenting Health Services at the University of Notre Dame; I trekked across campus for two-hour visits, twice a day, for six weeks to receive treatment after fallout from a surgery that nearly took my life.

While chasing my NFL dream, some notes were taken, then the book was shelved. While entering the next chapter of life and partying my butt off — making up for lost time sacrificed to chase an athletic career — the book remained shelved. From time to time, I would reexamine the chapters and build: installing electrical, adding insulation, and hanging the drywall. Then more life, more things ... the book was shelved.

After Covid-19, things (or rather, I) felt "off," so I began searching for the pre-pandemic me. I thought, "What better way to remember who I am than to finish what I started so many years ago?" So, I found the dusty shelf of yesteryear — relocating the "worksite." I added finishes, installed fixtures, and laid the hardwood floor. When it all felt "just right," final inspections were made by third parties and I conducted my final walk-through.

It is now time to put my work on the market for all to see. It's time to tell my story, to show you the past and let you walk in my shoes to experience one of the most — if not the most — unprecedented times in college football history for one of its most storied programs.

In reading this labor of love, I hope you find inspiration and entertainment. May you too remember who you are, and that you have the tools to adapt and overcome. May you find smiles, laughs, and those imperative tiny details hidden within the folds of memory. Thank you for taking time to remember the past with me. From my shelf to yours, I hope you enjoy.

# THE INTRODUCTION

THE UNIVERSITY OF NOTRE Dame. What is the first thought that comes to mind? Academics, Private School, Research, Service, Catholicism, the Cathedral of Notre-Dame de Paris, Ireland, Leprechauns?

No, it is FOOTBALL ... at least it is top of mind. Maybe it was Knute Rockne, the Four Horsemen, the Gipper, National Championships, Heisman Trophy Winners, or even the cinematic classic that is *Rudy*. One way or another, for better or for worse, Notre Dame Football comes to mind. It could almost be said when you think of college football, you think of Notre Dame.

"Notre Dame Football." The thought alone can send waves of emotion through your body. Those three words evoke feelings of tradition, excellence, values, history, family, friends, God, tailgates, and Saturday afternoons in the fall. The start of a new football season unites individuals spread across the world for one massive family reunion, both figuratively and literally.

Whether you are watching from the comfort of your own home, or your favorite bar down the street, you are reconnected with a sense of belonging, family, and friends. If you make the trek to cheer on your team in the stands, either to a home game or away, you are rejoined by people you have not seen or contemplated in years: old roommates, classmates, teammates, professors, staff members, priests, monks, etc. Regardless of where you watch your team, you will meet new friends who immediately become family simply because of the bond that is Notre Dame and Notre Dame Football.

During all the fun and excitement created by a football weekend, have you ever taken a moment to think about what the players go through? Have you wondered what their week, their weekend, or their gameday is like? Most likely not. Or, if so, the thought was fleeting and dissipated as quickly as it appeared.

While loyal fans are having the time of their lives, the players are doing what they always do, preparing. For a player, it does not matter what day of the week it is or what time of year; they are constantly doing whatever it takes to get themselves ready for gameday.

Under the stadium, in the locker room, pregame rituals are afoot. Some players sit in their locker with headphones on, as they gather their thoughts with a towel covering their head. Some will take a quick nap on the floor to bring serenity to a chaotic day. Some shoot the breeze with teammates, trainers, or team managers. A few will grasp a special picture that reminds them of who they are or why they are here. Some listen to music while singing and dancing. And a couple players visit every single teammate to shake their hand or give them a fist bump, almost saying to their brothers, "I have your back, we got this." Without fail, these routines take place before every game. These small, but distinctly meaningful, moments occur prior to kickoff.

Now, imagine an entire college career of four or five or even six years for a single player. What other moments take place during the week or year that you, the fans, have no idea are taking place? What are the compounding and competing events that result in the fully realized, finished product seen on a beautiful Saturday afternoon?

All students have a lot on their plate: from the normal family and relationship issues, to navigating their way through college, and juggling the stressful academic standards of an institution like Notre Dame. These pressures alone are plenty for any college student to manage. College life in general can quickly become overwhelming.

Now, add to the equation the rigorous demands of a big-time Division One college football program that requires almost as many hours as a full-time job. There is no "after the show special" or a "behind the scenes" of these players' lives. You do not know how they ended up at Notre Dame or what they expected when they got there, or how their journey at the university affected them. There are ups-and-downs you do not see, unless observed on a gameday. You do not see the pains they go through daily, the early morning workouts, the sacrifices, or the enormous amount of time singularly devoted to football.

Compile everything described within this introduction into a cartoon flipbook in your mind. Add to that flipbook your various college-life elements and events which appeared to you while reading. As you flip through the book you have created, see how the story changes with each page passing by your thumb. Take note of how the story develops as adjustments are made in the lives of your characters. See how the slightest alteration to your drawing changes the story.

Make one small adjustment — change a teacher, change a roommate, add a bad decision, add heartbreak, add an injury, add a surgery, add a setback of any size — and the entire storyline could unravel before it even starts. See how the life you created on paper, or in your mind, is affected by the previous drawing and how the next drawing will change due to present events. As your story unfolds, the stickiness of life holds a few pages together, creating an unexpected entanglement of uncertainty. You scramble to sort through the new chaos. What happened? How did I get here? Why did this happen to me? How much doubt has slithered its way into your mind? How cloudy has your future become? Where do you flip to next? How do you even continue?

When a student-athlete attends a university of Notre Dame's caliber, they are expecting consistency and some semblance of normalcy. They are expecting the flipbook that is their life to remain on track, with negligible drama and small course corrections. Twenty-two recruits in the 2001 recruiting class (eight who stayed with the team for five years) experienced anything but normalcy during their college football career.

This is a "**RISING thru <u>every</u> FALL**."


"D.L.Y.D." (Don't Let Yourself Down)


"Learn to appreciate both the 'Good' & the 'Bad.'
Without one, you can never truly understand the other."


"You have the ability, simply remember your courage."
— Matt Shelton

# PART ONE

## THE PATH

# THE SNAP

1

SNAP!

Falling to the ground writhing, screaming in agonizing pain. My left leg gives way, I reach for my knee. Laying there, yelling and cursing at the top of my lungs. Will I ever be able to play again? If I can, will I regain all my capabilities? Will I ever be able to walk normally again?

All questions I do not have answers to; I am petrified. For most anyone else, in a similar situation, the physical implications are creating this panic. But for me, the stakes are much, much more dire than the potential of a torn ligament and lifetime limp.

Grass coats my tongue as I spit dirt from my mouth with each gut-wrenching shriek. The football falls from my arm, sputtering end-over-end out of bounds. Dust kicks up from the ground. Sweat from my arm and body stains the ball; the collecting dust quickly cakes into patches of mud. Blades of grass begin to layer on the muddy leather.

As the ball comes to a stop, my mind is just beginning its tailspin. My thoughts are racing at a hundred miles an hour. Was all the hard work, sweat, and pain to this point wasted? Will colleges retract their scholarship offers? My future, once full of potential and opportunity, is disintegrating before my eyes.

I slowly fade back into the reality of this fall Friday night under the lights. I hear our trainer trying to settle me down, and stop me from moving, so the doctor can assess the situation. "Matt! ... Matt! Listen to my voice. Focus on me. I need you to calm down, so we can decide how to help. You're gonna be okay."

The doctor lifts my leg, saying, "I need you to relax your muscles." He begins pushing, pulling, and shifting my knee — eventually confirming my worst nightmare. "Matt, we'll need to do more tests, but it looks like a torn ACL."

For a football player, in the early 2000's, it is a death sentence. Amongst the unbelievable bolts of pain rippling throughout my body, panic sets in and a fear of an unknown future spills onto my face. I'm at a loss for words. It takes every bit of strength I have to hold back the tears building in my eyes.

The medical team helps me to my feet. I hobble to the medical cart. We ride off the field to the solemn clapping of concerned fans who hope for the best. We drive up a concrete hill, and through the silent dark parking lot. The roar of the crowd fades like the sound of a distant storm dissipating into nothingness.

The cart arrives at our old rundown high school locker room and weight room facility. The doctor and trainer edge me off the cart until my feet hit the ground. As cleats smack the pavement my left leg involuntarily recoils with uneasiness. The leg cannot hold much weight, so the doctor is my crutch as we slowly walk inside.

We cross the threshold; my already heightened senses are overwhelmed by the aroma of sweaty football equipment and the pungent musk of an overly used workout area. We make our way through the maze of lockers to the training table where the medical team performs more tests. Again, they are pushing, pulling, and stressing my knee. Each poke and prod elicits more pain. Doubts bleed into every crevasse of my mind.

With each heart-wrenching provocation by the doctor I think, "Why? How could this happen to me? Am I dreaming? Is this real? There's no way I have a torn ACL. They've made a mistake." The medical team steps out of the room to discuss the situation. The instant they are out of view I clutch my knee. Compression seems to ease the pain. Compression turns to rubbing. Slowly at first. Then faster. And faster. And even faster, as though I am attempting to reverse the wheel of time itself.

The path to Notre Dame (ND), to any university, is now entangled in uncertainty. Until this moment, the path was clear, the world was at my fingertips. A small-town kid from Collierville, Tennessee has a full scholarship to the University of Notre Dame, and other schools, to play football. Growing up in the South, football, and sports in general, is a way of life. Southerners live, eat, and breathe football.

*1985: A Ball Player in the Making.*

Hundreds, sometimes thousands, attend football games every Friday night in the fall. The thought of having my way of life taken from me, before I step into it, is devastating. Hopes of a college scholarship gone. Dreams of a college football career up in flames. Visions of an NFL career dashed in an instant. Or maybe ... not.

# HICCUPS & HIGH SCHOOL

## 2

GROWING UP, I AM a good athlete, but do not realize this until Middle School. I always play on teams where I am the youngest by a year or two, which means I'm not as developed as the competition.

Come to find out, playing more advanced competition at an early age probably isn't a bad thing. I learn how to take a butt-whooping and get up to try again. My competitiveness grows with each loss incurred. I become an athlete fueled by a drive to prove himself. I relish people doubting my abilities and thrive when facing adversities thrown my way. These are a few ingredients of the fuel propelling me to never give up.

Another component of this fuel, my parents — Ed and Shirley Shelton. They are there for me each time I fall, always supporting, and always allowing me to find my own strength to push myself from the ground. They allow me to focus on sports year-round, though it is made clear from day one of my introduction to sports that school comes first. Balancing academics and four sports a year in middle school is easy because of their discipline and guidance. The strength I find in these early years will continue to serve me well, both in competition and in life.

The balancing act isn't difficult because I have willing and able parents who support me in all that I want to do in life. They encourage the idea of playing football but will not allow me to play until they feel I am old enough. It's decided, without my input, I am too small and underdeveloped to participate in football until at least the seventh grade.

So, until I am "old enough," I play soccer and become a decent little player. I am the smallest on the team and the youngest by a couple of years. But I am quick and feisty, which helps during my soccer days. My aggressive play catches up to me during the sixth grade.

I play forward, I'm always looking to score, I never focus on defense during practice and sparingly during games. The last time I play soccer competitively is on a cold winter night in Germantown, Tennessee. Shortly after halftime I find myself playing defense, which is not what I would call a strength of mine. But I'm feisty so I give it my all. I slide-tackle the kid with the ball and end up breaking two toes.

My sweet parents navigate their way to the sideline to check on their boy. They barely begin their concerning questions when I blurt out, "This game is too rough, I'm playing football next year!" Maybe not my brightest decision, since football is — perhaps obviously — much more dangerous and injury-ridden than soccer, but what do I know? All I really know is that I have to play football.

Seventh grade, at last! The world as I know it is changed. The sky is the limit! Football is all I can think about. During seventh and eighth grade, I develop into a good football player. I learn a lot in these years: how to play real football instead of backyard football, the rules of the game, that I do not like getting hit, I am not very good when it comes to tackling, I am better suited for offense, and I absolutely love football! By the end of Middle School, I establish myself as a player with a lot of potential, with decent speed and quickness. When I begin playing against more age-appropriate competition my skill level becomes unmistakable.

High School, here I am and hello ninth grade football! I am ecstatic to step into the "big leagues." High school football. Is there anything better? For me, the answer is no. As a little punk kid, I have always dreamt of going to high school and playing sports. I could not wait to blaze my own path amongst the other awkwardly developing puberty-stricken youths.

Our ninth-grade football coach, Shawn Abel, is salivating to get his hands on this freshman class, since we are undefeated in eighth grade. He sees great potential in us and knows he will win a championship with this team. The ninth-grade team wins every game this year, until the championship game. We are defeated by a touchdown and our perfect season is lost. Disappointing, no doubt, but the future looks bright for this group.

To this day, Coach Abel blames me for the loss and missing out on an undefeated championship season. But I did not even play football freshman year ... I am the water boy. A couple of months before our first game — my big and hopeful announcement to the high school that I am here to be a football star — I start having discomfort in my lower back.

I'm lifting weights and conditioning with the football team, while playing summer basketball with the freshman team. In the middle of a summer basketball scrimmage the discomfort escalates.

After picking up my fourth foul, I dive to save the ball from going out of bounds. I crash to the ground. I push myself from the floor and get back into the offensive mix. I make a cut toward the rim, looking for a pass. The bounce pass hits me in stride. I leap from the ground for a layup and throw the ball off the backboard — moving too fast I can't slow down in time to do anything with the ball ... classic me.

As I land, I feel my back tightening up. I slowly get back to my feet. I begin running down the court to play defense and my left leg isn't participating in this couple's activity. I glare to the floor with confusion to see what is going on. I see my right leg carrying the weight of my entire body. I can't lift my left leg at all — it's just dragging behind me. I think, "What the hell?! This can't be good."

I stop and stand still, looking for a reset. With all the focus and strength, I can muster, I try lifting my "lazy" leg. Nothing! It still does not want to participate. After a few more attempts at running up and down the court, Coach Justice yells to get my attention. "Matt! What in the hell are you doing?! Pick it up. Let's go!" Something is glaringly wrong with my body.

My parents drive me to the doctor for evaluation and tests. The doctor discovers I have a broken back, a hairline stress fracture in my L4 vertebrae (the second to last vertebrae of the spine, located in your lower back). The L4 vertebrae — with L5 and the attached disc, joints, nerves, and soft tissues — provide a variety of functions, including supporting the upper body and allowing motion in multiple directions.

For me, especially at such a youthful age, this is a confusing injury. There is no singularly big event that causes the crack. And there is no chance that crashing to the ground to save a basketball from going out of bounds or slamming to the ground after a missed layup broke my back. So, what happened? The doctors conclude that a combination of events must be the culprit; there must have been a moment in the weight room I shrugged off as "no big deal" that was exacerbated by the daily pounding of running on the hard surface of a basketball court.

In any case, I am forced to shut everything down, no sports, and no running, so pretty much no fun. I begrudgingly conform with the doctors' orders and wear a back brace for the next six months. The form-fitted hardened plastic back brace stretches from the middle of my butt to the tip of my shoulder blades and clasps in the front with three Velcro strips. A perfect start to high school ... a broken back at the ripe old age of 15.

To that date it is the longest six months of my life. But at least my posture improves, and my friends have fun punching the brace daily to test its efficacy. Spring arrives. The time has come for me to break free of the brace. This is when I discover something new. Something feels different. My life is changed.

I'm fast! And I do not mean faster. I mean *really* freaking fast! Before the injury, my 40-yard dash time is 4.90-seconds, which is good for a kid my size going into the ninth grade. After the confinement of a brace, and after a few weeks of strength and speed training, I am beyond excited to see what I can do.

After the injury, as I line up for my first 40-yard dash test, I just know I will be "flying" today. I can feel it, even though I have no reason to believe I will run much faster than a year ago. Maybe this feeling is simply because I'm free of that ridiculously restrictive back brace.

Collierville High School's head football coach, Paul Cox, looks at me from the other end of the track. He yells, "Matt, you're up!" The clock starts on my mark. I walk to the line and kneel into a three-point stance, with fingers behind the white line. My fingers are barely holding the weight of my forward leaning body. My knuckles turn white, they begin to hurt and crumble under the pressure. I take a deep breath, then very deliberately raise my butt to the sky and pause for a beat at the top. BOOM!

Blasting out of my stance, a sense of calm and quiet take hold — much like the feeling you have before the snap of the football. The howling wind and chatter of teammates in the background are replaced with the sound of my toes tap dancing on the track. I scream through the finish.

The run feels good, but not great, which is always my feeling after running the forty. As I walk back to the finish line, Coach Cox gives me a peculiar look. He looks at me, open-mouthed with bewilderment, then down at his stopwatch and back at me. This cycle continues a couple times, I ask, "How did I do Coach?"

"Pretty darn good Matt, you ran a 4.48!" My jaw drops, and I cock my head to the side in shock. A 4.4-second anything is a great time for an NFL player, let alone a high school kid going into the tenth grade who recently recovered from a broken back. I have always been quick, but now I am fast. I guess I have finally "developed," and the gift of speed is one of the developments. Puberty is treating me well.

As tenth grade arrives, so does a lot of buzz about my 40-yard dash time within the football community. In these days, as a sophomore you are expected to play on the junior varsity team. It is rare for any sophomore to step foot on the field during a varsity game. The speed I now possess makes for one of those rare exceptions.

I land a job as a backup cornerback and a reserve spot on the offense. By the middle of the season, I am splitting time with the starting cornerback and eventually become the starter. As you know, I learned in my first year of football that I am not a good tackler, so imagine my surprise when playing on defense is my first big chance to shine. Every tackle I make this year is a shoestring-tackle.

I build a solid football foundation full of experience in tenth grade, and I have high hopes for the eleventh. Junior year does not disappoint on a personal level. I become an "Ironman" on the football team — starting on offense, defense, and special teams. I never take a break during a game. I love every moment on the field and enjoy every challenge that comes with never leaving the field. I know, if everything falls into place, our team has a real shot of making an appearance in the state playoffs, and there is an outside chance I will receive scholarship offers.

The team has a good season, we make it to the playoffs, but unfortunately are knocked out in the first round. I am comforted by the fact I have my senior season remaining and next year I will have another crack at the playoffs.

Junior year is a breakout season with 1,212-all-purpose yards as a wide receiver, running back, and kickoff returner: 17 catches for 305 yards and five touchdowns ... 62 carries for 325 yards with four touchdowns ... 15 kickoff returns, averaging 39 yards per return, with three touchdowns. I have six blocked kicks, returning one for a touchdown. On defense I have 61 tackles, four interceptions, and one touchdown. Scoring five different ways, I have 14 total touchdowns.

This type of versatility is extremely valuable to college football programs. It showcases the athleticism of a player, the work ethic and passion they possess, along with the willingness to do anything to help the team. This versatility is a huge help to me since I am neither the tallest nor the heaviest player on the field.

The 1999 season was a good one for the team and for me. I am fortunate enough to receive several full-scholarships offers and gain a ton of interest from universities around the country. Now it is time to bust my butt in the offseason to prepare for my final year of high school football ... senior year can be bittersweet under any circumstance. But mine, like so many others, is more bitter than sweet.

# Summer Showcase

## 3

**Summer 2000.** The summer before senior year arrives. My journey is not the same as the other students at Collierville High School. The other students are relaxing, partying, or working during their time off from school. Meanwhile, I attend summer football camps to show college football coaches what I have to offer their programs.

Before hitting the summer camp circuit, my cousin Brandon and I spend hours creating a highlight tape to mail college coaches around the country, all in the hopes they will offer me a scholarship. The crisp, early 2000's highlight film is a few minutes long and rocks "No Leaf Clover" by Metallica for every visually intoxicating moment. It showcases my junior season stats, best plays, and a new forty time, which most people do not believe until watching me run in-person ... 4.23-seconds (for perspective, a 4.21-seconds by Xavier Worthy in 2024 is the fastest ever recorded at the NFL combine[1]).

This summer I am on a mission to secure more scholarship offers and demonstrate I have the talent to succeed at the next level. I also need to prove the 4.23-forty-time is real. Some recruits push the truth on their testing results — bench press, squat, 20-yard shuttle, 40-yard dash, or other metrics — to make themselves more attractive to recruiters. So, I have a lot to prove before the senior campaign.

If you do not know, the 20-yard shuttle measures an athlete's quickness and ability to change direction. Imagine yourself in a three-point stance — right hand on the ground, your left is tucked and resting on your left thigh — straddling the 5-yard line on a football field. Your toes cheat to the right, as you slightly lean in this direction. Ten coaches stare you down, with stopwatches in hand. The clock starts on your movement.

You wiggle your left fingers, as you mentally prepare for your start. It's time. After one last deep breath, you leap to your right with a huge cross step, jumping out of your stance as quickly as possible. Sprint to the 10-yard line … keeping your head down, staying as low as possible. As you slam your right foot into the ground, do not cross the 10-yard mark, and start shifting your momentum back to the starting line and toward your next stop at the goal line. You swipe the front of the 10-yard line with your right hand — careful not to touch the ground with your left. Keep your balance!

You blast out of this crouched position, and sprint to the goal line … staying low and almost falling to the ground with each step. Your left foot slams into the ground just before the end zone, your momentum is already shifting back toward the finish line. You swipe the goal line with your left hand — keeping your right from touching the ground. You explode from this coiled position and finish through the 5-yard line where you started.

All in less than 4-seconds. In addition to the 20-yard shuttle, there are other agility tests football coaches conduct — 60-yard shuttle, X-drill, and 3-cone drill to name a few.

This summer, I attend the University of Notre Dame, University of Memphis, University of Mississippi, Mississippi State University, and Vanderbilt University summer camps. Along with a local Pepsi camp to prove

I am in fact the lightning-quick "little" guy we are advertising. In all these camps I am able to run my forty somewhere in the 4.2-range, the best being 4.23. After showcasing my speed, I just need to verify I can catch a football. Basically, showing coaches I can walk and chew gum at the same time. If you can run like the wind but you cannot catch a football — that tells coaches, you are a defensive player or better suited for track and field.

The Notre Dame camp is different from the other camps I attend. The camp is scheduled to last a couple days, but I can only attend the first evening and the following morning due to family commitments. So, I have to quickly make an impression and ND needs to do the same.

The impression ND makes the first time you step foot on campus is hard to describe. Former Irish head coach Lou Holtz made famous the following about the mystique of Notre Dame: "Those who know Notre Dame, no explanation's necessary. Those who don't, no explanation will suffice." My father attends the camp with me. He can't pass up the opportunity to visit the University of Notre Dame for the first time. He has always been a Notre Dame Football fan and loves everything the university represents.

When we step off the plane, early in the morning, we are immediately hit by a gust of wind I have only felt once before while on vacation in the Windy City of Chicago. It is a chilly breeze that lets me know I am not in Tennessee anymore. We jump into the rental car and drive to campus.

The drive isn't anything special — a normal-looking middle-America small town. We arrive at our hotel, which is a mile from campus, drop off our bags and decide to take a walk around campus before reporting to camp. Dad wants to make the most of this trip. I'm not happy about this upcoming walk. I don't want to walk around all day when I need to be ready for testing when camp starts tonight. I want to rest and prepare for the showcase to come. Dad does not think twice about my legs (I recently reminded him of this story, he laughed and said, "Yeah, that's my bad." Thanks, Dad.). We head to campus to see what this place is all about.

We hop in the car, drive toward campus, and turn left onto Notre Dame Avenue. The first structure I see at this earlyish morning hour, off in the distance, is the Golden Dome. The dome radiates a majestic glow fashioned by rays of sunshine whimsically dancing from its crown. It is stunning. We park and start our exploration of the university.

Still exceedingly early in the morning for a teenager, dew glistens from each blade of grass that has been meticulously manicured. Patches of fog linger, fighting to remain a part of campus for a little longer. The sun inches higher into the sky with each of our steps, creeping over the tree line revealing more and more of the beauty Notre Dames has to offer. The buildings are magnificently constructed with an old-world feel of elegance, tradition, and history. Every step you take seems to awaken more of the essence that is Notre Dame. Looking at these structures, you find yourself imagining the people who walked the halls, the traditions, and the stories each building holds.

We eventually make our way to Notre Dame Stadium. We walk from the south side of the stadium to the north. Each step gradually exposes the giant, spectacular mosaic that is Touchdown Jesus. It is a marvelously unforgettable mural of Jesus that will never leave the depths of my mind. To this day, it haunts me. It brings a smile to my face with each exquisite thought of its grandeur.

As I stand between the stadium, which held 80,795 people at the time, and Touchdown Jesus, my senses rouse. I begin to imagine thousands of people flocking toward these omitted Wonders of the World on game-day like a lighthouse guiding alumni safely ashore and home to their old stomping grounds. As a cool breeze brushes against my face, I can almost smell the popcorn in the air and hear the band playing in the distance. My imagination runs wild as I think about what the gameday experience would be like at Notre Dame.

From Touchdown Jesus, we make our way west to find the Grotto of Our Lady of Lourdes on the other side of campus. The grotto is a powerful sight; it's elegantly carved into a hillside, with a small forest as its backdrop, and faces a neighboring lake. Ivy paints itself into each boulder crevice, many of which weigh two tons or more — a small piece of the original grotto in France sits below the statue of Mary. Hundreds of candles flicker and fight against the unrelenting wind, as they await their prayers flaming into existence to be answered. After a prayer and few moments of tranquility, we take our leave along the main path — accompanied by rows of vivid flowers, six deep, on each side — to view the nearby water.

Even to this day, this sight, this Holy place, still blows me away. It gives me chills. It gives me an overwhelming feeling of togetherness and hope. There is a gravitas, a presence, a weight that dwells within this iconic sanctuary for prayer.

Everyone's first experience when visiting ND is different, but in each story, one word will invariably be there: "Chills." It is hard to explain the chills you feel when walking on campus, but they are there, and they are as real as the campus itself. This campus is more than beautiful, more than amazing, and has no equal, with few rivals. I've visited numerous campuses in my life and not one induces chills or feelings in the way Notre Dame does — I may be biased, but there is no denying this place is special. I feel *everything*, and see so much more, in my day and a-half on campus. I know if they offer me a scholarship, I will be hard-pressed to turn it down.

# Smoke House

## 4

THE EVENING EVENTUALLY ROLLS around after a long day of walking. Thanks again, Dad. Yes, I am tired from our exploration of campus, but I have work to do, and I plan to shine. The campers are herded together to be weighed, measured, tested, and timed. My weight and height are exactly what we represented in the highlight film, six feet tall and 170-pounds.

Now, it is time to run. We are running on old-school AstroTurf — concrete with a coarse, thin, rug-like covering — which makes for a perfect running surface. I run well, but not my best. I still blame Dad for making me walk around all day. I run a 4.27- and 4.29-forty, which are very respectable times. Do not get me wrong, they are great times, but I walk away knowing I can do better and wishing I could take another shot at the sprint. Not the end of the world, just frustrating because of the big stage.

After all the testing is complete, and before we wrap up camp for the night, Mickey Marotti — ND's head strength and conditioning coach — gathers all the campers. There is one more thing we have to do. Coaches are always looking for ways to create fun and energy; at camp these are found with the "Smoke House." The Smoke House is a 40-yard dash race between the six or so fastest players at camp. After Mickey announces the finalists, we break from the group huddle. I am in!

In short-order I get another shot at beating my 4.27-second run. We jog to the middle of the field for a race to see who will be crowned the Smoke House champion. As I am preparing for the race, I look around to see campers on each side of the runway, two-deep in spots, from the starting line to the finish line. The campers are yelling. Many of them are picking their horse and some are helping runners get amped for the race.

I settle into my spot on the starting line. I look down the line at my competitors and think, "I am the smallest here, and I'm the only white guy." I take a deep breath to center my focus, shutting out the noise of the moment, and kneel into a three-point stance. At this point, I am fairly certain no one is picking me to win, unless they happen to see what I clocked moments ago.

For as long as I can remember, there has been a stereotype that white guys are not as fast as Black guys, which isn't entirely untrue. A handful of university programs glaringly adhere to this stereotype when recruiting me. Weekly, after becoming aware of my forty-time, these universities send letters and brochures outlining their support of Black culture on campus. I am all for this support, but find it funny they see a number, 4.23-seconds, and assume this recruit is a Black guy. Umm, sure film is grainy back in 2000, but you can't take time to know who you are recruiting?

Needless to say, these colleges did not make my top-10. This stereotype works to my advantage at the Smoke House — and on the field throughout my career because opponents always view me as a possession receiver until they watch me run by them in person.

As I wait for the countdown to begin, sweat dripping from my brow, a nervous and excited energy pulsates through my body. I know this is a moment ... one of those points in time where you know "your path" could truly be reshaped and life as you know it may change forever.

A coach yells, "On your mark, get set," and blows the air horn. We're off! I burst out of the "starting blocks." My feet start wide to quickly generate power, with each step my shoes inch closer to one another. Staying as low as possible, shoulder and head no higher than my waist if I were standing, I surge through the 10-yard mark. My start feels solid, not great but good, so, "par for the course." About 30 yards into the race, I glance to each side to see where I stand — think Usain Bolt style — and I do not see anyone. I fly through the finish line to become the Smoke House Champion! And another sub-4.30-second forty is in the books!

A year later, during two-a-days at Notre Dame (I know, spoiler — I attend Notre Dame), I listen as running back Marcus Wilson recalls this Smoke House race.

"When we lined up for the final race, I looked down the line at the competition, and knew I was gonna win. I didn't see you run at all but didn't think you had a chance of beating me. What I didn't realize is you were a 4.2-guy ... I've seen fast white dudes before, but never a sub-4.3 guy. I was on the defensive side of things all night, so I didn't see you run before the finale. The horn blew and for the first 10 steps I thought I had the race, my start felt great, and we were all pretty even. Then, all of a sudden, out of the corner of my eye, you took off and won by a few steps ... I was so shocked bro! And, the next day you were smoking everyone in seven-on-seven drills ... honestly, I'd never seen a guy run that fast. You and Reggie Williams (a future University of Washington wide receiver) were killing everyone that morning."

As Marcus is telling this story, I can hear in his voice that he still could not believe I was faster than him — than everyone at that camp.

The following morning, I wake up at the crack of dawn with eagerness for the day to come. Dad and I will be leaving camp early today, but I still have something to prove before I can go home. Can I catch the football? Can I "walk and chew gum at the same time?" If I am extremely fast but can't catch the football, then that changes how coaches think about me and what they see for my future. This isn't necessarily a bad thing, if you do not mind playing defense. But the offensive side of the football is where I want to be next year when I step onto the college field. I need to establish I can catch the football when their eyes are on me.

Again, nervous energy takes hold as I have a lot to do in very little time during the morning camp session. I do not drop a ball, I run good routes, and catch a lot of deep balls — mostly Hail Mary's, Posts, and Corner routes.

Shortly after the morning session finishes, Coach Bob Davie calls me into his office for a meeting. I am anxious about meeting with Coach, but also eager to see what happens. My nervousness blanks most of this conversation from my memory, aside from the following. He says, "I'd like to offer you a scholarship to the University of Notre Dame to play football." Internally I shout, "AHH!" I'm overcome with joy, relief, and excitement all in one! Success! I thank Coach and shake his hand, as my goal of having a great camp and walking away with a scholarship offer is achieved.

The goal is accomplished at camp with only one evening and one morning session. I thought this was amazing because until this point I just knew I needed to stay for every minute of camp. If I had only known obtaining an offer was this easy, I would have gone to a lot more camps and spent less time at each one. Hindsight is 20/20.

For any aspiring college athlete who isn't on the radar of college programs, I recommend sending videos to everyone and attending every camp you can afford. If you are not the caliber of an elite player, which I was not, then you must get your name out there for people to take interest in you as an athlete. Camps not only get you in front of college coaches, but you will take away valuable information from these camps. You can learn what your strengths and weaknesses truly are when compared to others your age who are from various parts of your city, your state, or other parts of the country. Camp will also help you prepare for the next level of coaching and provide you with a better understanding of how college coaches motivate athletes.

Make sure the coaches see your strengths as much as possible when you attend camp and do your best to minimize your weaknesses until, through hard work, they become strengths. You must show them something that makes them want to take a chance on you, a gamble if you will. If your best asset isn't speed, then use your size, your jumping ability, your hands, your mind, your ability to process information, or any other ability in your arsenal that helps your cause. Show them you have heart, a high motor, or a strong work ethic. Find a way to show them these abilities. Take extra reps during drills, compete against the bigger and stronger players, or simply refuse to give up regardless of what is thrown at you.

Make them notice you. Intrigue them to such a point where they come find you, instead of you seeking them out. Easier said than done, yes, but not impossible. Each one of us has strength inside, waiting to be tapped in times of need, so dig deep and unleash every ounce of heart and energy you command. "You have the ability, simply remember your courage."

# Senior Recruiting

**5**

Summer ends and school rolls around. I'm a senior, a "king" of high school. The dream of playing college football moves closer every day, and the lights of high school begin its fade into memory. At the time I could not wait to get out of high school, to move on and be on my own. Looking back, I rushed it.

Sometimes, don't you wish you could go back to senior year to do it all over again? There are no real worries, we have our parents taking care of the "grown up" things, our jobs are easy — if we even had jobs — and we have little responsibility. Oh, to be young again. Everyone looks up to you as a senior and wants to one day be as "cool" as you are. You feel invincible. At least that is what we think to ourselves.

Senior year for an athlete is a huge year in their life. For many athletes, this year will be their last year playing sports and their last chance to impress college scouts. Luckily, I'm fortunate enough to already hold scholarship offers, so the pressure that comes with trying to obtain an offer is not on my shoulders.

Entering senior year, my goal is to win as many games as possible and have fun. In my mind I already know where I am going to attend college, but I have not told anyone yet. I want to explore my options to ensure I am making the correct decision for me. Also, recruits are allowed to go on five official visits. These visits are weekend trips with all expenses paid, and the university has an opportunity to truly impress you and your family. Official visits are a ton of fun and I want to take full advantage of all five. Can you blame me?

The recruiting process brings an amazing amount of pressure for student athletes. There are grown men, adults, whose livelihood depends on recruiting the best of the best teenagers in the country. Convincing one five-star recruit could save their job. Getting the commitment of a "blue-chip" recruit could start a flurry of commitments that turns their program around. These adults visit high schools year-round seeking out the players who can help build and rebuild their program. The coaches will randomly appear at your high school campus or at your football game. Coaches will visit your home, appreciate a home cooked meal, and enjoy the company of your family.

They promise you things, big and little. Before Name, Image, and Likeness (NIL) money, there were shoeboxes of cash and other "grey areas" that some coaches navigate while chasing a "big fish." No shoeboxes, or other treats, for me. But Coach Davie promises I can wear jersey number eleven, which I want but do not receive ... thanks Bob. And he promises that in 2002, two years from now, there will be a brand-new football complex for the team.

This type of attention can become overwhelming. If you are a five-star recruit, then you are receiving this attention from everyone. You can't "beat them off with a stick." Every big-time university in the country is hounding you. At 17 or 18 years old, it is difficult for any student to know what they want to do with their life.

High school students, who are non-athletes, apply to multiple schools in the hopes of admittance, just hoping their favorite school will allow them to attend. On the other hand, student-athletes, in some cases, have the pick of the litter. They have representatives from the universities and coaches begging them to join their programs. The athlete doesn't start applying to colleges months and months in advance of his or her high school graduation. They instead apply after committing, as a formality. Before a scholarship is offered, the university does its homework on the student-athlete to ensure he or she has the grades to get in.

I know, it sounds awesome, it sounds amazing to have so many people battling it out for your signature. Pause to think about how uncertain, how immature, how anxious of the unknown you were in high school. This wealth of possibility can be nerve-racking. One decision, just one, will dramatically affect the entirety of your life. Uncertainty grows, causing headache and heartache as you attempt to decipher which school is the "right" choice. I can only hope these kids have the support system in place to help guide them through this tumultuous time.

I am fortunate to have family around me who genuinely care during recruitment. Mom and Dad are with me every step of the way, ensuring I make the "right" decision. They tell me to take my time. They help me view options with more objectivity, clarity, and understanding — talking through the pros and cons of each scholarship offer. If not for them, looking to a future after football is not something I would be considering. Long-term success and happiness are the direction they nudge me toward. With their hands-on approach, they provide a lot of input and guidance, while ensuring I know the decision-making power is 100% mine. After all, the university I choose will be my home for a handful of years.

For me, it's more important to find a university that "feels right." This "feeling" is different for each player. Some athletes look for a school with tradition, recent on-field success, great education, good coaches, where their friends are going, how quickly they can play, distance from home, or something they cannot fully describe. Many players search for a combination, not just one factor.

Personally, I'm looking for a place with great football, great academics, and a place that feels like home. I want a place where football is life, not just for the players, but for the entire university. I need a school with a good education because I understand my athletic ability will not last a lifetime. My choice must give me a sense of family, unity, and provide a certain comfort when I am on campus. If I am mindful of these during my search, I know my parents will be happy with my decision and so will I. Mom and Dad always say, "It's up to you."

The recruiting landscape and the mentality of recruits has wildly changed since the early 2000's. And I'm not sure it is for the better.

Does anyone else hate how ridiculous recruiting has become? Sure, this decision is difficult and life altering, but come on. *Athletes, when you make the decision to commit to a university ... COMMIT*!

A recruit's word, these days, must be taken with a "grain of salt." It happens all the time. A recruit commits, decommits, commits to another school, and then decommits — continuing this pattern even after signing day. In today's college football landscape, many athletes have well over a year to vet a multitude of scholarship offers and their own feelings toward this decision. So do not commit until you are absolutely sure.

And when you arrive on campus, keep a few things in mind. Coaches are mean and unforgiving no matter where you play football. Academics are difficult and stressful no matter where you get your education. Homesickness can occur when you go to school in your hometown. "Man up" and stand by your word! And when you do remain steadfast, and things do not go your way, remember the "why" of it all. Lean into your reasons for picking this school over all the others that gave chase.

Do not jump in the Transfer Portal because your feelings are hurt. If you choose to leave, make sure it is for the "right" reasons. That said, if a coach leaves (head or position coach), I believe every player has the right to leave; I've never understood why coaches have so much flexibility with their loyalty, but players do not ... at least they did not until the Transfer Portal.

Aside from all this distraction, senior year is a momentous year! For most, it is full of excitement and fun. You are kings and queens of high school, finally. Nothing will stand in the way of you having the time of your life. The football players are bursting with anticipation of the season opener. You walk the halls taking note of the signage with your name plastered all over it, urging you to victory. The cheerleaders decorate each football player's locker, and one of them wears your jersey in support. The senior class has their caravan route planned for each game, and they are ready to paint their chests and faces to show love for their football team.

"Matthew 4.23" t-shirts, with "Need for Speed" printed on the back, pop up all over the school (a buddy was selling them, I am still waiting for my cut). Everything is going great; you are a senior ... what's the worst that can happen?

# Moments Before the Snap

## 6

**September 2000**. STACKING LAYERS of sound build in the night sky: coaches yelling, players jawing and panting, fans screaming, wind howling, and a lone band member's beating drum. The play clock winds down. The huddle breaks. I step to the line of scrimmage; the noise gradually fades with my intensifying focus.

I settle into the wingback position, on the right side of the ball, slightly offset behind and to the right of our massive offensive tackle. The stadium lights shine brightly from above as sweat drips from my chinstrap. I glance at the scoreboard; it's the first quarter, two minutes into the game. A sense of calm comes over me with the snap of the ball.

"Hut! Hut!" The ball snaps. I drive my right foot into the ground, pivoting to the left, and dash toward my quarterback. I take the handoff and I immediately begin looking for space to run. My eyes are darting left and right, scanning for any opening.

The left side of the field is crawling with offensive and defensive players colliding into one another, fighting to win their individual battle. There it is! I spot the hole I've been searching for and hit it as fast as possible. Sprinting through the opening without so much as a graze from the swiping hand of an opposing player. Running down the field, angling toward the sideline in the hopes I can outrun the final defender. He has an angle on me.

I have two options: continue this path with the hope of outrunning him or try to juke him. The defender closes in, corralling me toward the sideline. I'm nearing the boundary and running out of field. With each step I assess the situation, I realize he will cut me off before I can break free for a touchdown. He lunges to make the tackle. I plant my left foot in the ground as quickly and violently as possible, cutting to the right, juking him before impact and choosing to not run out of bounds.

SNAP!

The fifth game of my senior year comes and goes. The excitement and energy for the season have all but disappeared. The team's fortune, as well as mine, is now irreversibly altered. I am certain, at some point in your life, you have been asked, "If you could go back and change something in your past, would you?" My answer, "Yes, 100%."

Tonight is it. This is the moment. I would go back and run out of bounds. Taking away this injury, this single event, would my life have been any different? I will never know, but this is a thought I will always contemplate. Alas, I do not have the amazing senior season an athlete dreams of having during their last go-around on their high school field.

SNAP! Things are changed. Everything is changed. In a flash I am writhing in pain on the ground, screaming profanities at the top of my lungs. My ACL is torn in an instant. My future, once full of potential and opportunity flashes before my eyes, then fades into an ether of uncertainty.

The first of many tears do not fall upon my ghostly pale face until halftime in the locker room. Tears do not fall from the pain. Tears do not fall because of this difficult situation. Tears fall because of my teammates. The love and concern they show as they check on their injured brother overwhelms me. After halftime, with my knee wrapped in ice, I return to the sideline to cheer my teammates on to victory. I carefully jog up and down the sideline. Chest bumping players in the excitement of the game. The game is over ... we win.

The team puts a "W" in the win column, and I take an "L." As I leave the field, my eyes begin to swell as friends and fans come to see how I am doing. Their compassion and thoughtfulness are appreciated but seem to only make me feel worse in the moment. The concern and solemn looks painted on their faces bring to the forefront a realization this was my last football game as a Collierville High School football player. I will never don maroon and white again. A postgame walk to the car has never felt longer. Mom helps me inside the car and closes the door, thus closing the doors of my high school football career.

With help from the media, Notre Dame and every other college jousting for my commitment hear the news in short order. The following week I receive phone calls from coaches with their condolences regarding my injury. Some call to let me know they are standing by their offer to have me join their team, their family. Others call to wish me well and inform me they are pulling my scholarship offer. In the weeks to come, many universities just stop calling and move on without a word. The business side of sports is already rearing its ugly head.

The week after my injury I receive a phone call from ND. Head Coach, Bob Davie, calls to reassure me the University of Notre Dame is standing by its offer. They are standing by their word ... it works both ways, recruits. Coach Davie goes so far as to say, "If you never step foot on the game field or the practice field again, you'll still graduate with a degree from the University of Notre Dame." WOW! I've never been more excited or relieved in my life. He doesn't "tuck tail and run" like most of the schools. He stands by his word and his recruit.

This is the news I was hoping to hear. ND was my number one choice coming into the season and the commitment Coach Davie shows only reaffirms the decision I ultimately planned to make. The university, and Coach Davie, show loyalty to a severely injured 18-year-old kid, which brings about an earlier-than-planned announcement.

I decide to forgo all other official visits and all considerations for other schools. While most schools run from me like I am a disease-ridden, decrepit, tainted athlete who will never amount to anything on the field again, ND stands by my side. ND shows an unwavering commitment during a very uncertain time. After speaking with my parents that evening, we all conclude Notre Dame is the right choice for me.

The following day I call Coach Davie to pledge my commitment to the University of Notre Dame. My dream of attending a Division One school and playing football is well on its way to becoming reality. The stress and uncertainty brought on by the recruiting process comes to a close.

The future makes itself known. A new chapter is about to begin, not the one I hoped for at the start of the season — celebrating a state championship with my teammates and riding into the sunset with pure excitement for the future. Instead, I move forward with hesitation about who I am, who I will become, and how I will get back to being the athlete Notre Dame wants. It is time for me to get to work.

# More Fall Pain

## 7

THE SAME WEEK I get phenomenal news from Coach Davie, our team doctor confirms the nightmare of having a torn ACL, with several tests and imaging scans at his clinic. Now we need to drain my knee to remove the fluid and pressure buildup causing me extra pain. The doctor reaches for a syringe with the biggest needle I have ever seen. Its size rivals that of a straw you use with a Big Gulp. It's huge!

He grasps the barrel of the syringe with his left hand, like you hold a dumbbell, and jams the needle into my knee joint. My entire body jolts into the air. With his right hand he pulls the plunger away from the knee to extract the blood and fluid from within. The doctor slides his left hand down from the barrel to the needle and uses his right to unscrew the barrel. As he turns his attention to the bowl, to squirt the fluid into a basin for testing, it is as though he forgets he has a left hand.

The once steady hand of a doctor transforms into a bodybuilder using a Shake Weight. He moves the needle in every imaginable direction. Hitting everything in its path. Each slight movement causes a new, more intense pain. I try not to move, but my body has other plans, as I uncontrollably jump and wiggle on the examination table.

After reviewing the test results, my surgeon decides to wait a month to perform surgery. The thought process being, it will be best to rehab and strengthen the leg muscles, especially around the knee, before I go under the knife. Get as strong as possible pre-surgery, so when atrophy takes hold post-surgery, my road to full recovery will hopefully be shorter. This improvement in strength and leg mass will lessen the amount of atrophy and jumpstart rehab. The logic makes sense to me, and I am not a doctor, so we work and wait.

Nearing surgery day, three days and counting. It's a beautiful Saturday; I spend the day with friends riding four-wheelers and having a blast before life is slowed by surgery. It rained last night, which is perfect for a fun day of riding with the crew.

At the end of our ride, just before sunset, we decide to take a group photo with mud caked from head to toe. My hands, feet, and most of my body are frozen from speeding through the countryside on a chilly November day. I climb down from the four-wheeler, being very careful with my injured left leg. My feet hit the ground; I can feel its slipperiness, as the soles of my shoes search for stability. Streams of lumpy muddy water cascade toward the gathering pool at the bottom of the small hill. Caution is a must. I got this!

I carefully saunter across the soupy mud-smeared slope toward my friends. WHOOSH! BAM! I slip. I crash. I fall. And I don't got this! My healthy right leg abruptly slides out from underneath me and is en route to the marsh below. All hope of balance and safety is abandoned. The full weight of my body crashes down onto my ACL snapped leg. As my butt slams into the heel of my foot, I scream, falling to my right side and tumble down the embankment until splashing into the murky swamp below. I hysterically roll from side-to-side thrashing in pain.

Since the injury, I have barely been able to sit in a chair with my knee bent. Imagine, without being prepared, someone takes your index finger and slams it all the way back to the top (dorsal) side of your wrist. Take that feeling, multiply it by a hundred and that is close to the kind of excruciating pain I am in. The original injury itself was painful, but not even close to the pain I feel on this day.

**November 14, 2000**. Surgery day arrives. The nurse uses a permanent marker to identify my good leg and my bad leg. As the anesthesiologist puts a mask over my nose and mouth, he tells me, "I keep this good stuff in a shed behind my house ... I best not catch you back there looking for it next week. Now, count backward from a hundred."

The unmistakable industrial cleaning, antiseptic, slightly bitter, stuffy scent of the hospital filling my nose is replaced with the sweet vapory smell of chemically laden gas. I am knocked out almost before I start counting. I can only imagine the doctor's surprise when he cuts open my knee to find a churning pool of blood. After all, he drained fluid from my knee only a few weeks ago. The surgery goes smoothly, but due to the late start I stay overnight for observation.

The following morning, my physical therapist, who is also our high school team trainer, wakes me up at 6:00 a.m. to start rehab. Before we start, she punches me in the arm and says, "How in the world was there blood in your knee!" I walk her through the accident, and she isn't all too pleased with her patient, punches me again, and simply says, "You're an idiot."

Then, she shows me all the funny drawings and words of "encouragement" she wrote in permanent marker on my legs when I was out cold during surgery. That is the type of relationship I had with Marylyle Boolos. Marylyle shows me the basics on crutches, so I do not fall when going up and down stairs and gives me a few exercises to begin at home. Normally these exercises, these daily movements, are easy, but they are unbelievably difficult post-surgery. Simple things such as lifting the leg straight up in the air and flexing my quad. Atrophy is real. Strengthening my leg before surgery makes a lot more sense now.

*2000: Matt Shelton as part of the Collierville High School Dragons.*

I have a long way to go before resembling my old self again and, at this moment, it seems as though it will be impossible to get there. My first hurdle is simple, walk normally without a limp. Two weeks after surgery I will be on the campus of Notre Dame for my official visit. I need to show the coaching staff I have the determination and work ethic to get back on the field next year.

# Official Visit

## 8

**December 1, 2000.** I cannot wait for my official visit; the time is upon us. The plane lands in South Bend and Coach Lou, not Lou Holtz, is there to greet us — myself, and my parents. One of Coach Lou's first comments is, "Wow, you're not limping, and it's only been a few weeks, that a boy." Yes! First hurdle, passed.

I have been working extremely hard from the moment I opened my eyes after surgery to the moment I stepped foot on the plane to South Bend. The hard work is paying off. During this visit, I prove to every coach and every player I meet that I have the strength and resolve to be a Notre Dame man.

The official visit is amazing. The coaches set me up in a huge suite with a kitchen, living room and bedroom. That is something special to a kid from a small town in the South. My parents are in a room just like mine, but on the floor below me and on the opposite side of the hotel. This way I can have a blast and my parents will not get in the way.

Current player, Chris Yura, shows me around the university to give me a player's perspective. Each evening my parents and I are wined and dined by coaches and players. Parting ways with my parents after dinner, Chris takes me out for a "night on the town." I do my best to keep up, have a good time, and not slow the party down. Seeing as I am just a few weeks out of surgery, it is a tall order.

The first night out we pre-game in Tony Fisher's dorm room at Carroll Hall on the far west side of campus. Afterward, the group of guys sneak me into a few bars to continue drinking and start mingling with the ladies of Notre Dame. Never have I been so overwhelmed by a scene. This is my first time in a bar. Women are everywhere, drinks are flowing, music so loud I can barely hear myself think, and strobe lights put on a show in every room.

To kick night two off we play poker with Jeff Faine, Rocky Boiman, and others before pre-gaming at Chris'. We end up at a house party in an apartment complex near campus. Kegs on every patio as far as the eye can see, students seemingly dangle from overloaded balconies, and again college girls everywhere. Every night when I return to the hotel room from going out with the guys there is an extra-large pizza waiting on the counter. A late-night snack is the perfect ending to most drink filled nights, plus I think they were trying to bulk me up even before freshman year started.

This weekend the team has their end of the year banquet, which is very touching from an outsider's point of view. There is a lot of emotion in the banquet hall. You can feel how much everyone cares about the team and the university.

The afterparty is the best party, to date, that I have ever been to before. In high school we don't have these kinds of parties — I am guessing because we are underage, and mostly have our parties in a field, with bonfires encircled by trucks. We crash a student's apartment, and it is astonishing to see how many people can be packed into one apartment unit. There are red solo cups in everyone's hand, people shoulder-to-shoulder and hanging from the ceiling; college kids being, just that, college kids. I wish there were more details for you than these, but I unfortunately am unable to stay out too late with my knee. I am in an extreme amount of pain after being on the go the entire weekend and trying to "hang" with the big kids. It is the right amount of partying and drinking with the right amount of control, for me at least.

All good signs, considering I chose this school for academics and football. I know I need a place like Notre Dame that can both show me a fun time and allow me to excel with minimal distraction. "Know thy self."

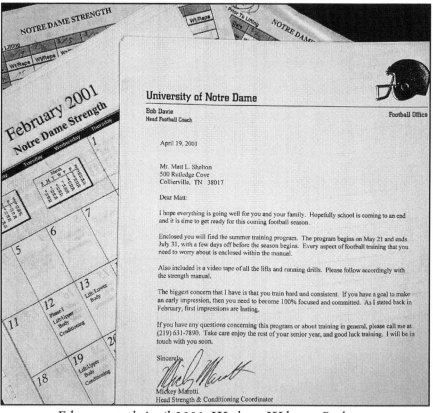

*February and April 2001: Workout Welcome Packages.*

# Rehab Revelations

## 9

WITH MY OFFICIAL VISIT in the books, it's back home to continue rehabbing the knee. Two-a-days at Notre Dame will be here before I know it, and I have a long way to go before I am fully healed. Rehab is an uphill, grueling battle I knew was coming but I did not anticipate how difficult the small things would become.

Curious how we tend to take them for granted — the little things. Especially ones which allow us to function daily without thought. Getting into bed. Rolling over in bed. Getting out of bed. Doing anything in the bathroom. Lifting your leg to get up from the couch. Walking to the fridge. Flexing your leg muscles to stand your ground. Taking a stroll through the park. Riding a bike. Driving a car. It's only when a basic daily function is taken away, or hindered, that we truly see how much we take our bodies for granted. The little things ... cherish them.

With fortune on my side and a lot of hard work, the loss of these capabilities will not be permanent. Soon, the "little things" and, hopefully, the full array of my abilities will return. For rehab purposes, a few months after surgery, Marylyle allows me to join the track team. I am running again. I am competing, and even winning at times.

Then, WAHOO! The next thing I know I'm running full speed straight ahead and doing extremely well (side-to-side activity was much more restricted at this time). I'm winning almost all my races. Marylyle has me on an accelerated rehab program and she is extremely aggressive in her approach. Her goal is to prepare me for the upcoming freshman year of football as quickly as possible. I view her goal slightly differently.

She is in full control of my rehab, and I'm glad to have her ... most days. She has the knowledge and experience to quickly return me to full health. She pushes my limits and makes the entire process almost like a game. Without proper training and supervision, I wouldn't be able to overcome every hurdle on this path to recovery. That said, I truly feel her singular goal is to make me cry due to the pain she is inflicting.

Her favorite way to torment me is by having me lie on my back, put the heel of my injured leg on the wall, and slowly allow gravity to pull the sock-covered foot down toward the ground. Once gravity has done its job, she measures my progress by the degrees of my bent leg. If I do not surpass my previous session's measurement, then her approach changes.

She grabs my ankle with both hands and jumps with the entirety of her 99-pound body; pushing and pulling on my leg with all her strength to force me past my current limitations. And every time the same excuse for doing so; in her Southern belle twang, with a mischievous half-smile, she says, "We have to break up the scar tissue." I still do not believe that one, she just enjoys tormenting me.

To this day, I have not forgiven her for all the pain she inflicted upon me, but thank her every day for the life, once thought lost, that she returned to me.

# PART TWO

## FRESHMAN EXPECTATIONS & THE UNKNOWN

breathe    you got this !

# Summer to Prepare

## 10

In life, what you expect to happen and what happens are very often two different things. Such was my Notre Dame experience. I expect to have a consistent, normal, out-of-this-world college experience. I expect kind-ish treatment by coaches. I expect an okay fan base. I expect academics to be difficult. I expect workouts to be relentless. I expect to graduate with the coaches who recruit me to the university. I both overestimate and underestimate the college experience I am about to have.

I graduate from high school, now fall camp and two-a-day practices are around the corner, along with the start of my college journey. My introduction of what is to come begins with a piece of mail. Mickey Marotti sends a summer training program to prepare the freshmen for a fast-approaching fall camp. In these days, players are not enrolling early to jumpstart their college careers. Hence, this summer before freshman year, preparations for the journey ahead must be made at home.

I expect the relentless nature of working-out to increase from high school to college. But as I scroll through the binder, I come to the realization that I am not ready; I was not expecting workouts to be as intense and demanding as these pages portray. Page after page of daily training: what to do, how to do it, what to eat, what to drink, etc. The schedule and amount of challenging work I see in my future is intimidating.

Don't get me wrong, I worked out extremely hard in high school. But nothing close to the intensity laid out before me in this book Mickey calls a "Strength Manual." Looking back to this moment, I realize this is the part of a movie when the music becomes ominous and eerie ... foreshadowing the "tortures" to come.

Fortunately, and unfortunately for me, my injury still does not allow me to train the way I need to each and every day — the way Mickey outlines. I am still on the road to recovery. I have a lot of physical and mental healing left to do. The doctors say my knee will be 100% recovered at the eight-month mark, but it will take two additional months for my mind to accept this as truth. So, after about 10 months I will know if I have the capability of being my old self.

During rehab and training a lot of inflammation develops in my knee, patellar tendonitis. Tendonitis only heals with time and rest so, unfortunately, I will battle tendonitis every day of my athletic career. There is no rest for the weary or a college football player. To this day, I battle knee pain daily and always will, until my body can take no more and I am forced to have a total knee replacement ... or two.

Since pain will not let me lift weights or condition as often as Mickey's workout program requires, I develop an abbreviated summer training program. I do most of the lifting and running activities, but I cannot push myself as aggressively as I need and want. When it's leg day in the weight room, I cannot do many reps or lift heavy weights. When conditioning, I can't run for long periods of time without risking a setback.

Pain tolerance and management are key, a hard balancing act for anyone, especially a soon-to-be college athlete who has something to prove. I cannot afford for anything to go wrong. Best to err on the side of caution until on campus, where I will have more hands-on training and daily support to deal with any missteps.

Honestly, I am naive to think workouts will be the same on campus as they are at home this summer. Really, how can workouts be more difficult than Mickey has already made them?

Oh, workouts can get harder, a lot harder. Again, I am wrong. The summer workout program is just a warm-up, an "ease you into it" introduction to college football. From the moment you step foot on campus until the moment you leave, you are training — you are literally eating, sleeping, and dreaming about football. The coaching staff never take its foot off the gas and never allow you to give up. You will get bigger, stronger, and faster during your time at Notre Dame, at least most do.

Workouts, aside from academics, are the most time-consuming aspect of a football player's college life. A close third is actual football: practicing, studying film, learning your playbook, internalizing the X's and O's of the game, etc. We are with the strength coaches more than we are the football coaches. Yes, during the football season, August to January, we are with the football coaches pretty much all day, every day, but we still have three, four, and sometimes more training sessions per week.

If you happen to be one of the unfortunate injured, then the strength coaches have full reign to absolutely kick your butt every day, or at least five days a week. You may not be able to practice, but no matter your injury there is always, and I mean always, something you can do in the weight room.

# FRESHMAN HELL

## 11

**AUGUST 12, 2001.** TWO-A-DAY camp arrives. I am leaving home to follow my own path in life — free of parents, siblings, family, and friends. At the airport, Mom gives me the hug of all hugs before I board the plane, squeezing me tighter than ever before, as her chin quivers and tears stream from her eyes. Her baby boy is setting out to become a man. Throughout college, Mom cries every time we part ways for any amount of time. There is sadness in these tears, but in this moment they are mostly tears of happiness and hopefulness from a mother full of pride.

As I take my seat, looking out of the plane window, a feeling of optimistic exhilaration pulses through my body with each heartbeat; I am leaving everything I have ever known behind to begin a new life with my new family.

We touch down in South Bend. I exit the plane and, yet again, a brisk gust of wind punches me in the face. I'm home. A student-manager greets me at baggage claim, helps load my luggage into the car, drives me to campus, and helps carry the bags to my new dorm room. Campus is much calmer than it was at summer camp, as the football team and staff are the only people on campus for a few more weeks.

As I get squared away in my dorm, I run into my fellow freshmen teammates, trainers, staff, and coaches. At this point, the coaches are all fun and games. They ask if I had a good flight, they ask about my parents, and even call me by name. They seem sincerely excited to see me. I think to myself, "This is great — they're such nice guys." Then it happens.

Here I am at my new home, Notre Dame. A small-town kid from Collierville, Tennessee making his way in the world. A football player, playing at the mecca of college football. I am a great football player; coaches all over the country wanted me to attend their university. Sure, nothing will be handed to me, but I have what it takes to succeed. I am hardworking, dedicated, and tough. I am on top of the world, and nothing will bring me down. These are a few of the confident thoughts brimming within my mind as I walk into my first team meeting as a Notre Dame Football player. I quickly learn my place on the team, with the wake-up call and side of humble-pie that are two-a-days.

Our first team meeting! Excitement is in the air. All the freshmen are joking around, laughing, and looking forward to the start of their new lives. Coach Bob Davie welcomes us to the University of Notre Dame with a smirk and a smile, then everything changes. A fast-approaching storm is barreling directly at me, ominously darkening the once clear skies, and opening my eyes with a thundering howl within the walls of this meeting room.

The Coach Davie I know fades from the fold and a stranger emerges in the blink of an eye, The once charismatic and soothing cadence of his voice transforms to that of an intimidatingly intense and scary creature. The trustworthy, friendly feeling he exudes evaporates; being replaced by more of a "you better not cross me" threat-like energy.

Our coaches go from warm and fuzzy to cold and callous. Never daring to utter the words "good job." Never calling me by name, and rarely yelling the correct jersey number at me. Instead, they will soon opt to grunt loudly and point their finger in my general direction to communicate. The "hey how are you" is replaced by a "do you know your shit [the basics and the playbook] yet?" The nice, father-like figures who recruited me — once full of smiles and cheer — over-night turn into angry grumpy old men who will become extremely angry at the tiniest of slipups.

Funny how all the coaches seem to display these new characteristics once there is no need to convince me to attend their university. During the recruiting process, these same coaches love you ... and show it. They would do anything for you — call just to chat, hangout with you, visit with you and your family, pick you up at the airport, and show you an enjoyable time during every encounter. The veil of niceties is lifted. The coaches, seemingly, forget who I am, forget my name, and forget why they wanted me to sign with ND in the first place.

Why should they care about me? Few freshmen step foot onto the field for meaningful minutes at this time in college football. Plus, I'm coming off a major surgery that almost guarantees I will not play during my first year. Their job isn't to be your friend or hold your hand. Now, they are your coaches. Meaning you respect them, and they will show you how to play football, bottom line.

Two huge changes already — my perception of the coaches and a promise broken. Going back on his word, the promise of number 11, I am assigned jersey number 82. Come to find out, freshman running back Marcus Wilson is promised jersey number one, then handed number 11 ... at least I am not alone in the shell game of deceit that is recruiting. With promises already broken on day one we have quickly learned coaches will say almost anything to get a recruit's commitment.

So, it is just us freshmen for two days. We are all alone with this unrecognizable coaching staff of grunting creatures. The idea is to give us extra time to learn as a group before the upperclassmen report for camp. In these two days we need to learn the playbook, how to practice the "right way," and the foundation of how to play football the Notre Dame way.

Remember, at this time there is no early enrollment to jumpstart a college career, so the coaches get the freshmen on campus at the earliest possible date in the fall. If we don't have the basics down before the upperclassmen arrive, then we will slow everything down at practice and in meetings. No one wants to waste time teaching freshmen on the fly when the "big dogs" are on the field preparing for the season.

**REPORTING SCHEDULE**
**PRACTICE & INSERTION 2001**

August 12, 2001

| SUNDAY August 12 | MONDAY August 13 | TUESDAY August 14 | WEDNESDAY August 15 | THURSDAY August 16 | FRIDAY August 17 | SATURDAY August 18 |
|---|---|---|---|---|---|---|
| Doll/DeFelippo | Addazio/Moynihan | Phillips/DeFelippo | Rogers/Moynihan | Mattison/DeFilippo | Robinson/Moynihan | Lockwood/DeFilippo |
| **Frosh Report**<br><br>1:00-4:00 - Report JACC - Meet Manager<br><br>Head Shots Coat/Tie<br><br>5:00 - Dinner<br><br>6:00 - (Frosh meet) at O'Neill<br><br>6:15 - Compliance meeting<br><br>7:30 - (Physicals and Equipment) at Joyce Center<br><br>11:00 - Curfew | Frosh Practice (Day 1)<br><br>6:30 - Wake up 7:00-(Cont. B'fast) at SDH<br><br>8:00-9:00-(Meet) **Off/Def**<br>9:05-9:30 (Meet) **Special Teams**<br>9:45 - Pre-practice<br>9:50-10:00-Stretch 18 Periods<br>**10:00-11:30- Prac.**<br>11:30-11:40 - Spec.<br><br>12:30 -Lunch (SDH)<br><br>3:00-4:00 - (Meet) **Off/Def**<br>4:15 - Pre-practice<br>4:20-4:30-Stretch 18 Periods<br>**4:30-6:00 - Prac.#2**<br>6:00-6:10 - Spec.<br><br>**7:15 - (BB-Q) Coach Davie's**<br><br>11:00 - Curfew | Frosh practice (Day 2)<br><br>6:30 - Wake up 7:00-(Cont. B'fast) at SDH<br><br>8:00-8:30 -(Meet) **Spec.**<br>8:30-9:30-(Meet) **Off/Def**<br>9:45 - Pre-practice<br>9:50-10:00-Stretch 18 Periods<br>**10:00-11:30 - Prac.**<br>11:30-11:40 - Spec.<br>12:15 -Lunch (SDH)<br>**VARSITY REPORTS**<br>**1-4 P.M.**<br>2:00-3:00 - (Meet) **Off/Def-Frosh**<br>3:15 - Pre-practice<br>3:20-3:30-Stretch 18 Periods<br>**3:30-5:00 -Practice**<br>6:00 - Team dinner (SDH)<br>**6:45-Team meeting at O'Neill**<br>7:00 - Compliance<br>7:45 - Physicals Varsity-Joyce<br>11:00 - Curfew | 6:45 - Wake up 7:15-Welcome Mass<br><br>7:45 - Breakfast<br><br>8:30-Frosh Meeting<br><br>9:00-(Varsity Meet) at O'Neill<br><br>11:30-Lunch (SDH)<br><br>1:30 - Media Day (Head Shots)<br>3:00-4:00 - Fan appreciation<br><br>5:30-Dinner (SDH)<br><br>6:00 - Leadership committee meeting at O'Neill<br><br>6:30-(Admin Meet) at O'Neill<br><br>**8:00-11:00 - (Meet) at O'Neill**<br><br>11:00 - Curfew | 6:30 - Wake up 7:00 -(Cont. B'fast) at SDH<br><br>7:45-8:30-(Meet) **Off/Def**<br>8:45 - Pre-practice<br>8:50-9:00 - Stretch<br>**9:00-11:00-Practice** 24 Periods-Shorts<br><br>11:45- Lunch (SDH)<br><br>**3:15-4:15 - (Meet) Off/Def**<br>4:30 - Pre-practice<br>4:35-4:45 - Stretch<br>**4:45-6:25 - Practice** 20 Periods-Shorts<br><br>7:00 - Dinner (SDH)<br><br>**8:00-9:30 - (Meet) Off/Def**<br><br>9:30 - Snacks<br><br>11:00 - Curfew | 6:30 - Wake up 7:00 -(Cont. B'fast) at SDH<br><br>7:45-8:30 -Spec. teams meet<br>8:45 - Pre-practice<br>8:50-9:00 - Stretch<br>**9:00-11:00- Practice** 24 Periods-Shell<br><br>11:45 - Lunch (SDH)<br><br>**3:15-4:15 -(Meet) Off/Def**<br>4:30 - Pre-practice<br>4:35 - Stretch<br>**4:45-6:25 - Practice** 20 Periods-Shell<br><br>7:00 - Dinner (SDH)<br><br>**8:00-9:30 - (Meet) Off/Def**<br><br>9:30 - Snacks<br><br>11:00 - Curfew | 6:30 - Wake up 7:00 -(Cont. B'fast) at O'Neill<br><br>7:45-8:30 -Spec. teams meet<br>8:45 - Pre-practice<br>8:50-9:00 - Stretch<br>**9:00-11:00-Practice** 24 Periods-Shell<br><br>11:45-Lunch (SDH)<br><br>**3:15-4:15-(Meet)**<br>**Off/Def**<br>4:30 - Pre-practice<br>4:35 - Stretch<br>**4:45-6:25- Practice** 20 Periods-Shell<br><br>7:00 - Dinner (SDH)<br><br>**8:00-9:00- (Meet)**<br>**Off/Def**<br>9:30 - Snacks<br><br>11:00 - Curfew |

ised 8-01-01 #3

We have offensive and defensive position meetings geared toward teaching us the playbook and review practice film. Hours and hours of studying are required. I have never been more lost in my life than I am during these first couple of meetings. The playbook is four inches thick, with hundreds and hundreds of plays to learn in a short amount of time.

There is no way I, or anyone, can learn it all before the upperclassmen arrive within days ... staying vigilant, I do my best.

Freshman camp also allows the class to bond with one another, without the pressures that come with the upperclassmen being around. I have already met many of the freshmen during previous visits to campus, but I really do not know much about them. During this mid-week freshmen football orientation, "Foundations of Success," we are given a short quiz to help us learn something about each of the twenty-two classmates. Think *Jeopardy* or questions on a dating app.

This is the question about me in the *"Irish Football Class of 2005: Who's Who*: 'When this Tennessee-special-teams-terror is not inventing new ways of getting the ball in the end zone, you'll find him stealing bases on the diamond.'" Not bad.

The 2005 class has players from all over the country, as it is with every ND football class: California, Illinois, Indiana, New York, Minnesota, Tennessee, Florida, Wisconsin, Massachusetts, New Jersey, Washington, Georgia, Virginia, and Alabama. The bonds formed during these weeks, and this season, will be crucial in helping each of us deal with the struggles to come during our time at Notre Dame. Where you are from, how you were raised, your ethnicity, your religion, etc. do not matter to us. We are family, and we will overcome any adversities thrown our way, if only we trust and support one another.

Adversity number one, waking up. For the next two weeks, the days will begin the exact same way ... panicked frenzy. At daybreak — throughout the entirety of camp — we awaken to the harmonic sounds of an eardrum-rearranging air horn shrieking through the hallways and banging at our doors, with the accompaniment of smooth screams, "Get up, get up, get up," and "Let's go!" I fight to not fall from my dreams, to remain just a little bit longer, until I can cling to imagination no more; rolling out of bed, I wipe the sand from my eyes, toss on some clothes and a pair of shoes, hustle to the cafeteria for a quick breakfast, and sprint to our first meeting of the day.

After our morning ritual — wake up, inhale food, struggle to stay awake at meetings — it's time to hit the yard. During these two days of learning and training we practice without football pads. Instead, we wear thin foam shoulder pads. These pads provide little protection and are meant for small accidental run-ins during practice. When I say little protection, I mean no protection. The foam pads will not protect you from a collision with a 250-pound linebacker barreling down at you full speed, trying to crush the life out of you.

Switching to these foam pads simply keeps the extra weight of football pads off you, helping to keep our legs fresher in the long-run, and lets you know this is a practice where we are *not* hitting or tackling. The coaches need the freshman class healthy and full of energy when the upperclassmen arrive. If I were wearing football pads at the start of camp, ones that actually protect a player, the ensuing story wouldn't have occurred in such dramatic fashion.

College football has already greeted me with a difficult summer work-out, rude awakenings at our first freshman team meeting, and the wrong jersey number. Once we put the "pads" on, I find that I am one of two wide receivers, so there are no snaps off and very few moments to breathe during practice. Yet still, there is another surprise in store — another greeting.

At our first freshmen-only practice, coaches tell us there will be no contact whatsoever, no tackling allowed as we learn how to practice the "right way." Learn how to form a huddle, break from a huddle, line up in the correct positions, move together on the snap of the ball, get from drill to drill quickly, and, honestly, learn just how inadequate we are as football players. We are attempting to transfer knowledge from the meeting room and playbook to the field. Much of our learning today is "on the fly." Everything is moving so fast. My head is spinning with information overload. I am not the only one — running backs are running the wrong way on plays, linemen are pulling in the wrong direction, defensive backs are in the wrong coverages, and linebackers are HITTING.

Again, we are wearing these foam shoulder pads, and the defense is told *not* to hit. I'm expecting everyone to listen to the coaches and that no collisions will occur on this day. This is my expectation. The reality is the opposite. In the heat of the moment our middle linebacker, Brandon Hoyte, is overtaken by his instincts, his training. Practice is faster, more intense, more difficult, and fatigue — mental and physical — is rampant.

Every day of practice, come hell or high water, we have seven-on-seven drills. In this drill there are no offensive or defensive linemen participating, only skill and big-skill players. Our quarterback Pat Dillingham breaks the huddle. I line up in a flank position on the right side of the field, a few steps away from the tight-end, and wait for the snap of the ball.

Hut! A coach tosses Pat the ball, I burst 5 yards toward the defensive back and plant my right foot in the ground to cut left into the middle of the field. Amid my 5-yard under route I avoid the outside linebacker, cutting under him. After crossing the linebacker's face, I lock eyes with the quarterback, as I look for the ball. Pat throws a perfect strike, as the ball inches closer I raise my hands at the last moment to catch the ball in midstride. The instant I catch the ball I turn to look for defenders in the hopes of gaining more yards.

Brandon is also tracking the ball as it leaves Pat's hand, setting him directly in my path. Brandon's instinct kicks into overdrive. He forgets the day's one rule ... *no* contact, *no* hitting. Football now in hand, my eyes and head go from catching the ball to looking for space to move up field. At the same moment, Brandon lowers his center of gravity positioning himself to deliver a monstrous blow. KABOOM!

Releasing his ferocious attack helmet first, hitting me just underneath the chinstrap and squarely in the throat. My feet launch from the ground. Upended as though I am attempting a backflip and midway losing confidence, then slam to the ground head and neck first. The collision is that of a semi-truck steamrolling through a stop sign and crashing into a compact car whose driver is obeying the law. After the "oohs" subside, the practice area goes silent — I'm told.

Floundering about. Clutching my throat. Gasping for air. My eyes swell with tears. Fear is setting in. Training staff and doctors race in my direction to evaluate the situation. Their words are gibberish as panic, once again, takes hold. I struggle desperately to find a single breath. After what feels like forever, the gasping subsides, and a single breath is finally found. Wheezing like an eighty-year-old smoker with each attempt to breathe. Not yet able to swallow or speak, I grunt and give a head nod to let the staff know I am okay.

Seeing as this vicious hit is to the throat, it's decided my second night on campus will be at a nearby clinic for testing and overnight observation. Doctors fear there has been damage to my esophagus, an unknown injury to my neck, or that my esophagus might collapse at any moment.

My body holds strong, no further issues. The next morning, I am at practice like nothing even happened. Welcome to college football! You signed up for this.

# UPPERCLASSMEN MOVE

## 12

AUGUST 14, 2001. THE upperclassmen arrive, driving their cars to the doorstep of O'Neill Hall where the team is staying for two-a-day camp. They move their belongings to the dorm room at a pace not to the liking of our coaches, so coaches are encouraging players to get their butts in gear: "Let's go! We have a lot to do! Let's go! Hurry it up!"

The arrival of the older players disrupts the little comfort I've been able to find since arriving at campus just a couple of days ago. Yet again, I sense an uneasy energy flowing across my body, as I can feel and see a change is coming.

During this evening meeting, our first as a complete team, the pecking order becomes clear with freshmen moving from the first rows to the last rows. The first order of business is for everyone to turn in their car keys. There will be no hopes of escape or temptations to deviate from the team's schedule. The majestic campus is reduced to a single dorm of solitude — think prison-like solitude, not Superman's fortress of solitude.

The inmates are allowed to exercise in the yard a couple of times a day, read in the library when time permits, eat in the cafeteria when directed, but are otherwise confined to their cells. Logistics: directly behind O'Neill

Family Hall (our prison of choice) are the football fields and locker room tents (the yard), the meeting rooms are on the first floor of the dorm (the library), the dining hall is a stone's throw north (the cafeteria), and our rooms (the cells) are located throughout the four-story building. From this moment on, I know the tides have officially changed and thoughts of escape are no more.

Coach Davie speaks to the team. He discusses our camp schedule, the upcoming season, and his expectations, then looks to one of the vets for support. "This is a damn country club, y'all have it easy. Look at these facilities. I mean it's Notre Dame. The best of the best for you." With a chuckle he says, "You have it easy here. Courtney Watson, isn't that right?"

Courtney, sitting in the front row and within swinging distance from the warden's podium, has a different take. "Well, it's pretty hard for me coach." With these words, you can see Coach Davies' blood boil, face turning bright red with anger, and he loses it. Starting with a sarcastic laugh that morphs into yelling-at-the-top-of-his-lungs, he screams, "You gotta be kidding me! Really Courtney?! Really?!" Courtney's answer is clearly not appreciated, but at least it is honest. This meeting is a microcosm of things to come.

After seeing the keys taken from the players and Coach yelling at the slightest provocation, I am fearful to see how the rest of camp will unfold. Later that evening, a few vets begin telling horror stories from years past. Everyone seems to have a tale, which they are eager to share. Are these upperclassmen simply passing along the realities of past two-a-days out of the kindness of their hearts? Are they attempting to strike even more fear into the hearts of the freshmen? Are these stories warnings about what is to come? Two of these stories stuck with me.

First, a player's love of "locks." One year ago, late in the evening after the last team meeting, and just before the call for lights out. A leery freshman hides in his room awaiting a knock at his door, as are all of the freshmen. He sits intensely gazing toward the door. Knowing they will come for him soon — he's heard the rumors about what will happen on this night. There is a rattle on the doorknob and a thud from a shoulder trying to swing the door open. Next, there is a knock at the door and a voice. "Open the door," an upperclassman says. The freshman does not move from his bed. "Hey, open this door, right now," another veteran demands.

Still sitting on his bed, the freshman begins swaying back-and-forth, back-and-forth. He begins chanting, "You ain't gonna get me, you ain't cutting my hair off." Louder and louder, he says these words. Then, he alters his tone: "I will cut you if you try to take my hair!" He tells the upperclassmen he has a knife and isn't going down without a fight. The freshman has lovingly grown his dreadlocks for years, meticulously taking care of them. These "locks" mean a great deal to him, which make him a prime buzzcut-target for the veterans.

This standoff is surprisingly won by the freshman — the upperclassmen want no quarrel with the knife wielding youngster. This story is memorable in its own right, but I mostly remember it because during the middle of his story I have an epiphany — I too am about to have veterans knocking at my door.

Second, the "escapee." Two-years prior, the team is a little over a week into two-a-days. A mammoth of a man standing at 6'9" and weighing 300-pounds decides he is done with camp. He's had enough. He is sick and tired of the difficulty, the abuse accompanying two-a-days. It is time to leave. Time to get out and go home. The lineman walks out the front door, only telling his roommate where he is going.

After walking several blocks, he hails the first cab he finds. He jumps into the cab, leaving the rigors of two-a-days behind him, and heads to the airport. As I hear this story, I am astonished that a player makes such a brazen move after one week of practice but, then again, I am only a few days into this whole thing. Someone, the roommate, rats out the lineman and the coaching staff knows. Prison Break!

As the veteran player tells me his story, I envision two coaches and a manager sprinting out of the dormitory toward an SUV and jumping into the vehicle faster than you can say Fighting Irish. They are racing to the airport in the hopes of thwarting the fugitive's escape. The manager slams on the brakes, fishtailing the SUV into the airport drop-off zone.

All three guys jump out of the vehicle and dash into the airport. As an airport attendee tries to stop them, the manager tosses him the keys and says, "Keep it close. This shouldn't take too long." The keys hit the attendee's chest and crash to the ground; as the fugitive recovery team races by him, he turns and throws his hands in the air, as if to say, "What the hell?" The hounds are hot on the jailbird's scent.

It does not take long to spot the gargantuan. One coach approaches from the front. He tiptoes toward the beast, careful not to make any sudden movements — if startled he may bolt. His arms extend, with palms facing the runaway, indicating he is not a threat as he attempts to calm the player down.

Now face-to-face with the animal, the coach attempts to persuade the player to come back. "You haven't done anything too bad yet. We can overlook this if you come with us now. Everything is okay." This effort is met with an unwavering commitment by the escapee to leave this "hell on earth," and he refuses to go easily. When the manager notices this conversation is not going well, he puts plan-B into motion.

He creeps behind the player, climbs atop an airline agents' desk, leaps into the air, and throws a bag over the freshman's head. Just as the manager does this, the second coach comes sprinting out of nowhere to tackle the player to the ground. The coaches and manager wrestle with the lineman, struggling to get control of the situation. Eventually the prison guards subdue their prize — hogtying the trophy and dragging him out of the airport. Some bystanders point and laugh; others cheer on the courageousness of the captors.

The recovery team exits the airport and looks for the prison transport ... umm SUV. My mind conjures this vision while the senior recalls this tale. Surely the reality of this story was less dramatic, but who knows.

After the upperclassmen's stories, I know that hazing is coming for me, and I can only hope for tolerable trespasses. The first team hazing event leaves me with a brand-new hairdo. Having my head shaved isn't *really* a big deal, but still, it isn't cool! Think about it, school is starting soon, and you want to put your best foot forward. You want to look your best for the ladies, your fellow classmates, and your professors. Instead, I show up for the first day of my college career with a bald head and looking like I haven't had a decent meal in weeks. The night the upperclassmen come to my room, I learn that even close friends — of three days — are willing to throw you to the wolves, just because.

I know upperclassmen are on the hunt, looking for prey; that is me. My roommate, Pat Dillingham, doesn't worry at all. He has his feet up and laughs at the fact I do not want to have my head shaved ... Pat already has a shaved head. So, here I am, locked in my room hoping they will forget about me or not find me. Then, I hear it. A knock on my door. It is another freshman, Dan Stevenson. So, I should be safe right? Dan does his best to convince me he is alone and says he is only at my door so he can hide with me. If the subpar acting chops are not clue enough, Dan must have forgotten dorm room doors have peepholes.

Looking through the peephole, I see three linemen salivating. Can you believe another freshman gives me up? They just shaved his head, so he figures I should have my hair removed too. What a pal! So, after a myriad of "encouraging" words, I open the door. You know, the usual — "We're gonna make your life a living hell ... you can't hide from us, we'll get you ... it'll be worse if you don't let us do this now." Eventually, I give in to these tree-size men. I make a business decision, hoping this will be the end of it. The vets, and Dan, encircle me for the long walk down the prison hallway to the bathroom — think John Coffey in "The Green Mile" — and there goes my hair. Adding insult to injury, they force us to clean up the mess they made.

The second hazing episode is fairly off-key. There is a commotion in the air, as I take a seat in the cafeteria for lunch. A couple bites into my meal I look across the table to my right to strike up a conversation with Chris Yura. Curiously, I see Chris is already looking at me. Puzzled, I tilt my head to the side and furrow my brow. The grin on his face gives pause, I'm slightly frightened.

Bang! He pounds the table with a fist. Bang, Bang! He pounds the table with both fists. Bang, Bang, Bang! The pace accelerates. The entire cafeteria joins his efforts. I think to myself, "Well, this can't be good." He yells, "Shelton!" ... and gives me instructions, as the noise trails off. My cheeks are bright red. I am smiling ear-to-ear, full of embarrassment. I push my chair back, the screech rings throughout the now silent mess hall. My mind goes blank as I climb atop the chair. I stand there for a few moments. "Boo! Come on, we don't have all day," someone shouts. The crowd grows restless, as I think. A light bulb goes off in my mind. I've got it!

Like a tuneless newborn songbird trying to sing and fly — with hand motions and all — at the top of my lungs, I belt out, "I'm a Little Teapot, Short and Stout."

# Dog Training

## 13

**August 16, 2001.** The upperclassmen are in the building! The freshmen mix with the veterans, and we practice as a team for the first time. The tide is changed. The winds are shifting. "I am always worried about the freshmen because they go from having all of the attention to none of the attention," Davie said[2]. It is clear the freshmen are officially forgotten.

My first on-field experience, in the "yard," against a veteran is memorable. One-on-ones, me versus him; in the backfield, Joker tells the QB and me what route to run. I sprint to the line of scrimmage on the 10-yard line, where a cornerback waits. Before we get into position, the CB says, "Timeout. Hey coach! This is what we got?! A small, white dude? Couldn't get *anything* else?" I smile.

We get into position; he is right on top of me, it's press coverage. The ball snaps, I slap his hands away from me, and fly by him on a deep fade route — plucking the ball from the air. Jogging back, he laughs while telling me, "I'm still warming up ... you ain't doing that sh*t again." Next time I'm up, he trades places with the CB who is set to go against me. Talking again, "Lucky ... ain't no way you do that again." I blast by him again, snagging another ball from the air. Jogging back to the huddle, he yells, "Hey coach! He good, he good. Fast as hell!"

Practice dynamic changes after warm-ups and one-on-ones. Just like we relocated from the front of the team meeting room to the back row when the veterans arrived on day one, we do so on the field. We go from taking every single rep during practice to participating sparingly, except on scout team. As I stand behind the other wide receivers, watching the veteran's breeze through drills I find to be so difficult, I have another epiphany. Football players are nothing more than trained dogs. Yeah, trained dogs!

The coaching staff is training us not to think but to simply react. You see a ball in the air, don't think, go get it. React! Never stop chasing until you catch what you are after. A fixation is created for the ball, the player you need to tackle, or whatever your goal is on the field. Football players are taught to go non-stop, 100%, 100 mph at all times until you are told by a whistle to stop what you are doing. Our anthem, played by all the coaches during practice, becomes, "Play until the whistle!" We become obedient pups who are somewhat scared of our masters, the coaches.

To this day, if someone fake throws a ball, I will turn and start running until realizing I have been deceived. We learn to do what we are told or else there will be implications. There are always consequences for your actions: extra running, less playing time, etc. They literally use the phrase, "He's in the doghouse." Coaches instill a fear inside that makes us, forces us, to do what they tell us to do without question, without thought. This type of "Dog Training" is essential for athletes; needing to think on the field will always slow you down, and not playing to the whistle, or through the whistle, will inevitably hurt the team or get someone injured.

The freshmen are demoted from the first team to the scout team. Scout team players play a pivotal role in the preparations of the team. Scout players wear yellow pullover vests to distinguish themselves from the offense or defense they are playing against. Their role is to play opposite the starters and backups (1$^{st}$ team and 2$^{nd}$ team) to provide them with different "looks," offensive plays or defensive coverages, of our upcoming opponent. During the season it is rare to have starters on offensive and defensive compete against one another at practice.

As a proud member of the scout team, I huddle-up opposite the starting offense or defense to hear and see the play we need to execute. The GA, graduate assistant, uses a meticulously detailed play-card to show scout players where to line up and what to do; they tell us the snap count, and strongly, sometimes creatively, "encourage" us to not screw this up. GA's must have spent hours drawing play-cards to make certain the scout teams operate efficiently during practice, so as not to slow the pace of play. The scout team isn't the worst gig in world because it affords me an opportunity to better learn defensive coverages. The downside to scout team is that I am not around my position coach; I do not receive vitally important teachings about our offense or how to become a better wide receiver in real time.

After a few days of practicing with the upperclassmen, I can hardly fathom how I will be able to play football at such an intense high-level for the next four years. I begin second guessing my decision to play college football. Not just at Notre Dame but anywhere. Look, these two-a-days are a real wake-up call for me. I now understand why there was a "fugitive" on the run a few years ago.

I expected college to be similar to high school. Do not get me wrong, I am not a complete idiot, I knew it would be a lot more difficult than high school. In high school we didn't have two-a-days. My high school head coach did not believe in them. He believed you can get all your practice done during one three-hour practice. Sports for high school athletes are fun; they are enjoyable. I viewed practice as extra time to hang out with my friends, not a lifestyle. In college, football truly becomes your life.

College football is my full-time job, and there is no time for a real job that puts money in your pocket. You can't afford to split your attention any more than you already are — football and academics. Fall camp drains you of everything you have inside. Your happiness, energy, excitement, joy, and love of the game. These two weeks of camp turn my life upside down.

As I struggle to adjust to college football life, there is one calming factor to lean on. Conversation. During the few breaks between meeting and practice, if I choose not to sleep immediately, there are conversations to be had. Speaking with veterans and other freshmen, my worries are subdued.

In the veterans I find assurances. This grim time will pass, but many more are to come. College football is not easy, but it is worth the sacrifice. I am told, whether I see it or not, there is light at the end of the tunnel and, when I make it to the light, my future will be brighter than ever.

In speaking with my classmates, I find I am not alone. I am not the only one who misses home, who misses his family, who wonders if I have made the wrong decision, who cannot understand why his coach hates him, or who wants to leave. We are all in so much pain, both physical and emotional. As we talk, reality sets in and 300-pound linemen begin crying as emotions boil over. This new reality, this new lifestyle does not provoke a single tear in my eyes, but it does shrink my confidence to an all-time low and create copious amounts of doubt.

I am comforted by the knowledge I am not alone on this journey. There are others who share my feelings and thoughts. Together the inmates press forward searching for clearer skies, hoping for change and greener pastures. There are many forms of change to come for this 2001 recruiting class, and these first few days are only the beginning.

# Funny, Finds Hope

## 14

During these challenging two-a-day sessions, I struggle to find hope. I do not see any resemblance of a light at the end of the tunnel, though the vets assure me it is there. I am 100% in a bubble. I have little to no contact with the outside world. I am searching everywhere for that hope to help me persist through camp.

I uncover hope in the small things, little things I again take for granted. It's in a two-minute phone call with loved ones that rejuvenates the heart. It's peppered in downtime with new friends, shooting the breeze about anything and commiserating about everything. And there it is, categorically found, the holy grail of hope that resurrects the soul ... laughter.

Looking to teammates for a laugh, anything to jumpstart my motor, I search for moments that will bring a smile to my face: funny stories, jokes, coaches, players, weirdness, or whatever else I can fashion into "light." I need something to help me get through camp, something to help me forget how much pain I'm in, something to help me see through the darkness.

A handful of days into two-a-days, I strike a goldmine of hope. The two "class clowns" on the team. Tight-ends Billy Palmer and Gary Godsey. Billy and Gary create hope with their perfect impersonations of coaches and players, hilarious caricatures they draw on the whiteboard, or by simply making others uncomfortable. They will do whatever is within their power to create levity, to make a person laugh, to take our minds off the "season" we all find ourselves in. If not for these two, creating an outlet at camp and shining light into the dark, the hope of surviving the perpetual agony of camp is fleeting.

Billy missed his calling in life, he should have been a standup comedian or jumped into the entertainment world. There is never a dull moment when he is around. Whether at practice, in the locker room and even during a game, he is always cracking jokes or somehow putting a smile on someone's face who needs it.

The walk from my cell to the yard — I mean, the walk from my dorm room to the locker room tent — somehow grows longer each day. I wonder, "Are the managers moving the tent away from the dorm every night? Why is this walk taking so long?" No matter what is going on, this walk turns into yet another "Green Mile" moment ... only the walk is daily.

With each step toward the tent my legs grow heavier, slowing my pace, as though unconsciously warning me or giving me a chance to turn back and make a run for it. Throughout my career at Notre Dame, this feeling is always present during two-a-days and many practices throughout the regular season.

Every stride to the makeshift locker room is a struggle. A battle of will. My body is driving in one direction and my mind in another — alternating between thoughts of going back to bed or hitting an exit door to bolt for the airport. But there it is ... with each step, the rumbling of laughter surges louder and louder.

As chuckles multiply, the heaviness in my feet subside. Instinctively, I know I am missing whatever Billy and Gary are doing to make camp tolerable. My legs become lighter with each belly laugh heard. My pace quickens in the hope of catching a glimpse of their antics. In that tent, the laughter becomes infectious, especially when the jokesters are on a roll. The effect Billy and Gary have on the entire team is amazing and cannot be understated. They bring joy to a team that is otherwise joyless during this grueling time of the year.

One of, if not the, biggest challenges I face during two-a-days is simply waking up each morning and getting out of bed to do it all over again ... though the air horn helps. I end up tricking myself daily — mind over matter.

Besides clinging to Billy and Gary, this single game is the most fun I have every day. As soon as I wake up (I really hate that stupid air horn) I jump out of bed to find my calendar. Sleep still in my eyes, I stumble around until finding it. Realizing I don't have a pen, I begin another search, pushing papers to the ground and knocking a water bottle on its side. As the water bottle hits the floor ... "Got it!" Pen in hand, a smirk curls my left cheek. I draw a giant "X" through today. My smirk springs into a smile and a feeling of peace rolls over my body with a warm embrace. The day has only just begun, and yet at almost the very same time it is officially over. I am one day closer to the end of fall camp.

A small win, a little bit of joy, and a sprinkle of hope. Then, I count the number of remaining two-a-day sessions, throw on our school uniform (workout clothes), and head to breakfast trying not to surrender to temptations of an airport bound taxi.

# CAMP CLOSING, GET OUT

## 15

FALL CAMP SLOWLY COMES to a close, as students begin to bombard campus. Two-a-days open my eyes to the reality of playing college football at Notre Dame. This is not easy, I am officially at the bottom of the barrel, my place is in the back, I cannot do anything right, the playbook is my best buddy, the coaching staff hates me, and I am generally a useless person. Yep, that pretty much sums it all up.

These 10 days have been an eternity, each day crawled and flew by at the same time. I thought camp would never end. Literally, I thought this hell on earth would last forever. Light at the end of the tunnel? Never saw that — unless you count a doctor's penlight. At least my time at prison is over; I am moving from O'Neill Family Hall into my own dorm. Freedom at last!

The team disperses, but two-a-days do not. We still have a few two-a-day sessions remaining before shifting into game week and regular season practices. As we move, so do practices, meetings, and meals. Practices move from the yard behind O'Neill Hall to the Loftus Sports Center on the east side of campus and its practice fields to the south. Meetings move to Notre Dame Stadium, along with meals for the time being.

**August 22, 2001**. Students are on campus, classes begin soon, and excitement is in the air. Anticipation builds as we inch closer and closer to the start of the football season. As I leave my prison cell on the south side of campus, I am thrilled to set up my new home in the north. It's a new beginning ... again.

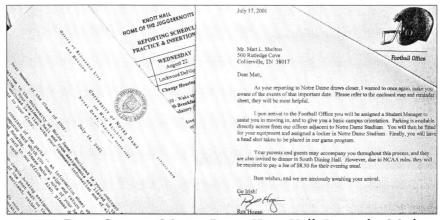

*2001: Dorm Contract, Moving Day to Knott Hall, Reminder Mail.*

On my walk across campus, it's a borderline miracle to see non-football people, real students on campus. The students are all smiles, buzzing about with the bliss of being back on campus or starting their first year at ND. Catching up with old friends or meeting a new roommate for the first time. Full of energy, ready for school to start.

There I am, lugging my life to the other side of campus — how did my baggage get heavier — frowning from ear-to-ear, depleted, and seemingly malnourished, wishing I were one of the happy students just arriving. Where is the VIP treatment that picked me up at the airport less than two weeks ago?

I finally find Knott Hall, home of the "Juggerknotts," and make it to my fourth-floor room — never have I appreciated an elevator more (some ND dorms don't have them). My new roommate is not here yet, so I claim the right side of the room and unpack my bags while eagerly awaiting his arrival. My door is wide open as I move my clothes into the dresser and begin setting up the room; I meet a few neighbors in the process, and they seem nice enough.

Then, with the door wide open, I hear a knock. I find it strange because everyone I have met up to this point just yells "hey" or "what's up," then walks right in without an invitation. I turn to find a slender Asian guy standing at my door with a backpack on his shoulders and luggage in hand. He is polite and timid when asking, "Are you Matt?"

My new roommate, Chong-Bok Lee, is in the building! He is a very unassuming, bright person and, come to find, a great guy. We hit it off the best we can. He is from Seoul, South Korea. We have a bit of a language barrier to work through (Korean and Redneck), and we end up never being on the same schedule. He is up all hours of the night on the phone with his family and friends who are home in South Korea. No matter what issues there may be, we have to deal with each another's quirks for at least the first semester.

Notre Dame does not allow incoming freshmen to choose their roommate. You are randomly paired with another freshman, or three if assigned a quad dorm room. This ensures students interact with new people and not someone they already know, or a teammate. ND wants the campus to be full of vibrant, active, and friendly people, not cliques who do not branch out. It is a straightforward way to encourage new friendships.

No matter how badly you dislike your roommate or desire to live with a friend, you're stuck with whomever you are assigned — at least until the end of first semester. After the first semester, if there is a major issue with your current roommate that cannot be resolved, you can make an appeal to the Residential Life council for a roommate change. Most roommates stick together and changes, if any, are made after freshman year.

You can also change dorms after the first year. Notre Dame doesn't have the Greek system, so there are no fraternities and sororities. Your dorm is considered your fraternity or sorority, consisting of all males or all females. The dorms are run by a university employee, a rector, who lives in the dorm amongst the students and has a rector assistant, an RA, who is a student and the right hand of the rector. Dorms throw dances, compete with one another in sports, and host pep rallies.

The idea is to create a bond, an attachment, to your dorm and the people who live there with you. When "Domers" meet for the first time, one of the first questions is, "Which dorm did you live in?" Whether we lived in the same dorm or opposing dorms a bond is instantly created through memory. The interaction between dorms, stories, the loyalty, the love for their dorm is always with them, along with their love of Notre Dame. Hence, I am a "Juggerknott" for life. I reside within Knott Hall for four years and love every minute. Chong-Bok Lee and I make it through the first year, but switch roommates afterward and lose touch over time.

Soon after wrapping up two-a-days the coaches take the entire team to dinner at a local restaurant. A relaxing bonding experience for the team outside of our normal football environment. I am beyond excited for a night out on the town. I have been cooped up on campus for the last couple of weeks. It's time to get away. It is all you can eat, and it's awesome! The restaurant treats the team like royalty. Patrons gawk as the team gets rowdy, lets loose, and has fun.

I thought we were going to be treated to meals like this all the time; I am wrong yet again, and we never overwhelm a restaurant as a team like this again. It is definitely a great way to cap off a long, difficult two-a-day camp though.

After a grueling, intense two-a-day camp, school starts in the worst way imaginable. Every incoming freshman is required to pass a swim test. If you fail the swimming test you need to take a semester-long class to learn how to swim. *Nobody* wants to do that.

As I stand in line waiting for my opportunity to perform a few different swim strokes in the Olympic size pool, I become less and less enthused about what is coming. My body aches and I'm freaking tired. I step to the pool, toes dangling from the edge, and dive into the pool with positive thoughts, "I got this ... it'll be easy."

I glide through the first three legs of the test, but then it happens ... bolts of lightning strike my legs. Then my arms. My ability to success-fully complete this test comes into question. My kicking becomes erratic, I struggle to continue moving forward. All form is lost as my seamless swimming stroke turns to a barely manageable doggy-paddle. Each breath is accompanied by water. My focused confidence turns to a medium-high panic. Water splashing the end of the pool. I thrash about feverishly search-ing to find the edge before I can keep my head above water no more. With a final push forward, by all four paws, I propel myself far enough to strike paydirt. And cling for dear life.

Two testing personnel rush to my aid, pulling me up from the water, and putting me into a nearby chair. Every muscle in my body contracts, pain erratically fires from head to toe. The cramp of all cramps is in full control. Overworked muscles and dehydration from two compounding weeks of nonstop punishment lead to this heart-racing moment. The testers quickly provide hydration, and fortunately for me understand why I struggled so much at the end.

Contractions wane, I delicately walk to the testers table to collect my passing grade.

# "Spies" & Fans Meet the Animals

## 16

Every day in the afternoon before practice, to get our house in order, we have a team meeting with position meetings to follow. In our position meetings, just as we did during two-a-days, we review the previous day's practice on film. Coach walks through it frame-by-frame critiquing our route running, asking us what we were thinking before and during the play, and yelling at us when we had even the slightest miscue. We also study film on the upcoming opponent. Coach points out their weaknesses, strengths, tendencies, and "tells" to give us every possible edge for gameday.

At this point in my career, these meetings take a lifetime. There is no film of myself to view; I am on the scout team, so my film is being watched in the defensive meeting rooms. I certainly do not need to watch film on the upcoming opponent, I am not playing. I will redshirt this year. When I have free time, which is rare, I watch the defensive film to review my technique and think about the learning points coach told the other guys during our meetings. This is the only way I can see what I'm doing wrong and what I need to improve upon as a player.

Honestly, it is difficult for me and other freshmen to keep our eyes open during meetings. Sleep is a valuable, rare commodity. Most coaches don't call on us at meetings, they don't coach us on our technique — like they do the vets — and we are simply exhausted from, well, absolutely everything. College life, academics, and football have caught up with me.

My mind is overloaded. Brimming with X's and O's and concepts from our dictionary-like playbook; plays tumble in my mind like a lopsided load of laundry stuck to one side in the wash. Perfect timing, let's add academic classes; each day my schedule becomes more unmanageable. Each bit of new information jumbles with the rest. The machine bangs into the wall and pounds the floor with each study lesson. Louder and louder, the machine thumps.

My forehead consistently rests upon the palm of my hands, as headaches are a frequent partner in my new routine. Though academic classes are challenging, the unofficial class of football is the most grueling. I need to somehow find balance between academics, football, and sleep. Classes and football create my schedule. I hope to find sleep after evening practice and dinner — during my "free time." Dammit! Mandatory evening study hall.

My life feels as though it is not my own. Every waking moment is created and accounted for by others. Every freshman football player is put into study hall and the only way out is through. Maintaining good grades is the singular avenue to secure freedom, but not even straight-A's will attain release in this first year. So, we are all stuck for now.

Four nights a week, two-hours each session, for the entire freshman year we must meet with our tutors at study hall. University counselors, who run the program, appoint student tutors to support players in their studies. Each student-athlete has a counselor who oversees all aspects of their academic career. This counselor — who works with a double-digit number of athletes, if not more — helps to create a productive study environment, sources the perfect tutor for specific curriculum, and ensures you are indeed attending all your classes. You are probably asking yourself, "How can one counselor check if you're in every class?" Spies!

We are warned, but "spies" in every class feels more like a scare tactic than an actuality. After one of Mick's 6:00 a.m. workouts I'm dead tired, so I press my luck. I skip class, crawling back into bed. The same day, before practice starts, my position coach calls me into a meeting room. I think, "Finally, we're gonna talk one-on-one about football," but I'm wrong. He scolds me for skipping class. I ask, "How do you know?" He replies, "I know everything. Don't miss another one." Then, after practice and dinner, the counselor calls me into his office to discuss why I missed class. As I walk into his office, I think, "How in the hell does everyone know?!"

I take my seat. He reminds me of how important every class is at ND and missing just one could set you back a week or more. He tells me again that I must work hard and stay focused to keep my grades up. He threatens to schedule daily morning check-ins with me if I make missing class a habit — even saying he will include my position coach. He reminds me if I don't have good grades, I will be ineligible to play on Saturdays. Got it. Message received. I push my chair away from the desk and say, "Thanks. I won't miss another class." Before turning to leave the office, I ask, "So who's the Snitch?" He points to the door with a sneer, "Get out."

From day one of classes until I graduate, student-spies are among us. Lurking in the back or sitting in the front row ... who knows. But they are always present. We never know who these "spies" are. But if we make the decision to sleep in or crawl back into bed after a 6:00 a.m. workout, we may be ratted out — snitches are among us. This is how important grades are at Notre Dame. There are no "free rides" because you are an athlete.

I quickly realize busting my butt inside and outside of the classroom is my only choice. Failing in the classroom can result in failure on the field. As much as I dislike mandatory study hall and the watchful gaze that comes with it, I need this type of structure to conquer the classroom. With the help of an amazing university support system, I learn how to manage my time. This system will not allow me to fail. I got into ND because of my football abilities, but it is success in the classroom that will keep me here.

Walk-throughs every day. Team and position meetings involve so many walk-throughs. After a meeting, or sometimes during, we walk out of the meeting room, take a left, then a U-turn right and head down the tunnel onto the stadium field. We walk through multiple plays to ensure everyone knows their role within each play and what adjustments to make depending on what type of formation the defense shows us.

During the walk from the meeting room to the field we pass the north gate of the stadium. Fans stand at the stadium gates in the hopes of glimpsing the field, the coaches, or the players. I feel like a caged animal. I say to myself, "We need to put up a 'Do Not Feed the Animals' sign." People do one of two things: stare and point but not say a word, or they stare, point, and yell out their favorite player's name. There is no wrong way to be a fan.

This also happens when the team walks from the stadium to the practice field and back. This walk feels a mile long most days. It's as if the spectators are scared to say something to the big bad caged lions, tigers, and bears. Never be afraid to say hello to the athletes. Notre Dame Football players are extremely friendly, and most will go out of their way to show appreciation to the fans — as all athletes, at any level, should. Like anyone else, players have bad days so forgive them if you catch them during a particularly bad one and they are not as friendly as you hope.

Most days, while the animals are in transit to or from practice, autograph hunters and fans alike are waiting in the hopes of obtaining the illusive ND football player autograph. If you have ever attended a game, then you know there is always a crowd of fans waiting outside the north stadium gate after a game and everyone is trying to get an autograph or a picture with their favorite players. Procuring these treasures after the game is not an easy task, due to the other hundred like-minded people.

The fans who are fortunate enough to arrive on campus during the week have much better odds of getting a signature or picture around practice time. Fans and autograph hounds usually look for the big names to fill in their football or Mini Helmet. It is impressively moving to see the love and passion fans have for the team. The team deeply appreciates their loyalty, so the least we can do is sign something or take a picture.

The only time I ever witness a player not sign something is because the autograph hunter wants three or four or five items signed. Players don't have all day to sign autographs for "hounds" who are only looking to make a profit. Most of the time we sign one item for the hunter and kindly say, "That's all for today."

Kids on the other hand, they are a different story. Players take time for the kids. Autographing something for a child brings a smile to every player's face. Seeing a kid smile from ear-to-ear and jumping around in excitement really makes you feel good. It can quickly turn a bad day into a good day. Personally, I will go out of my way to sign memorabilia for kids, and most players do. So, do not be shy. Just say hello and ask if you can have a signature. Odds are you will walk away with a win and a memory.

Players, it's your responsibility to make a kid feel special. That child remembers his or her courage as they approached a big, bad football player. Remember, you have the ability to make a child's day and, possibly, even change their life in a meaningful way. Football player, or not, we all have moments in our lives where we can impact someone's future if we only take the time. So, remember your ability and find your courage to help others.

# COACHING ENTERTAINMENT

## 17

ONCE REGULAR SEASON PRACTICES start, I realize Coach Davie is a pretty entertaining person. I do not notice this during two-a-days, since camp was a whirlwind, but the guy is funny.

Our practice fields are directly below the flight path of airplanes landing at the South Bend Regional Airport. Coach Davie has a fascination with planes. Bob can be yelling at a player, talking to the entire team, or simply sipping a cup of water; when a plane flies over the field, he stops and stares at the plane as it zooms overhead. He watches until it is just out of sight. In an instant the head coach at the University of Notre Dame reverts to a six-year-old kid with dreams of becoming a pilot one day. Small, yes, but it's another one of those "funny, finds hope" moments for me.

The day is rare when you don't see Coach Davie driving a golf cart on campus and at practice. He is practically attached at the hip with his cart. At the beginning of practice, as the team is stretching, Bob drives up shouting, "Are you kidding me, it's a *damn* country club round here!" Hilarious. You are the one in a golf cart. Maybe he means stretching is like a country club? I guess every coach feels this way because they all howl about how easy we have it, as they walk up and down the warm-up lines. Well of course you think it's a country club and it is easy — Bob drives a golf cart, and we do all the running.

The notion of practice being easy must be handed down from coach to coach in envelopes on their desk. Every regime I had at ND voices this same belief; maybe they were all simply fond of mind games. Practice was the opposite of easy.

The best golf cart moments entail Bob's dismounts — oh, they are something to behold. A few times a week we witness a "full send" dismount. It can happen anywhere, anytime, during any drill. Typically, Bob is wrapping up a conversation on the other field and watching the team as we start 7-on-7 drills. A few plays into the drill, Bob hops into his cart to hurry our way. Usually, he races over to yell at a player for screwing something up or to have a "teaching moment" while not leaving the cushy confines of his cart. Kind of fishtailing into conversations. But when he gets out of the cart for a talk, things become hilariously dangerous.

Set, hut! The ball snaps. The quarterback drops back to pass. The wideout sprints to the end zone. Bob speeds from his field to our field. The quarterback steps into the throw and flings the ball toward his wide receiver. The golf cart hits the back line of our end zone. Bob pumps the breaks just enough for him to safely leap out of the moving cart to have a teaching moment with a defender. The unmanned cart continues barreling toward the middle of the field. Out of nowhere a student manager bursts onto the scene. Running full speed and somehow in slow motion at the same time, the manager does his best to reach the cart before someone ... WHAM!

It is too late. The wideout leaps into the air, snags the ball, and the cart records a bone-crushing tackle. He flips over the cart and crashes to the ground. The manager is too late this time — though usually he arrives just in time to leap into the cart, slam the brakes, and ruin the freshly cut grass with a Nike checkmark fishtail of his own. Bob looks back toward the end zone, after making his point to defender, to see the result and yells, "Nice catch. Next play!" And we move to the neighboring field to continue practice while the wideout is attended to by doctors.

I continue searching for "funny, finds hope" moments and good times. On this occasion a "sleight of hand" name game makes a moment. Realistically, I know it is difficult for a coach to know every player's name on a 100-plus-man-roster. But Coach Davie has a real knack for knowing names and faces ... unlike some coaches on his staff.

He knows my name but decides to only call me by the nickname he gives me ... "Opie." Every time we see one another, he says, "How ya doing Opie?" I am not sure if he gives me this nickname because I'm a southern kid from Tennessee or if he thinks I look like Ron Howard's character, Opie Taylor, in "The Andy Griffith Show." Ha! Is this how he sees me ... a redneck skipping rocks on the lake with one hand and a fishing pole in other? Either way, I'm glad to have a nickname.

I am not sure how he does it, but Coach Davie always makes me feel important when he speaks with me. I've become a somewhat insecure freshman, so when the scary head coach takes time, here and there, to see how I am doing — while occasionally using my real name — my spirits are lifted. My confidence rises from the grave. The feeling is momentary, as reality soon becomes stifling once again. Look, anytime a coach is speaking with me and not yelling at me, I am happy.

That said, Bob seems to rarely, if ever, know the names of the walk-ons — a player not on scholarship. He and his staff, in my opinion, treat the walk-ons poorly. It's as if the staff doesn't see them as team members, which is far from the case. In a recent conversation with D.J. Fitzpatrick, he said, "Walk-ons weren't allowed to attend team dinners after a win ... all of their equipment, from t-shirts to girdles, seemed to be secondhand — even though Adidas gave the team free gear ... and when a walk-on was injured

at practice the coaches moved the drill without checking on the player."
There go the equipment managers again ... being stingy with gear. Maybe
this is why I quickly bond with the walk-ons — I too felt unseen.

Every college football team in America would struggle without the
help of walk-ons. These guys have a true passion for the game, and our
walk-ons love the University of Notre Dame. They attend practice every
day, just like the scholarship players, but they do not receive much credit
for their efforts. Walk-ons are an integral part of the team. They are on
every scout team. They allow starters and backups to rest instead of being
on the field as a member of the scout team. They help the team in any way
possible, hoping to earn a scholarship and play in a game.

On occasion the walk-ons enjoy testing Bob's remarkable skill of re-
membering names. Before practice we are sitting in our lockers. Coach
Davie is walking around talking to his players. Creating bonds, building
and reenforcing foundations. A couple of the walk-ons, who have been on
the team for three years, decide to see if Coach Davie really knows who
they are, without the help of a jersey. Does he know their faces?

Every locker has a name tag overhead. The guy's spot Bob making his
way toward them, so they switch lockers. As Bob walks up to say hello, the
guys strike up a conversation. Mid-conversation Bob artfully glances at the
tags and blurts out the wrong names for each player. The guys give each
other the "told you so" look, with a slight head tilt, and smirk that barely
contains their snickers. I know, an extremely innocent interaction, but it
helps underscore the handling of walk-ons versus scholarship athletes. At
least Bob makes the guys laugh, and I get another amusing moment.

# THE TUNNEL

## 18

WITH A FEW WEEKS of college football and academia under my belt, I have learned one thing — I am equally ill-prepared for both.

The intensity of football exposes my thinly-shrouded veil of preparedness. The overwhelming difficulty in the classroom reveals a disconnect of educational readiness from high school. Both highlight my lack of time-management understanding. I find myself again contemplating the future. Did I make the wrong decision in choosing Notre Dame? Can I do this and, if so, how? Am I capable of handling everything being thrown my way? Do I have what it takes to become a Golden Domer?

With the passing of each day, I want to go home more and more. On each phone call with my parents, I ask to come home, and they always say, "Give it one year and we'll talk about it." I yearn for the familiarity and comfort of home. I need to find something to help me through the grind that has become my life. Then, POOF!

There it is. Gameday, with a side of me bursting out of the stadium tunnel. Racing onto the field in front of 80,795 hysterically screaming fans. This experience, this moment is unmatched. This feeling alone will propel me beyond my doubts and push thoughts of leaving from my mind.

**September 22, 2001**. Saturday morning, it is the first home game of the season. The travel squad stayed overnight in Plymouth, Indiana and now board the buses that will bring them to campus. The non-travel squad meets for breakfast on campus in the north dining hall. After scarfing down a meal, the group walks to the Basilica of the Sacred Heart to meet the rest of the team for mass service.

With each step you move forward into an ever-growing roar of eager fans who begin gathering on each side of you. Expectancy builds within your mind. As the "B-team" gets closer to each group along our path — this happens multiple times on this trip, every weekend — the cheers once full of exhilaration slowly fade, their vigorous clapping dwindles, and the crowd scatters with the realization "these aren't the droids you're looking for."

These football enthusiasts mistake your group of non-travel players for the "A-team." The feeling of pride puffing your chest moments before quietly retreats into a somber humiliation, as fans scatter from your path. An unfortunate "walk of shame" the "B-team" encounters before each home game. Over time your embarrassment vanishes once you learn to appreciate the circumstances and find humor in their confusion.

The "B-team" disembarks from their choppy voyage to the Basilica for an abbreviated Mass, just as the "A-team" pulls ashore. To much fanfare, the team exits the buses, merges with the riffraff, and enters the Basilica.

As you step from the light of day through the darkened solemnness of this entrance, your breath is taken away. A sensation that you are peeking into the heavens cascades down the nape of your neck — every hair stands to get a better look — as rainbowed lights, from all directions, twinkle into your eyes. A striking collection of 19th-century French stained glass-windows line the entire neo-gothic-inspired, cross-shaped house of worship — one of the largest collections in the world.

You look up from the scintillating lights to find angels and saints looking back at you ... floating through the starry sky and resting upon the glowing clouds painted above. Hovering and keeping watch, serenading patrons who enter their heavenly realm. An aroma of immaculate old-world refinement, with ambrosial floral and nostalgic notes, nodding to the divine seep into your lungs. This magnificent house of worship brings about feelings of a higher power, humility, and wonder as you take your seat with the team. The first of many moments this day imprints on your mind.

Whether at a home or away game, players are not required to take part in this mass service if, for any reason, they decide against participating. I am not Catholic, so I appreciate Notre Dame does not force Catholicism on their students and welcomes all religions to campus; yes, it is readily available, but it is not forced.

Shortly after the team is blessed by the Priest you are excused. Slipping out the backdoor of the Basilica, with approximately an hour and forty-five-minutes until kickoff, the team gathers waiting for each member to exit the Basilica before beginning the players walk. The team slowly makes its way to the stadium through a sea of a thousand-plus cheering Irish fans escorting you the entire way.

High-fives and handshakes all around. You can't help yourself: wide-eyed with wonderment, smiling with gratification, walking taller than ever. As you near the north gate entrance, you have an out of body experience. You see yourself from above, walking the last 10 yards: surrounded by fans nine rows deep, laughing at something funny a teammate says, waiving to a kid in the crowd, and getting one last high-five before stepping onto the sacred ground of a gameday at Notre Dame Stadium for the very first time.

The atmosphere in the locker room is far different from that of practice days. The lighthearted calm-like feel is now earnest, and laser focused. Moments before the game starts, after all the pregame rituals, you get the call — Mick shouts, "Five minutes!" It is time to introduce the 2001 University of Notre Dame Football team to the world on our home field for the first time this season.

Standing from your locker, you walk to the other end of the room until you find the stairwell leading down and into the stadium. Crossing the threshold — chest-high on your right — you see an old, dented, beaten-up sign that holds memories for every player who has ever made this gameday journey: the top shouts, "GO IRISH GO," the center depicts a Fightin' Irish leprechaun trying to fight one of the two flanking "ND" emblems, and below the mascot a scream, "FIGHTING IRISH." You make a fist with your right hand, hit both ND logos first, then the leprechaun. With your fist still on the mascot, you slash your hand through the furthest logo for good measure.

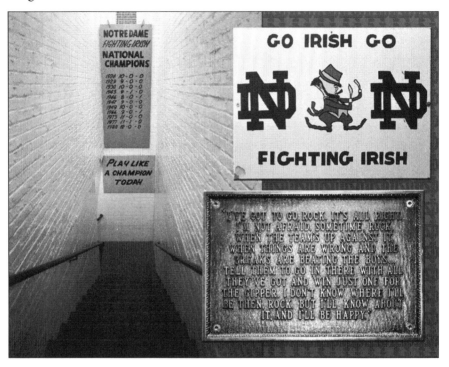

You canter down the stairs to find the iconic "PLAY LIKE A CHAMPION TODAY" sign at the bottom. You do another combination of bumps and a slash, then trot left down the old, rundown white brick hallway and through the final doorway into the tunnel.

You stand at the back of the pack. The team looks like a herd of cattle pushing at the gates, trying to break free into the next field. Coaches struggle to hold them back, attempting to keep the beasts pinned in until the field is ready for grazing.

Cleats patter to-and-fro on the pavement with eagerness. A tenacious roar from the stadium funnels into the tunnel to create a deafening echo that rings your ears. The air fills with an energy unlike anything you have ever brushed against. The smell of musky sweat, pungent mud, and buttery popcorn swirl through the packed stadium underbelly. Your senses are overwhelmed. With each heartbeat you feel the blood coursing through your veins, searching for a way to explode through your skin. A kaleidoscope of butterflies flutter and whirl about your stomach like aircraft caught in the turbulence of a storm. You hear the faint sound of a coach upfront, "Let's go!"

The clattering of cleats, once erratic, transforms into the coordinated beat of an army marching into battle. The cheers, once deafening, vanish. Your once anxious and jittery energy evolves into serenity. Butterflies scatter as you enter the eye of the storm. A stillness engulfs the atmosphere. You soak up every second, as the ticking of time beats slower within each step. A surreal moment. A fleeting moment. As you reach the 10-yard line, this feeling of time dilation dissipates, time normalizes, and you are hit with an acute awareness of how big this moment is. "Holy hell! I'm running out of the tunnel at Notre Dame Stadium ... millions of people are watching on television." Chills spread like wildfire across your body.

It is in this moment you know every pain, every decision, every stumble, every sacrifice you've made to be here, in this exact moment, has been worthwhile. You would do it all over again, if only to have this single moment in your college football career. This experience will eternally be etched into the mind of anyone fortunate enough to don a uniform at the most storied college football program in the country. It becomes a memory that will never be matched nor lose its shine. To this day, whether you are at the stadium or at home or at the bar, when Notre Dame runs out of the tunnel, you get goosebumps.

After a quick prayer in the south end zone, you stand, run to the sideline, and eagerly await kickoff. You continue to internalize the moment, turning in circles trying to see everything, as your excitement mounts. The kickoff return team huddles up just yards away from you; your toes inch onto the field, tiptoeing ever so closely, as you try to be a part of the group. Mickey comes running over, gets nose-to-nose, and yells, "GET BACK!"

You take two baby steps backward. Immediately start jumping into the air repeatedly, releasing your built-up energy, and cheer on the kickoff return team as they take the field. The players rush the home field for the first time this season. Everyone is in position. The referee blows his whistle to start the game. The fans roar louder with each cliffhanging moment of anticipation. As the football is kicked high into the air, fans unleash the most ear-piercing roar to celebrate the first play of 2001 at Notre Dame Stadium.

The game ends in a 10-17 loss to Michigan State. The team is now 0-2, as we opened the season two weeks ago at the University of Nebraska with a 10-27 loss. The season and my career are now officially off to a rocky start.

# SURPRISING COACH

## 19

As the season progresses, I come to the realization my position coach, Joker Phillips, has forgotten my name. At least it feels this way ... he never uses it. He seemingly detests my presence, rarely giving me the time of day. He doesn't take an interest in my life on or off the field.

In the meeting room, when he should be teaching everyone, I am left behind. Maybe he does this because he did not recruit me. Maybe he thinks I will never become a productive college football player. Maybe he believes I don't have the skills to be any good at wide receiver. Maybe he thinks or knows I will not play this year, since I am coming off a serious knee injury. Even if I do not play this year, is that a reason to not help one of your players get better?

With each passing week, I feel less and less a part of the team. I feel like more of a burden to Coach Phillips every day. I ask him questions about football and how to become a better wide receiver fewer and fewer times each day, until I eventually stop asking all together.

My knowledge of our playbook deteriorates. Joker knows not to ask me questions about our playbook, because I am lost and don't have his support. Without his teaching or help to get back on the right path, I am utterly and completely confused.

My practices now consist of reading play-cards and doing what I am told to do on the scout team. I don't really need to know our offensive plays because I will not see the field this year. I am a freshman and I do everything I am told without question. I am a semi-well-trained dog. I know my place on the team ... the bottom of the barrel.

Every day I wish Urban Meyer, the wide receiver coach who recruited me, chose to remain at Notre Dame. He is a great guy who believes I have real potential to be a good football player. After last season, he accepted the head coaching job for the Bowling Green Falcons. I have to say he makes the right career choice.

Bowling Green became a steppingstone to Utah, which became a steppingstone to the University of Florida, where he won a national championship in 2006 and 2008. Urban took a leave of absence, then accepted the head coach position at The Ohio State University in 2012 where he went undefeated in his first season, then won another title in 2014. Now, you can find him every Saturday afternoon, or morning, as an analyst for *Big Noon Kickoff* on Fox. The guy knows football, he recruited me, and during my freshman year I frequently wished that he stayed at ND.

That was my wish, but the veteran wide receivers were glad to see him leave. One of the veterans, Ronnie Rodamer, said, "I learned a ton about how to be a wide receiver from Urban. I ended up at ND because of him and how great of a recruiter he was. But on the field, he was very different ... almost Dr. Jekyll and Mr. Hyde. There are better ways to get things done and motivate players — no need to degrade players or call them names."

In discussing Urban and his coaching style, both in the early 2000's and when interviewing teammates for this book, many words were used by players that I can't write in the book. No matter what the older guys said, in college, I wish Urban stayed. I honestly believe he would have actually coached me, given me the time of day, and helped make me a better player. I know, at the very least, he wouldn't have forgotten I was on the team. Many years later I ran into Coach Meyer ... he still knew my name.

So, Joker is not teaching me much about how to be a college wide receiver, but somebody does take an interest in my growth. An unexpected teacher provides understanding. Shane Walton, a defensive back — a cornerback! Of all people, a sworn enemy of all wide receivers lends a helping hand. Who saw this coming, a CB helping a WR?

Maybe Shane sees some potential in me. Maybe he is simply helping a teammate. Maybe he understands by making me a better wide receiver he will benefit in the long run too. The better I am, the better I can prepare him for the games to come.

Shane is our starting cornerback; he is known for having quick hips and great feet — he's a former ND soccer player, so that tracks — plus a high football IQ. When I line up across from him, before the snap, nine out of 10 times he correctly tells me the route I am about to run. As soon as the huddle breaks, he starts gathering information. As I jog toward him, he notices where my eyes are looking, where I position myself on the field, where we are relative to everyone else on the field, and processes all the "tells" I am showing him simply from my stance at the line of scrimmage. I don't have the slightest notion I am providing him with so much information before the snap of the ball.

In between plays, Shane gives me pointers on how to be a wide receiver from his perspective. Know where you are lining up on the field — your spacing. When you are on the line of scrimmage, do not favor your left or right side — do not give the DB clues as to where you may be going at the snap of the ball. When running your route, do not lean into your break (the "cut") too early — do not show where you are going next. Do not let your eyes fixate on where you need to go — keep them guessing, never give the next move away with your eyes.

Not every lesson can be taught in between plays, so Shane stays after practice to get more detailed. He allows me to see the game from his eyes, which in turn helps me become a better football player. Shane lines up as a receiver and has me line up across from as a cornerback.

First, he shows me what he sees — from breaking the huddle to getting in position on the line of scrimmage. He shows me every "tell" and details better ways to conceal my plans. Second, he runs a route exactly as I do, then runs the route the way it should be run, so I can see the differences; he does this with multiple routes. The time, effort, and knowledge he provides me with in this first season is priceless for my growth as a wideout.

He is the only "coach" who shows interest in helping me become a better receiver. In his looking for better competition at practice, I unexpectedly find an amazing mentor. He gives me much needed confidence, along with a better understanding of the game. Shane cares, he is a class act, and I will always be grateful for his lessons and friendship.

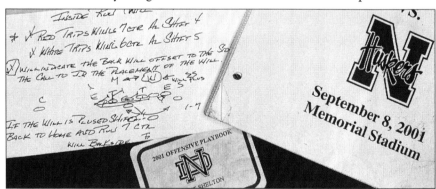

*2001: A Play, A Playbook, & A Gameplan.*

# 9/11 & PURDUE

## 20

**SEPTEMBER 11, 2001.** THE season opened at the University of Nebraska on 9/8/2001, as scheduled. Most of the freshmen traveled to this game in order to experience how the team travels. I did not due to my injury and instead stayed on campus to receive extra rehab.

Upon the team's return we begin preparations for the second game of the season against Purdue. On Tuesday September 11, 2001, the most horrifying act of violence in the history of the United Sates struck our great nation. Every American knows exactly where they were and what they were doing when they heard about the events on this terrible day. We remember, all too well, the feelings of sadness, panic, fright, and an overwhelming anger that grew throughout the day as more details emerged.

I finish my 6:00 a.m. workout, shower at my dorm, and walk to the stadium to ice my knee before class. The televisions in the locker room are on as usual. The TV show is interrupted by breaking news. Terrorist attacks on the World Trade Center and Pentagon. As I hear the news my jaw drops, my face loses all color, my body feels numb as I am overtaken with heartache.

This is another moment in my college career that is forever carved into my mind, but one I wish I had never seen or felt. The NCAA suspended all activities for the day, including practices. This cancellation is the appropriate human course of action allowing thousands of NCAA athletes to call their families, attempt to comprehend what has transpired, and to grieve.

Before I continue with this section, let me pause to recognize I do not know Bob's thinking on this day; nor do I know how he, or the rest of the staff, was affected by these horrific events or why he handled the situation in this way. I can only describe the event as I, and others, witnessed it.

I never doubted Coach Davie's intensity or desire to win. I never doubted his character until now, until today.

Coach Davie calls a team meeting to get everyone on the same page. As I look around at my fellow teammates, it is unmistakably clear each one is profoundly affected by these attacks. Bob starts the meeting by acknowledging the shocking attack, now simply known as "9/11." Bob informs the team of the NCAA's decision to cancel the day's activities. Everyone has been speculating about this already, so it really does not come as a surprise. Leave it to Bob to surprise.

He sees this as an opportunity. Saying, "This is an opportunity for us to get one day better than every other team in America. We're gonna have one more day of practice than Purdue this week."

So, practice it is. With our team meeting concluded, we gather for position meetings and position walk-throughs in the locker room. The air, the attitudes, the feelings are exactly as you imagine them to be in this moment, no descriptive words or adjectives are needed or could even do justice. The team walks to the stadium field, instead of the practice fields on the east side of campus — it's Tuesday, we always go to the practice fields, so afterward I wonder if this change is to conceal the fact we are practicing at all. On the field, we do not wear full pads, and again the energy and the effort of the players are as you imagine.

After practicing, the team gathers and takes a knee at midfield. Ronnie Rodamer earnestly remembers a few of Coach Davie's closing thoughts: "Jason Sapp, stop moping around." ... "Jared Clark, why don't you just transfer son?" ... "Vontez Duff, you're getting worse." While I may not know the coaching staff's mindset on this day, I do know these words are unproductive — given the events that took place a few short hours ago. A player should have been able to sit cross-legged in the middle of the field at this practice and still hear some communication of nicety or empathy on this day.

I don't believe practicing is entirely the wrong decision, but the messaging completely fails. The goal shouldn't have been to get one day better than the rest of college football. On this day, this notion sounds terrible, and it is sickening. A message everyone can support is that practicing today will provide us with a sense of normalcy, it will help take our minds off this tragedy for a small period of time, and it will allow for more understanding of the situation to be released. Hopefully, phone lines will not be busy. Hopefully, the news and our families will know more in a few hours. Hopefully, these hours will allow us to breathe and gather our thoughts. It will allow us to be there for one another, to support one other. This is a message, a plan that any team can comprehend and rally behind.

In the messaging of this situation, I believe many of the players — especially those from the northeast or those with family and friends in the northeast — lost some respect for Coach Davie and his staff. The week two game against Purdue is moved to the end of the season, but we got one day better ... I guess.

**November 30, 2001.** It's the end of the season, and time for our rescheduled game against Purdue. My first game away from ND. We have our standard Friday night team meeting before the game. Well, not standard for me yet. Even at home games I am not with the team after the pep rally on Friday nights, as the travel team (the "A-team") departed for a hotel in Plymouth, Indiana.

There I am at my first Friday night team meeting sitting beside my position coach Joker Phillips, who surprisingly acknowledges me by name. The team discusses the game-plan for tomorrow. I am of course lost since I do not know any of our plays. I know Purdue's playbook better than our own. After reviewing the game-plan, we honor the seniors who will be strapping up their gold helmet for the last time.

The student managers bring in large, framed pictures of each senior and place them on easels at the front of the meeting room. A couple of the seniors stand up to speak to the team. Each shows gratitude for their time at ND and expresses love for their teammates. Many tears are shed. Emotions run high as each senior knows this is his last game as a Notre Dame Football player.

Grant Irons, one of our team captains, wraps up his speech with tears flowing from his eyes. I am hit with chills, and warmth, as I hear his passionate words; I feel his love for this team. Joker nudges my leg, leans over, and whispers, "I'm glad you're here to see this." I am invigorated by the knowledge Coach Phillips may not have shown me too much warmth this year, but he does care about me and ... he knows my name.

**December 1, 2001**. The team ends the 2001 season on a high note with a 24-18 win at Purdue ... though the Purdue student section did everything within their power to distract us during the game. The student section is located directly behind our bench, and they are persistently in our ear until the end.

As we near the end of the game, the students begin throwing hot dogs and drinks at us. Coach Davie sees this, removes his headset, and calmly walks to our benches for a drink. Bob arrives at the water cooler to a barrage of offensive remarks from the enthusiastic students. The uproar catches my ear, so I turn to devote my full attention.

A fan yells, "How's it feel to know you're fired?!" Bob smirks and takes a sip of his drink. As Bob finishes, he lowers the cup from his mouth and a grin emerges. I swear there is a sparkle in his eye when I see the lightbulb brighten his thoughts — he has the perfect comeback. Bob reciprocates pleasantries, "Oh really, and how much money did you make this year?"

Hah! Well, what else can he say? His words need to stay PG, but still cut deep. As I laugh, Bob waves to his new biggest fan, tosses his water cup into the trash, puts on his headset, and returns to coaching.

The 2001 football season comes to a disappointing close, as does my freshman football campaign, with a 5-6 record. Watching my team's demise from the sidelines all season is disheartening; nevertheless, my first college football season is officially in the books. The incredible experiences outweigh the bad, making this undertaking worth every painstaking moment.

| 2001 Schedule | | | |
|---|---|---|---|
| **Overall 5-6** | **PCT 0.455** | **Home 4-2/Away 1-4/Neutral 0-0** | |
| Date | Opponent | Location | Result |
| 9/8/2001 | at Nebraska | Lincoln, NE | L, 10-27 |
| 9/22/2001 | vs. Michigan State | Notre Dame, IN | L, 10-17 |
| 9/29/2001 | at Texas A&M | College Station, TX | L, 3-24 |
| 10/6/2001 | vs. Pittsburgh | Notre Dame, IN | W, 24-7 |
| 10/13/2001 | vs. West Virginia | Notre Dame, IN | W, 34-24 |
| 10/20/2001 | vs. USC | Notre Dame, IN | W, 27-16 |
| 10/27/2001 | at Boston College | Chestnut Hill, MA | L, 17-21 |
| 11/3/2001 | vs. Tennessee | Notre Dame, IN | L, 18-28 |
| 11/17/2001 | vs. Navy | Notre Dame, IN | W, 34-16 |
| 11/24/2001 | at Stanford | Palo Alto, CA | L, 13-17 |
| 12/1/2001 | at Purdue | West Lafayette, IN | W, 24-18 |

# DAVIE'S DEPARTURE

## 21

DECEMBER 2, 2001. FOLLOWING the Purdue game, the team gathers at the stadium for our scheduled postseason meeting. We sit and wait for Coach Davie to address the team. Tension is noticeable in the players' faces. Uneasiness fills the room. Most of us already know the news to come ... Bob has been released from his coaching contract.

WHACK! The door swings open, slams into the wall, and Bob bursts onto the scene; he beelines to the podium. There he stands, visibly upset by the breaking news he is about to share with his team. He informs us he has indeed been let go by the university. "I'm in no way bitter," Coach Davie says. "No way will I have a chip on my shoulder as I leave Notre Dame. I'm not the least bit embarrassed. In fact, I'll walk out of here with my head held high and I'm really proud of what we've done."

The longer he speaks, the more strikingly upset he becomes. His well-thought-out words stray into more of a rant. He pounds the podium, "Joe Tiller, a better coach than me? That's a bullsh*t! You kidding me, firing *me*?"

Coach Tiller was hired by Purdue in 1997, at the same time Bob became head coach at Notre Dame. From 1997 to 2001 Coach Tiller had a winning record of 39-22. Coach Davies' record was similar at 35-25. Who knows why Coach Davie spiraled into a tirade about the Purdue head coach? I venture to guess it was one of the following: Bob coached against Joe in his final game — fresh on his mind, believed himself a better head coach than Tiller — who keeps his job this year, or he was simply enraged about being let go — talking about things can bring out some feelings.

In any case, Bob is entertaining to the end ... "That's a bullsh*t!" Bob's parting words to the team are, "I'm going to watch you next year and I'm gonna tape every one of those games and I want to see you win."

The firing of Coach Davie is not because of one bad season. People have their own opinions as to why Davie was let go by the university. I believe the two most popular out there are correct: the body of work was not satisfactory, and he was not prepared for the head coaching position.

An ESPN article on December 2, 2001, says: "What happened to Davie? He didn't win bowl games (0-3), he didn't beat top-10 teams, he started out 0-3 this season -- and he has the third-worst record (35-25) in the history of Notre Dame Football. There were just too many inconsistencies over Davie's five years." Something needed to change at ND. Football must get back on track. Notre Dame Football is a program that should be constant. Leading the college ranks. The article continued, "Assistant coaches should not be considered at all. To coach at Notre Dame, head-coaching experience is essential."[3]

I really hope this statement proves false in the long run, as current ND head coach Marcus Freeman didn't have head coach experience before accepting his current job — fingers crossed his tenure lasts even longer than Brian Kelly's.

Back to Bob. The bottom line is this: he did not win enough to keep university officials, alumni, and fans happy. As defensive coordinator for Lou Holts, 1994-1996, he witnessed the difficulties that accompanied the head coaching job, but at the time was still unprepared for a job of this magnitude.

The position of Head Coach at the University of Notre Dame is the toughest, most scrutinized job in college football. "Beano" Cook (1931–2012), an American college football historian & television commentator, once said, "The three toughest jobs in the world are: President of the United States, Mayor of New York, and Head Football Coach at Notre Dame."[4] When a team or a university is often described with terms like "storied" and "legendary" and "rich tradition," you had better win if you want to keep your job. This pressure to win has only increased since 2001.

In a 2001 press conference, the president of the university, Father Edward "Monk" Malloy said: "This is a very difficult job, maybe one of the most difficult jobs in the sporting area and yet there's a lot of rewards that go along with it as well. It's a [high-profile] position. It takes a person who knows himself well, who is not [exceptionally] sensitive, who can speak straightforwardly, who is not trying to impress the masses, but simply do a good job."[5] Coaching at such an elite level, you are either loved or hated. There is no in-between, no middle ground. The people who love you are demanding and expect only the best. No matter the cost, no matter the obstacles, and no excuses.

Ultimately, I believe Coach Davie was unsuccessful as ND's head coach for one reason: lack of offense. I am sure there are other reasons, and as an offensive player I may be biased, but Bob seemed like an out-of-touch CEO who did not pay attention to a third of his company, his offense. Billy Palmer, when asked why he thinks Bob was fired, said, "It's risky being a hands-off head coach. You are only as strong as your coordinators. He was hands-on with defense, but not with offense, which is where the team struggled most." Defense was his forte, he was one of the best defensive minds in the country, and he was very hands-on with special teams.

A Chicago Tribune article noted, "Davie, who made his reputation as a defensive coach before assuming the top job at Notre Dame. ..."[6] And this is where his focus remained as a head coach. He was not involved enough in the offense. While focusing on defense, Bob entrusted his offense to his COO (Chief Offense Officer), offensive coordinator Kevin Rogers.

After an 0-3 start to the 2001 season Davie even states, "I need to be involved with the offensive staff a little more," and admitted he "intends to devote more time ... to helping jump-start an offense whose battery [was] close to dead."[7] Bob's shift in focus to the offense was too late to change the tides. In 2001, the offense averages 19.5 points per game (ranks #100 out of 117 teams)[8] and 289.7 yards of total offense per game (ranks #111);[9] whereas the defense allows an average 19.5 points per game (ranks #22) [10] and 304.9 yards per game (ranks #14).[11]

There was no balance to the offense. We were one-dimensional and predictable. During the 2001 season, the team had 750 offensive plays, 532 rushing attempts (71%) and just 218 passing attempts (29%).[12] The 2001 national champion Miami Hurricanes ran 55% of the time and passed on 45% of the time[13] — that is balance.

Within our run-heavy offense, we tended to run our favorite play often, an option to the short side of the field. The short side of the field, the boundary, has the least amount of open space to run toward. The boundary is typically the weak side of the defense, meaning there are fewer defenders on that side of the ball and usually a smaller and quicker defensive end to block. There is logic to running the ball to the boundary, but not in doing so on back-to-back plays or even every other play, as we create a tendency that defenses can use to their advantage. Additionally, when you are a run-focused offense — think Navy — you do not practice throwing the ball as often and therefore there will inevitably be a lack of chemistry between the quarterback and receivers. This lack of chemistry is highlighted by our 52% completion rate (109 completions in 208 attempts).[14]

Also, by balancing the offense with more passing plays, we could have utilized a talented wide receiver like David Givens (one example of many). He had a good career at ND — 72 receptions for 800 yards and three touchdowns — but he could've had a great career if utilized more effectively. Don't get me wrong, David was a great blocker, but he also had great hands the ND fanbase didn't see enough. He was drafted during the seventh round of the 2002 NFL draft by the New England Patriots. During his six-year career in the NFL he had 166 receptions, 2,218 yards and 12 TD's. In 2004, with the Patriots, David had 56 catches for 874 yards with three TD's. In one NFL season he surpassed his career yards and equaled his career TD count at ND ... with 16 fewer catches.

David was given a chance to shine in the NFL and he did. He would've had a much more impactful career in college if Givens had only been given more chances.

**December 3, 2001**. At a press conference Bob says, "I want to do whatever gives this football team the best chance to win next year. If Notre Dame thinks that they can hire someone who can come in here and do a better job of winning games than I can, that's certainly their prerogative to do that. I accept that and wish them well."[15] In his five seasons as head coach at ND Bob Davie had a .583 record. He had three winning seasons during his five years. Yes, he had a winning record, but that is not good enough at Notre Dame.

University officials, alumni, players, and fans alike are not happy with being just an okay football team. The university's athletic director, Kevin White, voiced this sentiment at a press conference: "A year ago at this time, I believed that we had turned the corner under Bob, and that we were prepared to reclaim our traditional standing among the nation's elite college football programs ... Today I can no longer say that. I cannot stand in front of you and tell you we have a program on the verge of competing and hopefully winning a national championship."[16]

It is time to cut ties, time to move on, time to find a new head coach to lead Notre Dame Football. Bob Davie may not have been a fan favorite during his tenure at ND, but his players appreciated and respected him. I know I did. He took a chance on a physically damaged kid from Collierville, Tennessee not knowing if I would ever play football again, let alone be the speedster he recruited. I will always be grateful for the faith and commitment he showed me. A return to glory and a national championship were not in the cards during Bob's time as Notre Dame's head coach, but our university is a better place for him having been here.

I am not one of the fortunate handful of freshmen who took the field during this season. Lingering knee issues from the ACL surgery persisted, and I need a lot of work to become a productive wide receiver. I am lucky enough to make it through the season healthy with zero new injuries, and I add the notch of a college football season to my belt. I learn my place on the team, I fashion myself into college football shape, and know I will be fully prepared to compete for a position on the field next year.

When I signed on the dotted line to attend Notre Dame, I thought Coach Davie and his staff would be by my side for an entire career. Little did I know his firing would become only the beginning of many changes, many up-and-downs, and much uncertainty.

# "By George it's O'Leary"

## 22

Hindsight is 20/20. I guess it is a good thing I did not learn the entire playbook since I now have a completely new offensive system to learn. In addition, now I will have to learn how my new head coach and his assistant coaches operate. Who knows, maybe this time around my position coach will teach me how to be a wide receiver.

I am optimistic for this fresh start, and the new opportunity to improve and play on Saturday. We are coach-less from December 2$^{nd}$ to December 8$^{th}$. During this time players lean on one another, and our strength coaches, for consistency. After Coach Davie is fired, university officials have an open-door policy if we need to discuss the situation. These officials do not provide us with any clues as to who they are seriously vetting for the head coaching position — we are kept in the dark.

Davies' coaching staff, just like the players, are in limbo — not knowing who the head coach will be, or if they will have a job once ND finds a successor. Coaching names being thrown around include Oakland Raiders coach Jon Gruden, Stanford coach Tyrone Willingham, Oregon coach Mike Bellotti, Oklahoma's Bob Stoops and Steve Mariucci of the San Francisco 49ers, to name a few.

After six long days with an uncertain future, we hear the good news. The hire we have been waiting for is made. We know who our new head football coach is going to be, the man who will be here to guide me through my remaining four years of eligibility. Consistency here we come — and it's George O'Leary!

**December 8, 2001**. George O'Leary was named ACC Coach of the Year in 1998 and 2000. He compiled a 52-33 record (.612) in his seven years as head coach. In announcing the appointment, Athletic Director White notes that Coach O'Leary brings:

"An exceptional 22-year coaching career ... a pivotal figure with conference and national championship teams at both the professional and collegiate levels. He knows what championship football requires and how to coach young men to win at the highest level. His teams are exciting on offense, relentless on defense, and skilled on special teams. Just as important to us, George has a genuine passion for Notre Dame and for the qualities that make the university unique beyond athletics-our Catholic character, our high academic standards, our residential student life, and our traditions of community service and student volunteerism. I believe we've found a man who is ideally suited to become a part of Notre Dame, to energize our football program and to lead us, as someone once said, 'onward to victory.'"[17]

Amazing, I love it! Elated, I cannot wait to seize this new opportunity. The campus is buzzing with excitement ... the future of Notre Dame Football is secure, and it is time to meet our new leader.

**December 9, 2001**. On a frigid Sunday afternoon, with your new commander leading the charge, the team marches through the wide hallways of the Joyce Center arena. With each step, the music and cheer intensify. You funnel through double doors to an electrifying welcome from 1,700-plus screaming fans, the timeless sounds of the ND band, and cheerleaders flipping through the air — all waiting to meet the head coach who will marshal in a new era of Notre Dame Football dominance.

You step onto the basketball court. Coach O'Leary veers left to the podium and the team plays musical chairs behind him. As you find a seat in the middle of the back row, you pick up the commemorative t-shirt draped across and shake it open to see what it says. This face-to-face introduction to the ND family is marked by a tagline ... "by George it's O'Leary!" Listening intently to George's declaration, you hear a group of students in front of you and to your right, proclaim, "We love you, George!" O'Leary jokingly replies to the eager fans, "I hope you say that after mid-season." The atmosphere is captivating, and the fans love Coach O'Leary. What a way to welcome the new coach.

After this welcome to the family moment, it is time for our first team meeting with George. During introductions alone there are a few "red flags," for the players paying attention.

Flag number one. Coach asks each of us to stand and introduce ourselves. The seniors in the first-row kick things off. One-by-one, we move down the line, everything is running smoothly ... a player stands, says a handful of words, and sits back down before the next in line does the same. "I'm Jason Halverson, senior, play defensive line, and I'm a walk-o ... " George interjects, "Stop. Stop. Stop. Move to the back. Walk-ons never sit in the front row." Walk-on or not, Jason is one of the most beloved guys in the locker room, and George is off to a rough start at this meeting.

"Red flag" number two is raised in bunches. As introductions continue, I start to see a pattern. Justin Tuck stands up and almost before he starts, Georges belts out, "Stop. I know who you are, just sit down. Next." Justin sits. Darin Mitchell stands. "Stop. I know who you are, just sit down. Next." And Darin sits down. Nearly every player from the southeast is stopped before or midway through their introduction. The start to this meeting is choppy at best, and the team already has issues with the new head coach.

Okay, so there are multiple rough patches. These team meeting moments do not register with me until weeks later, because I am thrilled about having a new coach and just know that the program is back on track. However, there are several dissidents who are seriously considering transferring because George O'Leary is named their new head coach; almost all the players are from the South, which by my count is around 26 players, excluding seniors.

One of these players is ND's all-time sack leader (well, now 2nd all-time after Isaiah Foskey broke the record in 2019), a future All-Pro and Super Bowl Champion, Justin Tuck. George O'Leary recruited him to play football at Georgia Tech and thought George treated him poorly at the end of the recruiting process. Justin said George was a great recruiter — but when Justin told him he would not be attending Georgia Tech, O'Leary went "nuts." In a recent conversation with Tuck, I asked him to clarify, and he said, "It wasn't that he went 'nuts,' it was more that he was extremely sour I didn't choose Georgia Tech. He discounted even offering me a scholarship, and said I was a 'bottom of the barrel' recruit who was lucky to get an offer from Tech."

O'Leary shows no class in the situation with Tuck. Hence, Justin is planning to transfer anywhere in the country just to get away from our new coach. Other players have had similar encounters with O'Leary, and they too are planning to defect. Soon our team will be minus a double-digit number of players.

The decision by these potential defectors is even more understandable after reading an article published by Adrian Wojnarowski on December 12, 2001, entitled, "O'Leary brings some baggage to South Bend." The exposé outlines an incident at Georgia Tech that took place only one-year prior.

The article starts, "His crime was missing a block. ... 'A missed assignment, I forgot what I was supposed to do.'" Dustin Vaitekunas, an offensive lineman, allows the defender to reach his, and George O'Leary's, quarterback during practice. An innocent mistake countless players have made. A player forgot his assignment in a moment, a moment where things happen extremely fast — the snap of the ball. At the end of practice, while running gassers for conditioning, George calls out for the O-lineman. Dustin doesn't hear him, the players yell, "Dustin, go up there, go up there. The coach is asking for you." Dustin, says to someone, "What do I do?" "Just stand there," they said.

Next thing Dustin knows, "Four players started running for Vaitekunas, full speed ... they obliterated him." Dustin said, "Two guys hit me. I mean, you can't get four guys to hit one person at the same time." The colossal 6'7", 315-pound lineman crashes to the ground. "He stayed down for 15 minutes. Doctors rushed to his side. Physical and emotional problems trailed him. His mother considered filing assault charges against O'Leary but let it go. Vaitekunas never returned to the football field. O'Leary stripped his love of the game, his dignity. And no, he will never play football again. He gave back his football scholarship, left Tech."[18] An isolated incident should not define a person, and people make mistakes, but I venture to guess there were other occurrences where O'Leary disregarded players' safety and other norms of good sportsmanship. As they say, "it is what it is."

Back to Notre Dame. While several teammates explore and consider their options, Coach O'Leary schedules individual meetings. These meetings are meant to get his house in order: individually discuss the players' future, assess attitudes, obtain a general understanding on the state of the program, outline expectations (for the team and the player), etc.

I open the conference room door for my conclave with exuberant anticipation. From the moment I step foot into this royal chamber, the tension is palpable. The conditions feel immensely bleak and grim, as I take my seat in the first row of 20. His ivory tower soars above me. Its shadow slinks five rows deep. Brief pleasantries are exchanged. No smiles emanate from the dais upon which his throne is set. With this theatrical backdrop, the newly appointed tsar foreshadows the iron first mentality in which he plans to rule. The spectacle is only missing the effectuality of the "Iron Throne" that was forged by a thousand swords and three fire-breathing dragons encircling the prey seated in the front row. It appears he wants his new players to fear him rather than respect him.

Accompanying this holier-than-thou display is a message of how he will rule — an iron fist approach and a micromanagement style termed "O'Leary time." "O'Leary time," simply put, means if a meeting starts at 2:00 p.m. and you arrive at 2:00 p.m., then you are late. On time, according to our new tyrannical term, "O'Leary time," is five minutes early for all football activities. To this day I do not get it. You mean to tell me we have a meeting scheduled for 2:00 p.m. and if I show up four minutes early, I am late?! How about just shutting the door at 2:00 p.m. and anyone who opens it afterward is late and will be punished, or just schedule the meeting five minutes earlier than you want it to start.

Look, football players know being on time is not optional. If we are late there are always consequences like: early morning lifting or running, staying late after practice to run, or coaches yelling at you and embarrassing you in front of the entire team, etc. Whatever the punishment may be ... we do not want it! It strikes a nerve.

Why the new terminology? Why force such a meaningless scare tactic on your "subjects?" We are not little boys. We are growing young men. Do not complicate an already complicated college life. Trust and respect go a long way. Maybe I am an anomaly at this age because being on time seems like common sense. Punish us for being one-second late, not for being four minutes and fifty-nine-seconds early.

I walk away from this meeting less than enthused about the treatment and rules to come.

**December 13, 2001 – Part One**. George retains three assistants from the Bob Davie coaching staff. They will provide a great foundation from which to build his staff and help ease the transition. Greg Mattison, Bill Sheridan, and Steve Addazio will help with any player personnel questions or issues; plus, they already have good relationships with the players, and can hopefully help retain the recruits committed to ND.

**December 13, 2001 – Part Two**. Justin Tuck and a handful of other players have their transfer papers prepared. Meetings are scheduled with Kevin White. Justin is on his way to his meeting when he hears the news. George O'Leary resigns?! Wait ... WHAT?! Our new leader, our sovereign, who is to reign over us with a heavy hand is dethroned after *only* five days. The era of George O'Leary has met its demise. The team, the entire Notre Dame community, was recently without a head coach for six days, which ends up being one day longer than George was our coach. Coach O'Leary came to ND to make a difference, to rebuild the program, and bring Notre Dame back to glory. Instead, he brings something entirely different to the university:

*"For two decades, O'Leary, 55, formerly the coach at Geor-
gia Tech, exaggerated his accomplishments as a football player
at the University of New Hampshire and falsely claimed to
have earned a master's degree in education from New York
University. Those misstatements followed him on biographical
documents from one coaching position to another until finally
reaching Notre Dame, one of the most coveted and scrutinized
jobs in college football. When Notre Dame officials contacted
O'Leary, he admitted the inaccuracies first about his playing
career, then about the master's degree. Both he and university
officials agreed he should resign, and in a span of 36 hours
O'Leary tumbled from the high point of his career. "Due to a
selfish and thoughtless act many years ago, I have personally
embarrassed Notre Dame, its alumni, and fans," O'Leary said
in a statement to the university Thursday night, which university officials released today. "The integrity and credibility of
Notre Dame is impeccable, and with that in mind, I will resign
my position as head football coach effective Dec. 13, 2001."*[19]

Unfortunately, for all involved, our brand-new head coach is removed
more quickly than he was found. Some may not count George as a head
coach because his tenure was so brief. I get it. He never coached a game at
ND. Still, his time at Notre Dame counts, especially to the players.

Step back, envision his short-lived tenure with my eyes. A head coach is
announced and introduced to the family; if you introduce your girlfriend
of five days to your parents then breakup, is she not an ex-girlfriend?
Assistant coaches are retained; your new girlfriend allows you to keep
your ex's friends around because they are cool. Team meetings are a form
of group counseling; we have counseling together. He meets with every

player individually; there are multiple one-on-one therapy sessions. A pep rally welcomes him to the family; we throw an engagement party with 1,700-plus guests. A press conference is held; the marriage announcement is a national headline. Adidas donates t-shirts for the pep rally embrace; there are wedding gifts. Let's not forget the hope and other wide range of positive emotions snowballing within a struggling program, which are fully internalized once the future of the program is secure.

For better or worse, George O'Leary's name will always be associated with Notre Dame Football. Etched within its history books. A campus, a family, a team (well, most of them) — once flooded with excitement — see their hopes for the future spill from its cup and splash upon our pep rally shirts to become a coffee stain that can never be removed.

Stunned and in disbelief, I wait ... again. For the second time in 11 days, as a member of the most storied athletic program in the history of college sports, I am without a head coach. My first semester is in the books, two head coaches are gone, and a third is around the corner. The past four months have been nothing short of a real-life rollercoaster, with astonishing ups-and-downs and twists-and-turns.

When arriving on campus, I imagined a college career with Coach Davie at the helm and endless possibilities suspended in the future waiting to be discovered. Though my leader is changing, my hope for a bright future remains.

I have learned a lot in my brief time here and now fully comprehend there is so much more that goes into what people see on an idyllic college football Saturday afternoon ... I have so much more to learn. But for now, I wait, we wait, for our third head coach in 2001.

# PART THREE

## THE WAYS OF WILLINGHAM

# A Return to Glory

## 23

Mind swirling, lost and leaderless again. Two head coaches in the rearview mirror, with another in our sights. I've only been at the university for *four* months! In the immortal words of Bob Davie, "You kidding me? That's a bullsh*t!"

Bob's words describe my thoughts perfectly. Notre Dame stands for leadership, excellence, and football. ND is the best of the best. Yet, at this very moment, the football team is without a boss for the second time after an underwhelming season and a disastrous succession plan. I guess you can say there is only one direction to go from here ... up.

In a recent interview with Coach Bill Reagan, former Head Football Administrator at Notre Dame, we discussed O'Leary's exit, "The announcement was made ... that day all the coaches were instructed to not talk with anyone. Bernard Muir [the associate athletic director] called a team meeting with the players and told everyone to 'Sit tight.' Not a chance; later that evening I drove to Kevin White's house ... his wife answers the door saying, 'They're in the basement.' I walked down and find five athletic department executives huddled together with stacks of papers everywhere ... scrambling to sort through the situations and secure the future [of Notre

Dame Football]. That's when Rex Hogan and I were put in charge of everything recruiting and told to keep the class together."

Time is of the essence. The university needs to recover from its misstep in a timely fashion but can ill-afford another setback. Current players sit waiting — idle hands and whatnot — and high school recruits watch as they assess and reassess their options (I don't think Bill and Rex lose a recruit). We need to find a head coach who will force the football world to forget about the recent fiasco. Let's get it right this time.

**December 31, 2001.** Eighteen days after the era of O'Leary and 29 days after ditching Davie, the university finally ends its search for a new head coach.

It's the holiday season, presents have been under the tree since December 2, 2001. So many shiny goodies, full of history and hope, it's difficult to choose the best one. Mom and Dad gave us permission to open one gift before Christmas. We picked up each one, giving them a good shake before deciding on a singularly spectacular gift to unwrap. We pulled the bow and ripped off the wrapping paper. Before all the paper could hit the ground, our parents leapt from their seats, raced to us, yanked the gift from our hands, and told us it was the wrong model, then took it back to the store. Unfortunate, but these things happen. Mom and Dad get things wrong like everyone else. Equally tragic for the kids and a little out of the ordinary, Christmas comes late this year.

There are still various collectables under the tree — though some have said no, and others cannot compete. There remains one shiny gift under the billowy branches, surrounded by other polished presents, with wrapping paper debris sitting atop. This one reemerges from the rest. But the children hesitate ... we have been here before. Will Mom and Dad let us keep this one?

The kids cautiously approach and slowly crouch for a closer look. They pick it up, raise it to their ear, and give it a good shake. This is the one! They rip at the edges. With each tear of the wrapping paper more layers are revealed ... hope, loyalty, intelligence, confidence, strength, and integrity pierce through to the forefront. A sparkle in the collective eye of the Notre Dame family is seen as "WE" proclaim to the world Notre Dame has once again found hope of a promising football future in the form of a new head coach. We are back — and Tyrone Willingham is the gift!

His task is great. His resolve will need to be greater. His toughness and determination will be tested by everyone, both inside and outside of Notre Dame. The board of trustees, the students, the faculty, the players, the fans, the alumni, the competition, and the "talking heads" that are the media world. But who cares what they think? Guess what? We have a head coach! Just to be safe though, I will hold my breath until day six to ensure he lasts longer than O'Leary. It may have taken a little extra time to spot our gift under the tree, but from what people are saying about Coach Willingham, the wait is well worth our time and frustration.

**January 1, 2002.** Tyrone Willingham is officially introduced to the world by university President, Father Malloy, and Athletic Director, Kevin White. Father Malloy speaks very highly of Tyrone, saying:

> *"I felt a great rapport and a great sense of confidence. I really believe, despite all the speculation, much of which was idle and uninformed, this process has resulted in the selection of an outstanding coach for Notre Dame, who knows that we have a high bar of excellence here, that he recognizes what it means to work within an outstanding academic institution, for a meaningful education is our first priority, that he's comfortable and excited about working in a religiously affiliated school, where we use*

*God language regularly and meaningfully and in which
we expect that one of the things that will happen to the young
people entrusted to our care, is that they will grow in the life
of faith as well. "[20]*

Athletic Director Kevin White says:

*"To the people at the NCAA he's a man of impeccable in-
tegrity, to the recruiting gurus, he's among the very best in
attracting talent even while maintaining the highest SAT
scores in the nation. He's a disciplinarian whose players
love him. He's left one of the great universities and one
of the great athletic programs in this country to be part of
Notre Dame ... We have spoken to a great many people
about this man - people including the Commissioner of the
Southeastern Conference Roy Kramer, the general manager
of the Chicago Bears, Jerry Angelo, the general manager of
the Cleveland Browns, Carmen Policy, Baltimore Raven
head coach Brian Billick and former Stanford and San
Francisco 49ers' head coach Bill Walsh. Every one of them
regards Tyrone as one of the very top coaches in the game
today at the college or pro level. And they regard the job he's
done at Stanford as simply amazing. "[21]*

Clearly, there are many well-respected people who believe in Tyrone Willingham, the coach and the person. Though ultimately Coach
Willingham is not chosen by the university first, it is said he had risen
to the top of their list prior to hiring George O'Leary.

I heard whispers ND planned to hire Tyrone after his interview but decided to entertain one more contender — George. At this interview, I heard O'Leary dazzled with his strong fiery Irish background and a solid plan to succeed at ND. Our officials got caught up in the lure of O'Leary and forgot how much they liked Willingham. Naturally, after O'Leary's exit, the board sought the man who they originally fell in love with and decided to offer him the job of a lifetime. If this were the case, why did it take 19 days to hire him?

I asked Coach Reagan, "The delay may have been more about convincing Tyrone to come onboard ... because ND passed on him after the first rounds of interviews, but you'd have to ask Kevin [White]." I'm sure this was a factor — how could it not be — but my guess is that the search committee, and board, wanted to guarantee the process was more exhaustive this time around ... another error cannot be afforded.

Tyrone Willingham signs a six-year contract to become the 28th head football coach at the university and Notre Dame's first African American head coach in any sport. Rev. Jesse Jackson, who previously urged Notre Dame to consider Black candidates, stated, "It's a victory for fairness and equal opportunity to succeed or fail, to even the field for athletes, you have to be willing to even the field for coaches." Floyd Keith, executive director of the Black Coaches Association, said, "This opens up a lot of doors for a lot of people. We have minority candidates out there that just haven't been considered before. There are other Tyrone Willingham's out there."[22]

This hire is already viewed as a success by many, and on multiple levels. Now Tyrone needs to succeed on the football field, while ensuring academic triumph for the team off the field.

His standards are high, he knows how to win, he has an air of confidence about him. He *is* the man for the job. The team, and fans, need confidence after a rough couple of years for ND Football. Along with a

44-36-1 career record as the head coach at Stanford, he brings a track record of success at an institute with extremely high academic standards, similar to Notre Dame. "For the last seven years, Tyrone has led the program with the highest academic profile of all of major football, and over that time he's won two conference coach of the year awards and taken his teams to four bowl games,"[23] says Kevin White. The university is confident that his leadership, passion, coaching-style, and work ethic will transfer from Stanford to ND — he will bring our football program back to prominence.

Winter break comes to an end and students will be on campus soon. Tyrone needs to hit the ground running. He must make a strong push to solidify the 2002 recruiting class and quickly teach his new football team his football lifestyle philosophy. Coach Willingham brings with him a high-powered West Coast offense which the likes of Notre Dame fans thought may never be on display in Blue and Gold. For as long as fans can remember, to this point, Notre Dame has been an option offense that loves to "pound the rock" and occasionally throw the ball. Tyrone will bring most of his coaching staff from Stanford with him in the hopes their chemistry can quickly right the ship at ND.

Freshman year ... semester number two. Students return from winter break with a renewed sense of self after time at home with loved ones. We return to find campus covered with a fresh powdering of crisp white snow. Nature is rejuvenating itself for the year to come, and Notre Dame is along for the ride. Sunshine escapes from behind the clouds to create a layered, distorted beauty of light and dark only a perfect morning can create. Elongated shadows steal toward oblivion with each uptick of the sun. The foggy remnants of O'Leary and Davie, once hovering throughout the hallowed grounds, gradually begin to burn-off as sunlight rises above the trees. Rays of light melt the snow, shimmer atop the Golden Dome, and dance into every nook-and-cranny of campus, as it fully awakens from its slumber. The beams warm the cheek and provide hope of a bright day ahead. Hope of what the year will bring. And hope, that in Tyrone Willingham, we have found our perfect morning and a return to glory.

Like the rest of the family, I am happy we have our new head coach, but I'm even more thrilled to have a new position coach. Maybe my new position coach will give me the time of day and teach me how to be a college WR. A new beginning is about to start.

A team meeting is called, and we gather in the stadium conference room. We take our seats and wait to hear from our head coach, in-person, for the first time. To athletic director Kevin White's credit, he kicks off this meeting by recognizing mistakes were made during this lengthy head coaching search. Dr. White runs through a litany of credentials for Tyrone Willingham, then he calls Tyrone to the podium.

The entire team stands and starts clapping. I am sitting near the back, jumping, trying to see our new coach over the tall trees standing in front of me. Still not able to see much, I hear someone begin to speak, as clapping subsides: "Tyrone Willingham is excited to be here at Notre Dame ... Tyrone Willingham cannot wait to start coaching this team." As we take our seats, I think to myself, "Wow, this sounds great! This guy's saying all the right things. I can't wait to hear from Coach Willingham."

Several players are looking around in confusion, trying to piece together who is speaking. Didn't Kevin just introduce our coach? I don't see anyone else preparing to take the stage. I thought the guy speaking *is* Coach Willingham. I thought I knew what Tyrone looked like, but maybe the pictures I saw were of an assistant because this guy is talking *about* Tyrone. The speaker continues to tell us what Tyrone Willingham plans to do at Notre Dame ... "Tyrone" this, "Tyrone" that. Man, I am baffled.

Then, it dawns on me as I put two-and-two together — give me a break, it's only my second semester, and I'm on my third head coach. This is Coach Willingham, and he is speaking in third person. Peculiar and new to me, but I will go with it. Once I decipher this is indeed Tyrone, I think his way of speaking is kind of cool. It really grabs your attention with how different it is from the norm. At least at first. After hearing him speak in third person for a while, the novelty is lost, and I want nothing more than to hear him speak in first person. Coach Willingham has a strong, energizing message for his team, but for me the message misses the mark due to his mild-mannered, soft-spoken, and extremely deliberate words.

**January 28, 2002.** Coach Willingham introduces the 2002 coaching staff. Seven assistant coaches joined him from Stanford: Bill Diedrick — offensive coordinator and quarterbacks, Kent Baer — defensive coordinator, Mike Denbrock — offensive line and tight ends, John McDonell — offensive line, Trent Miles — wide receivers, Buzz Preston — running backs, and Phil Zacharias — linebackers and special teams. Greg Mattison, defensive line, is retained from the Davie era, and Trent Walters, secondary coach, comes to ND by way of the Minnesota Vikings.

Accompanying my second semester is the start of my first offseason. I admit, I am a little frightened about what is to come. The uncertainty of a new chapter gnaws at me with persistence. I know the offseason will be tough, although I'm eager to get this show on the road. A new coaching staff affords me a chance to make a second first impression at the university, which would not happen under normal circumstances; I'm determined to make it a great one. I need to learn this new coaching staff, our new playbook, and bust my butt to get this fresh start off on the right foot.

# The Forge, The Blacksmith, & The Internals

## 24

Head strength and conditioning coach, Mickey Marotti, is retained by Tyrone. Mickey is a man who knows how to motivate college kids and strike fear into the hearts of his players. Strength coaches are the backbone, the glue that holds a team together. Their iron-striking mentality forges the resilience and intensity a team must possess to win on this stage.

When strength coaches get their hands on an athlete, they have one job — to make the player better. At least this is what I thought. Come to find out, their real goal is to make you puke. Not to just make you puke once or twice, but every single time you walk into their house of pain. Their job is to drive you past the point of no return by any means necessary. You must get bigger, stronger, faster, and quicker no matter what. Workout sessions during the season were difficult, but I quickly learn they were child's play compared to offseason workouts.

Freshman year I am late once to an offseason morning workout. Mickey crushes my soul so thoroughly that from this point on, when I have an early morning workout, I wake up every hour on the hour, starting at

2:00 a.m., in a panic terrified I am going to be late — you will see why in a moment. Instead of three workouts a week, we start working out four to five times a week. The intensity is ratcheted up, splatters of blood drip from the weights to the floor, players dodge weights being thrown at their heads, and a thirst never quenched are a few noticeable changes seen in the offseason. This is where the magic happens. A team comes together here. They strengthen their bond of brotherhood for the trials and tribulations of football season.

The first thing you need to know about Mickey is he doesn't have an inside voice. Screaming to the skies, yelling, and spitting an inch from your face are his preferred methods of communication. Secondly, his two best friends are pain and suffering, and he relishes every opportunity to introduce and reintroduce them to you. Thirdly, the love of his life is punishment, and he will make sure you get to know her well. If a player isn't living up to Mick's standards, you will hear about it, well everyone will hear about it, and you will feel it dripping from your brow. He will not hesitate to introduce you to his best friends, and he loves to spread the love.

Now that you have a sketch of Mickey ... let's add some paint. As you step into Mick's world, rubbing sleep from your eyes with both hands, the picture blurs into focus. Lines of weights, machines, and benches string across the room. A fragrant concoction of dust and rubber soar from the tiled mats into your mouth with a yawn; your right-hand hurries to cover. Vision still hazy, you spot a shadowy figure moving quickly across the room to what looks like a weight tree, which holds hundreds of pounds. Jab, Jab, Hook, Jab, Jab, Hook ... as if on repeat until the battle is won and his message has been delivered. Mick wins!

The blood drenched tree tells a different story. Clear-eyed, you see him walk toward you. He pulls a paper towel out of his pocket, as if this were a premeditated moment of intimidation. Wrapping his bloodied hand, he stares you down, and ensures his point is received. "Wake up! Get your ass in gear!"

You can pull any former player's name from a hat, and they will detail an equivalent tale — a yawn, a lackluster effort, standing around talking to teammates for too long, etc.; it never took much for Mick to decide it's time to make an example of a defenseless plate tree.

When not in the mood to fight a weight tree, Mickey works with other diabolical tools in his belt of motivation. He sprints to the tree ... here we go again. "Mad Mick" is taking his frustrations out on a poor tree. He arrives at the tree but does not throw a punch — maybe they worked through their issues. The look in his eyes is still crazed, like a mad scientist whose lightbulb of torment has just been switched to the on position and his idea is ready to be released onto an unsuspecting world. With a menacing smile of bliss, he rips a 5-pound free-weight from the tree, turns, and throws it at your face. You jump out of the way, narrowly escaping impact as the weight hits the ground. Mickey screams "pick it up!" You bend down to pick up the weight and hear, "Not the weight, your ass! Get it in gear!"

Being part of these intense, off-the-wall, motivational-techniques, I am acutely aware of the situation I find myself in; results come with a no holds barred policy and are expected no matter how we get there. Never have I been so fearful of, or concerned by, another person in my 20 years of life on Earth.

The reality, as I came to know it, is that Mick has an unrelenting passion for getting the best out of his athletes. He will do anything humanly possible to make his players better, to help them reach their full strength and conditioning potential. Whatever it takes — screaming and spitting in your face, making himself bleed just so you know how important this is, or throwing weights at your face — Mick will see his players evolve into the athletes he knows they can become.

Once you elect to stand up to Mick, show him some backbone — when he sees you outgrow the tools holstered across his motivational belt — Mick knows his tactics are working and slows down his antics. Your newfound confidence and spirit will help you overcome all challenges along your journey. Even so, stay vigilant, Mickey still has a job to do ... while in his weight room you are never completely safe from his reign of terror. From day one to the end of your time with Mick, this Mater Torture Technician will be the bane of your existence, well, at least when traversing within his domain.

Torture technique number one ... weigh-ins, with a hint of water-boarding and overhydration. As soon as you step foot into Mickey's Manor, you walk to the scale to see if you are on track with your weight gain or loss goals. Some players walk confidently, some not so much, and some look hungover. You are almost always in the "not so much" category when it comes to the scale. The goal is to reach and maintain 175-pounds. You arrived on campus at 170-pounds, playing between 165-pounds and 175-pounds throughout your career.

As you step onto the scale, your shoulders somewhat slumped, you know ... you know because you are *always* underweight. With clip-board in hand, peering over your shoulder, Mick yells like a drunken upperclassman applying pressure at a house-party, "DRINK!" Side-stepping to the left, bending at the waist, you drink from the water cooler. After multiple giant chugs, you sidestep right back onto the scale, and again hear, "DRINK!" This back-and-forth process of "making weight" can take one minute or thirty minutes, depending on how much water you need to drink to "make weight."

On a normal day you drink 3-pounds of water and on occasion 5 to 6 pounds. After "making weight," and without fail, it's time to warm up for our workout session. And what is the perfect warm-up? Jump rope. When you jump up-and-down your stomach is usually in perfect unison. But these extra pounds of fresh, unsettled weight have a mind of their own.

Imagine having 6-pounds of liquid in your stomach right now ... the thought alone is aggressive. From the scale, you waddle to the warm-up area on your right and groaningly bend over to pick up a jump rope. Barely containing your new weight within its temporary residency. With a handle in each hand, you swing the rope over your head, accompanied by a half-hearted leap — no big deal ... yet. Your stomach and body begin this venture in tandem — one goes up and so does the other — until you reach the summit. Here we go!

With a gurgle in the back of your throat, your body seemingly detaches itself from your stomach to make its decent ... traveling downward, as your stomach continues to rise — roller coaster feelings hit while doing bunny hops. Your body makes landfall, as your toes touch down, while your stomach peaks and screams back to earth attempting to catch up. The transition bubbles a pocket of air to the surface for a loud, risky release. Nausea sets upon your face, paling with uneasiness; your workout partner takes a few steps away from the drop zone.

Your body launches back into the stratosphere, your stomach passes by like a ship in the night and bends past its bottom like a 300-pound person in a bouncy house — nearly breaking through. Two jumps completed. You drop the rope and sprint to the nearest garbage can. False alarm. You do this repeatedly until your five-minute jump rope warm-up is finished ... oh, and add about nine bathroom breaks in between.

Torture technique number two ... offseason "Harley" workouts every Friday. Mickey likes to name his workouts: 10-speed Bike, Mountain Bike,

Ducati, and Harley. These names give you an idea of what to expect from the workout — easiest to most difficult. Harley workouts begin like any other workout: a weigh-in and a warm-up. Today is the day you learn these workouts are all about punishing you — umm, pushing — your legs to their limits and beyond.

After surviving the torturous divergence of warming up, and the hasty releases of your newfound weight, you sprint to your first exercise in the back of the weight room. Leg Press.

You throw on a weight that will allow you eight to 10-reps, max. So, heavy, but not too heavy. You catch a whiff of something foul ruminating in the air, as you take your seat. You struggle to fight through your last rep ... 10! You start to get up from your seat. A kindhearted torture assistant throws a hand up at you to say, "Stop. Don't overexert yourself. Let me get this for you." Too kind. You lean back in the chair to watch him remove a plate from each side of the leg press. Psyching yourself up, you pull on the handlebars and sway to-and-fro, then push! Pushing until you fail at eight-reps. Again, allowing you to remain seated, generosity springs from the assistant who removes another plate from each side ... a pattern that continues until there are no weights on the machine. You labor through your last set with five-reps of plateless pushes.

Exhausted. Legs shaking with pain. Face pale and full of color simultaneously. You attempt to stand from the machine and crash backward into the leg press chair. As you sit, you stare through the floor in a lightheaded daze. The gurgle resurfaces to your throat, as the swirling foul stench is inhaled once again. You remember a conveniently placed trash can at the front of the leg press section. You look to your left. Contemplate a visit, and think, "Not today!"

You have never visited this container of waste yourself, but on many occasions have seen brethren make a stop to let it *all* out. Over the years you will see a few miss their target — provoking tinderbox conditions, driving the Torture Technician into a fit of excessive rage. The first exercise machine of the day, for in-shape college athletes, and some are already puking their guts out.

After pulling yourself off the leg press machine, you hustle a few feet to the nearby wall on your right. Wall sits! Wall sits from hell are next on your agenda.

Trying to catch your breath, you lean over and place your sweaty palms on the gold painted wall. Your friendly neighborhood assistant screams, "Let's go!" You push yourself from the wall, half-spin, slam your sweat soaked back against the cement, and slowly take your seat beside four teammates already "sitting" on the wall. Shakily, at the end of the row, you slide downward leaving a slimy trail in your wake — you take a break with hands on knees, stealing time to secure more energy. Ultimately, your knees hit their mark, bent to a ninety-degree angle ... perpendicular to the floor. You swing a 45-pound plate across your lap. The bigger guys to your left have more than 90 pounds each. You settle in for the long-haul, five minutes.

One-minute passes. Two minutes pa ... who are you kidding, you do not make it to two minutes. Your legs are on fire, burning and stinging as they uncontrollably shake. You crash to the ground in agony. Debilitating exhaustion commands you to remain crouched on the gym tile. Your thoughts entangle in argument. ...

Negative Self

We live here now, and ...

Haha! Wait ... what?!

No ... no, that's not true. You funny guy, you. Ha.

Stand up ... please, stand up. You got this! ... Here we go.

Negative Self

Shut up, with your stupid positivity. I'm home. I quit. I'm done. Go away!

Stop it.

You're acting like a child. Everyone's looking.

Who do you want to be? The person who "lives" on the floor? Or the person who RISES ... the person who pushes through the pain and adversity to victory?!

Decide ... I'll wait.

Mick spots your fall through the forest of weight machines. Like a lion chasing an injured buffalo, he charges toward you. Screaming words of "encouragement" for you to get your ass off his floor. He circles you from above. Attacking with pellets of spit that accumulate on top of the weight still wedged between your stomach and thighs. ...

Negative

Ugh! Fine ... you're the worst. Help me up.

Listening to your positive thoughts ... you rise — fear of the Technician's continued wrath does not hurt the cause either. You gather all the strength you can find. As you inch your way up the wall, Mick walks away. Composure gained, you are returned to your post and again aid in the efforts of keeping this *damn* wall from falling. After a couple of these rotations, up and down the wall, the weight room is safe from implosion; the torture assistant informs you that you've hit the five-minute mark ... with a chuckle. ...

Negative Self

Sh*t. ...

As you ready yourself for the next assignment, he yells, "Two more minutes!" Your face and body language tell a story. ...

Negative Self

Son of a B*tch!

F*ck this! I'm outta here. This is dumb ... with this bullsh*t ... ass ... BULLSH*T! Oh, "FIVE minutes," ...now it's SEVEN!

You go scr*w yourself.

Whoa! Wow!

A little aggressive, yeah?

Negative Self

F*CK YOU!

Stay outta this.

This isn't soccer ... you can't just randomly add time at the end!

Fine, fine, fine. I can do this ... AHH! DAMMIT!

Buddy ... figure it out. You're like two exercises in.

Your hopes for a reprieve are dashed. Your squadron reassembles on the wall. You look to you right. ...

Negative Self

> **What the F*CK is Mick doing?!**

He shouts, "Guys! Looks like you need a little help!" ...

Negative Self

> **Nah. We're good Mick! Keep your ass over there!**

As though he is Neo in the "Matrix," he drops his weight, pushes into the floor — ripples ring around him — he flies directly at you "sitting" on the wall. Just before hitting you, he leaps ... similar to a lead singer jumping off stage into the crowd. Laying across your laps, on top of plates weighing hundreds of pounds, Mick "crowd-surfs." The Man, the Myth, the Legend, the Master Torture Technician himself — screaming at the top of his lungs, "You better not f*cking drop me!" With a twinkle in his eye, he smiles and cackles with crazed pitches more terrifying than the Joker.

Next, you jog to the dumbbell rack. Pick up 45-pound weights. Then, hurry to the squat rack. Single leg squats! You stand atop a wooden box, with one leg hanging off the edge, and squat as deeply as possible. Your legs are still on fire, burning with fatigue. You lose all strength and barely catch yourself before crashing to the ground, unable to lift yourself with one leg. Slumping over with embarrassment, staring at the ground like a child scolded in front of the entire class, you walk back to the dumbbell rack to make an exchange for 35-pound weights. ...

Negative Self

> **REALLY?! You weakling. In front of everybody. Falling to the ground. Are you even trying today?!**

> **Stop it! You *need* to chill. It happens. Just pick up a lighter weight and try again.**

Negative Self

**"Just pick up a lighter weight." Meh, meh, meh.**

After your humbling walk back to the wooden box, you begin again with a more manageable weight. Resetting at the top of the box, bending deeply with one leg and back up ... success! Found it! Thirty-five-pound dumbbells are all you can manage on this day. You crank-out as many reps as possible on each leg during multiple sets until you can do no more.

Next up, the farmers walk! You pick up a set of dumbbells from the rack, walk the length of the weight room and back, about 50 yards. At the end of each trek you pause, stop, and set the weights down, attempting to recover. Still looking for breath, you start the next leg of this slow and excruciating walk. After finishing the sixth round, you pick up lighter dumbbells, and walk 50 yards to exit the weight room. After 35 yards through a winding hallway, you pass through a double set of doors and enter the indoor track. You complete a full loop with minimal stoppage and dumbbell slippage. You saunter back to the weight room for a rerack and a finish.

In between the aforementioned exercises, you also do hamstring and calf exercises, which feel almost like fillers before the next round of demolishment to your quad-muscles. After the farmers walk, you just know the workout is over. It has to be. You can barely move. You are on the verge of puking and passing out at the same time. As you set your dumbbells back on the rack, the ominous voice of Mick yells from across the room, "Board pushes!" ...

Negative Self

**The F*ck is that? What the hell, MICKEY?!**

**Doesn't matter ... you got this!**

**Negative Self**

> You're still here. …

After visiting the "torture device," known as the water cooler, Mick gets in your face and shouts, "All fours!" You take a few steps and fall flat on the floor. Your right cheek swims with the other liquid marinating on the surface. …

**Negative Self**

> Oh, this is nice!

> Gross! Do you know how dirty the floor is?

**Negative Self**

> It's cold and feathery like a bed. We live here now. …

> You. Are. An. Idiot.

Mickey continues with instructions; not fully understanding what is going on, you catch every other word. Mick kicks a two-by-four in front of you. It tumbles end-over-end, nearly kicking up and into your face. …

> Watch it, jerk! Damn, that was close!

**Negative Self**

> Relax … *you* need to chill.

Okay, here you go. You put a hand on each end of the wooden plank and lift your butt in the air. Ready to go! Mick screams, "Hold on!" He tosses a 45-pound plate in front of the two-by-four and yells, "Push!" At least he doesn't throw it at your head.

You start pushing and balancing the plate on the board. Head down, face flush, sweat streaming to the floor from all areas of your body, you push. Five yards in, considering what you've just been through, you are absolutely cruising ... WHAM! You fly forward over the board. Your face skids across a combination of the 45-pound plate and the ground. ...

Negative Self

**THIS IS BULLSH*T!**

Yeah ... this is some bullshit.

Since day one in the weight room, you have wondered why there are rows of duct tape evenly spaced the length of the 50-yard facility. Now you know! It literally hit you in the face. The tape is meant to stop your momentum, forcing an abrupt halt and restart multiple times during the final exercise of the "Harley" lift. After six sets of down-and-back, or an inability to finish due to pure exhaustion or vomiting, you are finally done. Success! You finish and retain all your water!

You walk outside, a brisk wind greets your arrival, and you starfish on the cold pavement. This cool down is exactly what you need. Early morning workout complete, your respite on the concrete is over, and it is time to duckwalk back to the dorm for a shower before going to class.

Told you we had this.

Negative Self

Yeah, yeah, yeah. ...

# BABYSITTERS

## 25

COLLEGE, FRIDAY NIGHTS! WHAT thoughts stir to the top of your mind? Dates, parties, relaxing, or something wild? Not for the Notre Dame Football team, at least not with Tyrone at the helm.

As if Mick's torment isn't difficult enough, Tyrone adds Saturday morning conditioning. Not the most popular activity at 6:00 a.m. following a Friday night. The only "silver-lining" is we will not have a "Harley" lift the day before Saturday morning conditioning — I will take whatever bright spots I can find at this point. Tyrone is taking away one of two nights a week, during the offseason, student-athletes and students alike across the country — the world! — live for. Friday Night! Is there anything better in college than a Friday night after a long week of class?

Whether it is relaxing, having fun, unwinding from a stressful week, partying with friends, or simply getting some much-needed rest, Friday nights are reserved — they are sacred. And no matter what you decide to do on a Friday night, there is optionality — a choice. Tyrone has taken choice away from many of his players by adding a sixth day to our work week. Saturday morning workouts are used as a babysitting mechanism to keep the team away from any potential troubles accompanying a Friday night. We are the university's children, and he is the highly paid babysitter.

Most players choose to stay home or keep things low-key on a Friday night before conditioning, but some guys decide against changing their partying ways. The majority of those who choose to go out Friday night are clearly sluggish before and during their 6:00 a.m. workout. But there are a lucky few who somehow can go out partying all night, conceal any signs of their late-night adventures, and still be ready to go. Those fortunate few are enigmas to me, and I have no idea how these outliers pull off this feat ... I need my sleep.

Saturday morning arrives, and you show up early (guess "O'Leary time" stuck) to find six stations assembled on the indoor field. During the team huddle, you are told each station will last 10 minutes, and each week your assigned group will begin at a different station. The group breaks. You sprint to your gameday stretching spots for warm-up. Equally spaced. Five-yard intervals. No talking. Mickey belts out commands and the stretching begins. After a long week of school and workouts, stretching on the ground is a tricky endeavor at this early hour. Lying there your eyes start to close, you are barely awake, but you know better than to give in to this temptation — facing the Torture Technician wrath is the last thing you need.

The whistle blows, warm-ups are over. Mick yells, "On the whistle, sprint to your station! If you aren't fast enough ... we do it again!" Another blow of his whistle and you sprint to the first station. Keep in mind, every station is a competition, winners and losers, and there are no breaks.

First up ... bags. The bags station consists of two rows, each column with six tackling dummies lined up evenly spaced on the ground. The horn blows. The first 10-minute session starts. Racing through the bags, different patterns each time, the drill seems to end as quickly as it starts.

You do alright. You are quick but stumble some, kicking the bags here and there. Everyone is struggling to pick up their feet this early in the morning. The horn blows again, station one is in the books. You huddle up with your group, get a pep talk from a position coach, break the huddle, and sprint to the next station.

Station number two ... jump rope. Without a few extra pounds of water before starting, you think to yourself, "This should be easier than usual!" You partner up with a teammate for this one. The horn blares. You frantically start jumping, while your partner begins with sit-ups (altering with pushups). With one-minute intervals between jump rope styles, and pushups/sit-ups, you bounce until the coach tells you to switch with your partner. Each set is a different variation, it is your choice: regular, both feet, alternating single foot, feet front to back, run in place, crisscross, etc. You choose whichever variation you think will help time go by faster and take your mind off the fact you should be in bed right now.

After the horn, your group runs to the third station ... hoops. This station is comprised of two giant rings resting side-by-side — looks like a figure eight or infinity sign. You line up at the marked start of one hoop and your competition does the same on the other. The whistle blows! You sprint around your hoop, not touching the ground with your inside hand, and scream through the starting (now finishing) line. Are you faster? Next, you run the entire figure-eight, with a carrot and rabbit approach. You line up at the marked start of the first hoop and the competition lines up a coach-determined distance behind you. The chase is on! If you are caught by the rabbit, then pushups are your punishment and the title of slowest in the group may be in your future.

Fourth on today's list ... the blocking station. You line up in your wideout stance. Across from another skill player (running back, wide receiver, or cornerback) holding a tackling dummy. And a third player lines up at running back, with a ball in hand. All three of you are in position, waiting for the station coach to blow his whistle. You hear the call and burst forward a few yards to engage. You shuffle your feet to mirror the CB, keeping him in front of your body the best you can. The CB tries to get around you to "tackle" the running back barreling toward you. Your hands shoot to the tackling dummy. Fight to keep the dummy (the pad ... not the CB) tight into your chest and directly in front of you — do not let it get away from your body, the referee may see your attempt to hold. This drill serves two purposes: it is meant to work on your physicality and create good blocking habits. You are evaluated on your ability to out-muscle the competition, and the coaches provide feedback on how to improve the blocking technique for your specific position. Cut-blocking (diving at the defenders' ankles to take his legs out) becomes your go-to move, until you become stronger and improve your technique.

Almost done! Station number five ... dots. You love dots! Here you work on quick feet. There are two rows of mats side-by-side on the ground, with plenty of space in between one another. Each mat has five dots on it, each set looks as though someone rolled double fives at the craps table. Each mat is in competition with its counterpart across the aisle. The whistle blows and you compete to see who has the quickest feet in the group. There are five starting points on the mat and multiple patterns for the coach to call out (each pattern includes the use of all five dots being jumped to with both feet from various directions). The process is always the same, no matter the pattern ... move fast, do not think, and win.

SIX! The final stop today ... shuttle station. Here, you compete with another player in the 20-yard shuttle and the 60-yard shuttle. The 20-yard shuttle was detailed in the "Summer Camping" chapter. Now it is time for the 60. You start at the goal line, sprint to the 5-yard line, swipe the front edge — careful not to put your other hand on the ground — and run back to touch the goal line (that's 10 yards). From the goal line you burst to the 10-yard line and back (another 20 yards), then you fly to the 15-yard line, touch the line, and sprint back through the goal line (another 30 yards). If this is the last station in your rotation on a Saturday morning, you are in for a tough finish. Last drill completed. You are done for the day and cannot wait to go home — that is when you hear Mick yell, "Line up! Warm-up positions! Move! Move! Move!"

Tired and cross that you have seen the sunrise on a Saturday, the team dashes into warm-up lines and await instructions — there is still more work to do. You can only hope abs and pushups are the final items on the babysitter's checklist. You lay flat on the ground and raise your feet six inches off the ground until Coach Willingham says to put them down. There are numerous variations to the six-inch abs workout — up and down (together and separate), circles, scissors, out and in, over and under, etc. — and you do all of them multiple times for what feels like an eternity.

After one set of abs, Tyrone blows his whistle. You flip as fast as possible to the pushup position. He blows the whistle again, and yells, "Not fast enough gentlemen, do it again!" By the fourth time the team figures it out, though this battle will happen most Saturday mornings — there are always a few people who just cannot get their act together before 10 a.m.

The whistle blows, you flip over again to get ready for pushups. Tyrone yells, "On the next whistle, push to the top and hold until every one of your teammates is in position." Some days this takes a lifetime, and you hold for minutes at a time, waiting for stragglers to join you all at the top for the first pushup. Everyone is exhausted. Fatigue shakes throughout every muscle. Falling to the ground. Players struggle to push themselves from the field. You are all *finally* in position. Coach blows his whistle, the team counts out loud, and proceeds to do pushups on Coach's whistle, together, until he is tired. This pattern outlined for abs and pushups alternates over and over until our babysitter feels the team can do no more. The final whistle blows, you fall to the ground for the last time today.

This may not sound all that intimidating, but trust me, it is no cakewalk. Saturday stations are non-stop mayhem from Mickey's first whistle to Coach Willingham's last. I will never forget the time Tyrone invites the entire campus to a Saturday morning workout for tryouts. He is searching for an undiscovered talent to join the team as a walk-on.

The whistle blows, warm-ups are done, and we race to our stations. The guys trying out for the team are sprinkled amongst all six groups. My group's first station is done, and bags are next. Competing with our normal intensity, we are more than halfway through the second station and one of the new guys steps to the line. The whistle sounds. He's off! Sprinting over the bags as quickly as possible, one bag, two bags, three bags, six, and races through the finish line. Wait ... he isn't slowing down. Tilting my head, I think, "What's he doing?" He beelines to Coach Willingham, shakes his hand, says he is grateful for the opportunity, but this is not for him this year and he will be back next year (a manager spills the tea afterward). Then, he scurries through the exit door, never to be seen again.

He peeks through the looking glass. He taste-tests the core ingredient, the foundation, of a college football team ... hard work. And realizes being a college football player is not as fun as it looks on gameday.

Our babysitters use Saturday morning workouts as part of this team's foundation. If you want to be a Notre Dame Football player, there are sacrifices. The goosebumps of running out of the tunnel on gameday are earned, not given. They come with a price, and you need to be willing to give it your all, no matter the cost.

# Probation & Control

## 26

Spring break is in sight, and it will be a welcome interlude from the offseason grind — though thoughts of the spring practice to follow subdue my enthusiasm. On a Saturday evening after an early morning workout, we pregame before our night out at an apartment next-door to campus. After having a couple drinks with teammates and friends, we journey to the lacrosse house north of campus.

Late into the evening, with the house party winding down, our group says their goodbyes and walks out the front door toward our designated driver's bright red Jetta. As the door slams behind us, an audible is called.

A teammate's friend says he has not been drinking and wants to drive. Our attractive chauffeur says that is fine with her; she wants to sit in the passenger's lap on the ride home anyway. From the porch steps to the car, I ask our new driver multiple times if he is sober and able to drive — each response affirms he is "good to go." He isn't stumbling or slurring his words, so I trust his cavalier confirmations. Plus, the drop off point to my dorm is less than a mile away. All signs say we are ready for our venture south. And with that, we cram into the car.

Our driver starts the Jetta. Four guys contort themselves into the back-seat and our original designated driver slides into a teammate's lap in the front. Seven people in total, four who are football players. And we're off! Just before we hit the campus line, sirens sound and blue flashes brighten the shrouded surroundings. We pull over to the side of the road in a panic. Was our driver speeding? Was he swerving? Is a blinker out? Or does the officer simply see too many people in a crowded car?

Crowded clown car! At the Douglas Road and Juniper Road red light, he sees a lot of people crammed into a compact car and two people in the passenger seat using one seat belt ... the math is bad. Perfect. Just what we need. As the officer walks toward us, a frenzy engulfs the car, "Shush. Shh-shh. Shh. Sh*t up! Here he comes." He knocks, and the driver rolls down the window. The officer asks, "Do you know why I pulled you over? ... Have you been drinking?" The driver responds to all questions with, "No, officer." He grabs the driver's ID and walks back to his car to run the license.

The officer ends up making multiple trips to his car. With every trip, our car erupts in chatter and multiple guys need to use the bathroom. I contemplate hopping out and running to the dorm ... they are right there, a football field away. There is no way a cop is going to catch a 4.2-forty-guy. Everyone encourages me to run, but I am just not that guy, so I take my medicine.

Everyone in the car has their license run, most walk the line and blow into the breathalyzer. I blow what amounts to mouthwash — though I am not sure how considering I've been drinking for quite a while — and our driver is legally drunk ... surprise!

Did I forget to mention two football players are in the trunk? Yep, and one of the guys is 6'3", 240-pounds ... that makes nine for a ride in a Jetta! Every time the cop walks to his car, the trunk-guys speak up. "I have to pee!"

"Are we there yet?" "Yeah Shelton, save yourself ... run! No way in hell he'll catch you!" "I'm about to pee my pants!" "Hold it, don't you f*cking pee on me!" Their bladder control is top-notch tonight, and no one is peed on during the making of this memory.

I have no idea how the cop doesn't catch the trunk-guys, they are neither quiet nor still at this stop. Tickets for the driver, the underage drinkers, and the doubles partners wearing one seatbelt. Fortunately for me, I take care of the ticket in court. I am handed a fine and probation before I leave town for spring break, so my name does not hit the news when the incident does ... unlike a few of my teammates.

Maybe the babysitters are correct, and we do need a little extra oversight.

*2004: A Few Wide Receivers Flexing for Fun.*

# The Stolen Passion of Spring

## 27

**APRIL 4, 2002.** THE start of spring practice is two days away. During spring ball, the NCAA allows for 15 practices, including the spring game. With a new head coach leading Notre Dame, the team needs to get on the same page and quickly.

Going into the spring practice Coach Willingham says the following about his master plan: "My thoughts on practice are let's not talk about it, let's try to go get everything in place ... For me, the main focus of our spring practice will be, first of all to try to make sure that our gentlemen understand that it is necessary for us to communicate in all areas: offense, defense and special teams, and then try to produce an environment that will allow us to be successful in the spring, and hopefully during that process, identify the young men and put them into right places to help us be the football team that we would like to be."[24]

**April 6, 2002.** Spring football begins on a Saturday. What is it with Coach Willingham and Saturday offseason workouts? My first spring ball in college is here and I finally have a chance to prove myself on the field to my new coaches. I am healthy (ACL surgery was more than a year and half prior), I have a working knowledge of the new playbook, I have acclimated to the college lifestyle, and I have a fresh start. Now it is time to make an impact on the field in a short amount of time, while learning how our new coaching staff operates.

To an extent, every player starts from scratch. Sure, the coaches have watched old game films and witnessed non-football drills, but they haven't seen us "live." I am anxious and a little nervous on this day, which are becoming emotional themes at college. I am still a very raw wide receiver, with much of my coaching coming from a cornerback. I need to prove I have the ability, the tenacity, and the work ethic to get the job done. The veterans still have a leg up on me, but my slate is clean. My actions will dictate my playing time. The harder I work, the faster I learn, and the more high-level ability I can show, the better my chances are of becoming an integral part of the team.

After warm-ups and stretching, all hell breaks loose. The whistle blows and the practice field turns into a madhouse as everyone's scrambling to locate their position coach. Everyone's a freshman today, the trained dogs are lost puppies: moving drill-to-drill — not knowing what to expect — there is an air of uncertainty. "Our practice[s] [are] intense and quick," Willingham says. "At the same time, we are not at such a pace that we don't have the opportunity to teach. We want to make sure that it is a major element of what we do. I thought it was a good first day, I thought the young men were eager to get started, as were our coaches."[25] The teachings he mentions are beyond quick, as the pace of practice has drastically sped up from what we once knew.

My thoughts on practice are … I am freaking tired! The pace of practice is so much faster than anything I experienced last season. The pace will only increase as we grow together as a team and grasp a better understanding of the expectations. We all learn a lot during spring practice, including a new peculiarity (in addition to speaking in the third person) and two new rules.

Coach Willingham takes no part in a time-honored tradition so many coaches prescribe. A rite of passage blatantly dismissed. Cursing. He does not curse, and there is no grabbing the facemask to yell with spit flying in the face of his players. Confusing, but I appreciate the novelty, at least at first; ultimately, I see that it becomes extremely difficult to motivate and coach grown men without cursing.

College athletes can be difficult to motivate. Cursing is a motivational instrument frequently used within the coaching ranks because it tends to work well. Maybe the words themselves are not important, instead the accompanying anger is the key? Perhaps the words are simply the catalysts for coaches to quickly source their display of rage?

Today I realize Tyrone does not curse under any circumstances, ever. A coach who doesn't curse is like a kid who doesn't like candy. Cursing is a cornerstone within the football coaching community. Most football coaches seem to curse every other word. That's how they get their message across to an exhausted, overwhelmed, and sometimes unmotivated athlete. Tyrone does have one "curse word" he uses when he is really upset, "DAMN!" "Damn" ... it doesn't strike the fear of God into anyone, but when he uses it, you know he means business; just like you know you're in trouble when mom yells your full name — "Matthew Louis Shelton!" — and I'm on the move with trouble rapidly approaching.

As we quickly work to learn how the coaching staff operates a practice, we learn a new rule. A rule I've never seen at football practices. No fighting. What?! No fighting? Last year there was a scrap at every practice. But Willingham doesn't tolerate fighting during his practices. One way or another, a reckoning is coming. Early in practice, a few scuffles breakout. Tyrone warns the team each time, visibly more upset with each interjection. His seriousness is at peak levels, an example needs to be made.

"Hut, Hut!" The running back takes the handoff for a 5-yard gain. "Hey, hey," I hear a coach shout. Jeff Faine, our starting center, is still driving a defensive lineman backward; he slams the defender into the ground, 15 yards down the field. Jeff stands, turns, and starts jogging back to the offensive huddle for the next play. The defender springs to his feet and pushes Jeff in the back — not smart. Jeff turns, pushes the defender, throws him to the ground, jumps on him, and they fight until a swarm of teammates pull them apart. The final straw. The reckoning is here. The entire team runs together around three practice fields. We run until Coach decides we have learned our lesson and it's time to resume practice.

Jeff is one of those players who fights at most practices. In games you see Jeff repeatedly driving his defender backward 10-plus-yards and body slamming him into the ground. Practice is no different for Jeff. He does this to everyone, no matter if the guy across from him is a starter or a walk-on, and no matter the size. He is a beast. With the implementation of no fighting, there is a noticeable change in Jeff (pretty sure he doesn't smile at practice again) and others on the team. Because of this new team rule, some players lose their aggressiveness. Asking a football player not to fight is like asking a hockey enforcer to keep his gloves on. It is a big ask!

The aggressive nature of players comes to a screeching halt. The entertainment of the game is lost for them, passion is lost, and fun is gone. Do not hit the opposing player, lightly bump them so you do not start a fight. Do not stand up for yourself, back down. Do not stand up for a teammate, let them be bullied. The natural order of football gets dismantled by this rule. Aggression, intensity, and sometimes fighting undoubtedly help athletes perform. Why completely remove it from the equation?

The second rule implemented during spring ball is about time management. If a player is late for any meeting, Coach Willingham makes not just that player run, but the entire position group. When a player is late, the position group meets the following Wednesday at the indoor field for a 6:00 a.m. run. This is a workout Tyrone does with us, if he decides against hitting golf balls into the netting instead. He is always energized for morning workouts and participates for enjoyment. We are the opposite — fatigued, miserable and do not want to be here.

*2003: A Few Wide Receivers Flexing for Serious.*

The only time the wideouts meet for a Wednesday morning run is because of Rhema McKnight ... next year. I get it, it happens, but dammit, Rhema is injured! He can't run, or practice, or even participate in the Wednesday morning workout — which we are doing because of his bad time management. I can't believe Rhema has the nerve to be late for a meeting; sure, he is on a scooter and crutches, and delays happen, but come on man! He isn't practicing so he is not tired. He knows he does not run if he is late. He laughs off his tardiness, even though his teammates are forced to do extra running because of his lapse. It is ridiculous that Tyrone makes our position group run because an injured player is late to a meeting. As I run around the track, watching Tyrone hit golf balls into the netting, I mutter a litany of "encouraging" words in his direction.

After our bonus workout at 6:00 a.m., during the middle of spring ball, all I want is to slip back into bed for a nap and skip class. I need a chance to recover before the afternoon practice. Hate to say it, but there is no decision. Sleep wins! I cross my fingers, roll the dice, and hope there are no "spies" looking for me in class. See you next week, teach!

**April 15, 2002.** Seven days into spring practice: the wide receiver unit is working hard, and the team energy is drained. The team's collective head is spinning with information overload. The first week of practice makes me feel "green" all over again. From football meeting rooms to the classroom, I have been in a constant state of learning since I first stepped foot on campus last year, August 12th. The coaching staff has been evaluating each position and player on the team to determine roles and strengths.

At this point, after only a few practices, Tyrone has the following to say about his vision for the wide receivers: "It's very difficult to judge and make decisions when you're going through as much learning as [the wide receivers are] going through. They're now totally involved in the football game. In certain styles of offenses, you're limited in terms of your role ... our receivers are not limited in terms of their role. They're going to have to execute in all facets of the game. So, they're learning how to get open, adjust routes and read coverages on the run. They seem to be doing a good job of that."[26] Each day of spring football the receiving corps makes improvements, both in our understanding and execution of our new plays. Our role on the team is expanded, with more opportunities to catch the football ... we are no longer underutilized!

**April 27, 2002.** Spring football culminates with a 3-0 victory for the gold team at the 73rd Annual Blue-Gold Game (our intrasquad scrimmage). I walk away from these practices feeling as though I have a real chance at seeing the field on gamedays in the fall.

# Summer School Soiree

## 28

FINAL EXAMS ARE COMPLETE! Freshman year is in the books. Summer has arrived! I am ready for a break and excited for time with my family in Tennessee. Maybe we will go on a week-long camping trip? Maybe I will visit my teammates in California? Maybe I will hit the beach in Florida for a week?

Two weeks? Summer break is only two weeks long?! "That's a bullsh*t!"

We are granted two weeks of semi-freedom at home. Mickey strongly suggests working out while away, as he informs us there will be a conditioning test when we return. That said, it is your break, and you can do what you want. I can ill-afford to fall behind, I have put in a lot of solid work with the new staff and do not need it cancelled out by a lazy two weeks. My time at home is quick but just what I need. I return to campus for mandatory summer school reenergized by the positivity of family and friends.

My airport taxi pulls up to campus. I unload the trunk and inhale deeply after setting my bags on the ground. The smell of freshly cut grass fills my lungs. I look around and see the rejuvenation of winter on full display. Vibrant, colorful flowers are scattered as far as the eye can see. The grounds are meticulously manicured. The tree canopy is brimming with wildlife. South Bend summers are incredibly beautiful. Maybe I view campus as being more picturesque because the winters can be brutally cold, or maybe it is because I am a southern boy who feels his roots when blades of grass are between his toes on a warm, sunny day. No matter the reasoning, these summer days here are flawless.

Yes, summer school sounds terrible, but it is awesome! I never thought I would say those words about summer school, but there it is. My responsibilities include two classes four days a week and football training. When I am not at football or in class, I am hanging out with the guys. We play pickup basketball, the team has an indoor basketball tournament (my team won the title, and Carlyle Holiday chose our team's name, "The 1954 Hoosiers and a Black Guy"), we have house parties, I sneak into bars with the older guys, we hit the beaches of Lake Michigan, and we have numerous other bonding experiences. One of the best bonding experiences this summer are the eight-hour "Halo" sessions deemed mandatory by Jeff Faine ... not a chance I am saying no to this guy.

Winter of 2001 the original Xbox console is released, and the world is in an uproar. My parents surprise me with one at Christmas, and the little free time I find in college becomes "Halo" time. For those of you who do not know, "back in the day" you could not just turn on your gaming console, connect to the Wi-Fi, and play with anyone in the world. But you could connect a maximum of four consoles through the university's network, via a wired connection called the ethernet.

The team spends the summer at Knott Hall, so I do not need to move far when dorm rooms are assigned, just down the hall. Thus, I am the first to have an Xbox up and running. Jeff Faine sees this, sits down, asks me politely if he can play as he resets the console ... I will allow it, I am almost done anyway (I was not almost done). From this point forward, Faine is a fixture in my room, the big bad senior stops by to visit the lowly sophomore almost daily. We are obsessed. Sixteen of us playing at once, four guys are crowded around each console, we play the days away. Bathroom breaks, no. Food breaks, no. Any attempts by the three of us playing with Jeff is met with a glove-like-mitt yanking you back to your seat, or a punch to the shoulder that says, "Sit your ass down until I say you can move." Oh, these are the days.

Another bonding experience is on the horizon. A road trip to Kalamazoo, Michigan. On a Friday night, post mandatory "Halo" session and after one of those perfect northern Indiana summer days on the ND campus, the boys hit the road. An 82-mile road trip north to Kalamazoo. We are hitting "The Zoo" and heading to "The Vu." Déjà Vu Showgirls, an 18 and up strip club, is the perfect way to unwind as summer comes to an end.

After an hour and a half drive, with mostly linemen in tow, our caravan reaches its destination. Fifteen football players pile out of their cars and head toward the door. Checking ID's, the bouncer says, "Not gonna have any trouble tonight are we guys?" One player somehow forgets his ID, so he is confined to the car with a buddy who eventually leaves the club to hang out. I have never been to a strip club, and it does not disappoint. Beautiful women galore, and all are seeking my attention. Yes, for money. Nevertheless, attention is attention and I am young, so a win is a win. Some of the guys have been here before and know there is a special treat for birthdays.

Happy birthday Johnny Drama! Yes, your birthday was months ago, but today is your birthday. The DJ calls Johnny to the stage, tells him to take a seat on the chair in the center. From his booth left of the stage, the DJ looks Johnny directly in his eyes and says, "Sit on your hands, and no touching of any kind." Simultaneously, the strippers line up in front of the booth. The first dancer walks on stage and does her thing, then the second, the third, and so on. There are only a few lap dances remaining. Smiling ear to ear, you can see the wheels turning faster and faster in Johnny's mind with each passing dance. The next lady walks on stage, puts her hands on the ground, does a handstand in Johnny's lap, and performs the splits.

Johnny looks to his right, then to his left. He looks at a few of his team-mates with a devious grin. His hands have never moved so quickly as he grabs both cheeks and "motorboats" faster than Joey Chestnut competing at Nathan's Famous Hot Dog Eating Contest. The dancer pushes away from the chair. Her feet hit the ground and she moves to the side, as she instinctively knows bouncers are running to the stage after seeing their one and only rule broken. Johnny, who stands over 6'4" and weighs around 250-pounds, jumps to his feet. Simultaneously, 12 teammates (minus the two outside in the car) do the same. The bouncers rushing toward Johnny freeze ... they have become keenly aware of the situation. A large group of men, both in number and size, are moving toward the stage too. Multiple 6'3", 300-pound men are in the group. An old-fashioned standoff!

All participants inch closer and closer to the stage. The bouncers lock eyes with one another, trying to decide what to do next. Is breaking the only house rule worth this kind of fight? Do the bouncers really want this brawl? Fortunately for all parties involved, the dancer steps in to say she is okay, and everything is fine. Cooler heads prevail. Johnny apologizes to the lady, her co-workers, and the bouncers. We all take our seats and the music plays. Next to the stage ... two-a-days! Summer is over, and the next football season is upon us.

# TY'S TRY, "TAKE ONE"

## 29

**AUGUST 31, 2002.** THE season opens at the University of Maryland and expectations are high. We don't disappoint too much. We get the win over the Terrapins 22-0. Looks great on paper, but we have zero offensive touchdowns. Nick Setta has five field goals, and Vontez Duff has a punt return for a touchdown. The wide receivers have 14 catches for 197 yards. Unfortunately, I don't have a catch. No surprise, I already knew I would be a reserve this year, hurdled by the two freshmen, though I was hopeful to have something thrown my way. I have zero "looks," but the two freshmen receivers, Rhema McKnight and Maurice Stovall, combine for three catches and 25 yards.

My role is official. Relegated to a reserve wide receiver and a special team's player. This will not become the season I hope for it to be. All my offseason hard work will need to carry over into next year, as I wait for my chance to shine on gameday as a wideout. This is not a setback, it is simply a setup for next year. There is more work to be done.

**November 2, 2002.** For the 19th time in school history, just the fifth time in the last 30 years, Notre Dame starts a football season undefeated with 8-wins. Now ranked #4 in the country, we travel to Boston for a matchup with the Eagles of Boston College. The old saying goes, defense wins championships. Our defense is the heart and soul of the team, and that is why our new head coach is winning during his first season.

Our defense has been sensational this season; at the end of the year, they rank #5 in scoring defense (13.5 points/game), #7 in rushing defense (81.75 yards/game), #8 in pass efficiency defense (94.08), and #12 in total defense (293.63 yards/game).[27] The defense continues to dominate in this game, but again the offense doesn't provide support. The offense loses three fumbles, throws two interceptions, and only finds the end zone once in six red zone visits. A brand-new offense, yes, but the ineffectiveness remains — the offense becomes an Achilles heel. Boston College wins 14-7 and we notch our first loss of the season. With a record of 8-1, we must regroup and find some sort of offense to help our elite defense.

*2004, Pep Rally at the Joyce Center: Matt Shelton, Tyrone Willingham, Bob Morton, Regis Philbin.*

With wins over Navy and Rutgers, the team regains its footing just in time for a huge matchup. We are ranked #7 in the country, with a 10-1 record, and travel to Los Angeles for a showdown versus the University of Southern California. USC is 9-2 and they are ranked #6.[28] This is our last regular season game, and a win keeps our hopes of a BCS invitation alive. The movie script of a first season is blown apart in a lopsided 44-13 loss to USC. They manhandle us with 610 yards of total offense to our 109. Our dominant defense has their back broken by the deadweight of an anemic offense weighing them down all season.

On January 1, 2003, we play in the Gator Bowl in Jacksonville, Florida against North Carolina State and Philip Rivers. The Wolfpack spanks us 28-6. After a spectacular start, the season ends with back-to-back losses.

| 2002 Schedule | | | |
|---|---|---|---|
| Overall 10-3 | PCT 0.769 | Home 5-1/Away 3-1/Neutral 2-1 | |
| Date | Opponent | Location | Result |
| 8/31/2002 | vs. Maryland | East Rutherford, NJ | W, 22-0 |
| 9/7/2002 | vs. Purdue | Notre Dame, IN | W, 24-17 |
| 9/14/2002 | vs. Michigan | Notre Dame, IN | W, 25-23 |
| 9/21/2002 | at Michigan State | East Lansing, MI | W, 21-17 |
| 10/5/2002 | vs. Stanford | Notre Dame, IN | W, 31-7 |
| 10/12/2002 | vs. Pittsburgh | Notre Dame, IN | W, 14-6 |
| 10/19/2002 | at Air Force | CO Springs, CO | W, 21-14 |
| 10/26/2002 | at Florida State | Tallahassee, FL | W, 34-24 |
| 11/2/2002 | vs. Boston College | Notre Dame, IN | L, 7-14 |
| 11/9/2002 | vs. Navy | Baltimore, MD | W, 30-23 |
| 11/23/2002 | vs. Rutgers | Notre Dame, IN | W, 42-0 |
| 11/30/2002 | at USC | Los Angeles, CA | L, 13-44 |
| 1/1/2003 | vs. NC St. (Gator Bowl) | Jacksonville, FL | L, 6-28 |

Our high-powered West Coast offense starts and ends the season in the same way — zero touchdowns in both the first two and last two games. The offense averages 22.3 points per game (ranks #91 out of 117 teams[29], 9-spots better than last year) and 313.5 yards of total offense per game (#108 [30], 3-spots better than last year); whereas the defense allows an average of 16.7 points per game (#9 [31], 13-spots better than last year) and 300 yards per game (#13 [32], 1-spots better than last year). "Coach

Willingham is honored by multiple organizations as national coach of the year in 2002 for becoming the only first-year coach in Notre Dame history to win 10 games."[33]

Again, not a setback: a setup for next year. I play in 10 games this year as a reserve wide receiver and special teams player. I notch one catch on a screen pass for a grand total of 18 yards that I fumbled out of bounds, tally one tackle on special teams, and 12 yards on a kickoff return against Michigan — which I stole from Shane Walton, my old "coach," when I did not hear him call me off (my bad Shane). I appear on special teams 51-times and play wideout for a grand total of 10:47 minutes — not even close to what I hoped to contribute. I did, however, make my way onto the field and that itself is a personal win. Small, maybe, but a step in the right direction that allowed me to gain valuable experience while competing on the national college football stage.

After the bowl game I visit Tennessee for a week of much needed family time before returning to school for the start of second semester sophomore year. Round two of spring football inches closer with every passing day. My goals for spring football are to ... 1. Show how much I have improved, both in skill and knowledge of the playbook, and 2. Show Coach Miles I deserve more playing time.

During spring ball, I give it my all, but to no avail. Coach Miles does not take note of my improvement as a route running specialist or even notice my deep threat ability. So, nothing spectacular happens during spring ball. I am exactly where I started at the end of my first season — still needing to prove myself. But how else can I prove myself? When will my real opportunity present itself? Will I ever have a chance to shine?

# "MIDNIGHT MASSACRE"

## 30

SUMMER SCHOOL IS BACK. That means summer workouts with Mickey. He decides it is time to shake up our lifting and conditioning routines. After an intense leg workout, an assistant strength coach leads our group to the practice field for a finishing exercise. As we turn the corner, what do we see?

Mick in the back of a mini-dump truck! He screams at us, "Let's go! Get your asses over here! Faster! Faster!" And it is awesome! The group is loving this changeup. A torture assistant sits in the driver's seat with the truck in neutral. Two players sprint to the back of the truck and start pushing. Mick stands in the truck bed, leaning over the tailgate. Hovering over us, ravenous froth falls on our heads from his "encouraging" words.

Groups alternate when Mick decides to blow the whistle. Rotating for what feels like an eternity, we push the truck around the field multiple times. Slipping. Falling. Scrambling to get up and not lose any of the truck's momentum. Teammates only stop to vomit. Maybe we don't love this change in routine? Years down the road, Mickey admits to removing the brake light bulbs and instructing his staff to lightly press on the break for the entire workout — as if it wasn't difficult enough. But honestly knowing would not matter to us because this type of workout counts as fun.

In another move away from the norm, Mick creates a weightlifting obstacle course with 12-stations for the team to tackle together in groups. He makes lifting an active competition, which in turn makes getting your butt whipped not as recognizable or terrible. The team navigates through the course. Each player is timed. Each rep is counted. And a coach at every station keeps score. After 12 timed lifting events, and running from station to station, everyone on the team is exhausted. This summer Mickey is doing everything in his power to ensure the team does not succumb to the monotony of workouts and school that is on repeat for weeks on end. Within the mutual struggles, competing with one another outside of football practice, a team's bond is deepened, and the family has fun!

The last workout of the summer is historically the greatest and most entertaining training session of the year. Mickey calls it "Midnight Massacre" — the least surprising title ever created by our Master Torture Technician. This workout is by far the most fun the team has together, other than gamedays. Every player looks forward to this workout: we plan for days, if not weeks. This lift is designed to create pain, pump, and fun.

At the stroke of midnight, dressed to impress, the team gathers in the weight room. My first summer, one-year prior, I look around the room: cavemen with clubs, astronauts fully suited, Hacksaw Jim Dugan — two-by-four in hand, a 320-pound man in a one piece woman's bathing suit, vampires with blood dripping from their last meal, a horse being operated by two guys, Jesus is wearing Adidas, a devil engulfed by flames, a priest and nun wearing less than holy accessories, a complete 80's rock band — hair flow to match, and clowns ... who I can only assume are here to terrify me. If you can find it, you can wear it — no questions asked.

In the days leading up to this workout the Technician's team measures everyone's chest and biceps for comparison. "Midnight massacre" focuses 100% on the upper body, destroying your arms and chest. During the workout, when ready to compare, you sprint to the strength coach holding the clipboard and a tailor's measuring tape. You curl your arm and flex your "gun." If you do not beat your previous measurement, you sprint back for a few more reps before measuring again.

This crazy, fun, nonstop workout ends with a killer ab session. Mick, the ever-constant motivator, leads the closing exercise by instructing the entire team to lay down in a giant circle on the floor. Ten minutes into the ab session everyone is moaning and groaning in pain. Trying to get the team going, Mickey begins "encouraging" some of the guys.

I'm too far away to hear exactly what Mick says to Gary Godsey, but I notice their exchange. Mick walks away, returning to the middle of the circle. As Mick hits the center, Gary blurts out, "F*ck you Mickey!" In a surprising turn of events, Mickey calmly replies — he doesn't throw a plate, fight a weight tree, or even yell. He simply turns and, in a deep foreboding voice, says, "No Gary ... F*ck *you*." Then tells the team, "We were so close to being done but thank Gary ... 10 more minutes!" Thanks again, Gary.

During my second summer on campus, Tyrone terminates the attire. "Midnight Massacre" lives on, but the accompanying fun is stripped from our Torture Technicians toolbelt without explanation. The sweat drenched, entertaining costumes that unify this muscle-pumping, summer-ending bonding session of torture — which the team embraces and loves — is sequestered to the toybox. After all, every kid knows that babysitters like to destroy fun ... this provocation is "par for the course."

There are teammates who are so upset they threaten to quit, to transfer. No, they were not likely to quit over this type of change — like many players who planned to leave after George O'Leary was hired; however, it does underscore how much the players relished the spectacle associated with the pain of "Midnight Massacre."

A pattern emerges under Tyrone's reign ... no fun allowed. Many coaches say football is not supposed to be fun ... they are wrong. A case in point, USC. Every time I see their Friday walk-throughs before a game, the players are having a ton of fun — laughing, joking with their coaches, and smiling (there are smiles); Pete Carroll seems to make and keep football fun for his players, and he makes it look this way in the NFL too. His fun coaching style works during his nine years at USC, as his 96-19 record and two BCS national championships (2003, 2004) indicate.

Football is a demanding, yearlong sport. Players must "put the pedal to the metal" at all times, well, almost all the time. Blood, sweat, tears, pains, injury, and utter exhaustion are just a few repercussions of this job. Athletes do not think about it, most officials of the sport do like to talk about it, but death is a very real possibility. The game brings risks and consequences. Football needs to have elements of passion and fun ... positive aspects that keep a player wanting to play the game. Without passion, will players risk their lives on the field? Without fun, will players expose themselves to the aftermaths of the sport? The positive elements this game brings to a player breed a willingness to put oneself in danger.

In under a year-and-a-half, Tyrone confiscates our fun, subdues our passion and collective fighting spirit, and commandeers the freedom of offseason Friday nights. Instead of a team wrapping up the summer with the excitement of "Midnight Massacre," the summer ends with one of our toys being taken away: a positive, team-building motivator is thrown in the trash.

# TY'S TRY, "TAKE TWO"

## 31

**FALL 2003.** JUNIOR YEAR is here! Tyrone's second season at Notre Dame begins. The Notre Dame community expects to witness major progress. A 10-3 team that ends the season with back-to-back losses will not suffice.

Fans are calling for a national championship. Anything short will be considered a failure. Many within the family, community, and media believe we have our return to glory in the form of Coach Tyrone Willingham — though not all share the same sentiment. Along with the optimistic excitement of many fans, pessimistic rumblings germinate into existence. After what some consider a meltdown at the end of last season, whispers in the shadows percolate.

**September 3, 2003.** You are done with two-a-day practices. You're in the middle of game week. Typically, during the season, Tuesday and Wednesday are the two toughest practices leading up to gameday. These weekly practices can be just as tough as two-a-days. The team still needs a bit of levity and fun to get through each week during the season. No matter the time of year, football generally brings challenging times to its players.

Below the stadium, you swing open the locker room door to get ready for practice. You step through onto hallowed grounds. Immortality is on the left, Heisman trophies and championship rings welcome you. You turn to the right and make your daily walk to the wide receiver lockers located along the back wall. A myriad assortment of light-colored bricks along the wall shimmer gold with each step. The full-bodied Notre Dame blue carpet — with a thick ND gold strip outlining the edges of the room — usher you to the middle, past the golden ND logo. After a quick conversation with fellow wideout, Omar Jenkins, you take a seat in your locker to get ready for meetings and practice.

After pulling up your practice pants, you take a seat to put on your ankle braces and cleats. You look around the room. A few players are running late, scrambling to get ready. Players are napping on the floor. Trainers are checking on injured players. With a deep inhale, you realize the musky locker room smell is stout today and wrinkle your nose. Commotion is everywhere. Laughter circles the room. Music is blasting from a locker to your left. The TV across the room has the volume turned all the way up.

Underneath the noise, a handful of lockers to your right, you sense the frustrated urgency in someone's heavy sighs. You look over to find Billy Palmer bent over, scavenging through his locker. Shuffling clothes and cleats around. Throwing things behind himself with his left hand. Then, his right. Shoes, clothes, and papers pile around him. You ask, "What are you looking for?" He glares in your direction, irritatingly sighs, and says, "Sock!" "Hmm," you reply. "Sock! I have one, and don't want to deal with them to get another." He points at his locker, as his lone sock dangles in his other hand.

The equipment room is on the other side of the wall, behind his locker. The equipment managers are notoriously stingy with the issued gear, which is unexpected at ND ... Adidas, the university's apparel sponsor at the time, gives the team anything and everything they can possibly want. Billy, like the rest of the team, gets pushback from the managers when asking for new issued gear or anything for that matter. His frustration stems from not wanting to deal with the back and forth of asking for gear. Then, you see it in Billy's smile. A lightbulb flickers on. An unusual tactic to get what he needs — opting for a big surprise.

With enthusiasm, Billy's walk to the manager's counter appears to be more of a skip. From your angle, it looks like he is jubilantly skipping along the "yellow brick road" — the gold carpet in front of the lockers. He hits the end of the road. As he suspected, the "front gates" to the Emerald City are closed to all — the window is covered by a metal drop-down door and locked. His smile widens, this is the exact scenario he wants.

He jumps onto the counter, contorting himself well enough to lay down on his left side facing the door ... he settles in, nearly falling backward over the edge. Regaining his balance, he places his elbow on the counter, and he rests his head on top of his left hand. He strategically drapes his other arm along his right side, with his found sock in hand. He forgot to knock. Bang, bang ... then, he redresses the presentation.

The guard flings open the front gate, with a clatter, to see who has the audacity to bother "the great and powerful Oz." Billy dares. The manager feasts his eyes upon the gloriously naked body of Billy — his gaze can't help but be drawn to the lone sock searching for its counterpart and covering Billy's "equipment." With an even bigger smile, Billy says, "Hey boys, I'm looking for a friend!" Mr. Palmer quickly obtains a complete pair of socks and, to his contentment, never needs to search for a pair again.

**September 6, 2003**. After a 29-26 overtime victory against Washington State, the post-game is like all the others. Recruits and families, males only, visit the locker room — peeking behind the curtain of ND Football.

After showering and wearing only a towel, Billy walks up to a tight end recruit near his locker and shakes the kids' hand, saying, "Let me show you a drill, we do this one every day. This is how it's done." Billy lines up with his feet staggered, knees bent, and ready to block any defender attempting to get by him. On his own count, he shouts, "Down, set, hut!" Exploding off the line of scrimmage, he kicks backward and punches the air with open fists to block the imaginary defender, performing naked kick-slides in front of all the visitors — welcoming them to campus. One shuffle, two shuffles, then three. And Billy barely catches the slipping towel before it drops to his knees. The recruit covers his mouth and chuckles, as he is taken off-guard by the moment.

Football and life really are about the little things. A little humor, something weird, anything that makes a person smile. Again, Billy provides uplifting moments.

# MILES APART

## 32

MY POSITION COACH AND I are not seeing eye-to-eye, and not just because he is shorter than me. Coach Trent Miles has taught me a lot since arriving on campus. He has a remarkable database of overall football knowledge, about how to be a wide receiver, and about our offensive system. He is a good teacher in the meeting room. He teaches great route running technique. On the field, he shows us the nuances of how to be an all-around wideout. Though, as there are with most coaches, for all the positives there are negatives.

Trent is not what I call a "players' coach." On many occasions, I feel degraded not only as a player, but as a person. Many times, I feel verbally abused and attacked as a man, instead of a player being criticized for his on-field play. Maybe some of these feelings are simply due to the player-coach dynamic, but maybe not. All I can do is show you events as they happened from my point of view. This is one of those events.

Recently, I asked a fellow wideout, Ronnie Rodamer, if he recalls the story I am about to share. He replies, "Hell yeah, I remember that happening to you. He did something similar to me. He put hands on me one day when I was walking away from him. He grabbed my shoulder pads and violently yanked me back to him. I got in his face and said, 'I'm not one of those freshmen, don't every put your f*cking hands on me again!'"

On this day, Trent and I go toe-to-toe on the practice field. The evening sun dwindles from the sky. Beams of light pepper through the clouds. The wind shifts, turning cool and crisp, as the night begins its stretch on this fall day. Mickey blows the whistle, and we break from the team warm-up that begins practice. With a pep in my step, I run to my right — from field number two to the inside edge of its neighbor, field number three — and meet the other wideouts on the 50-yard line for positional warm-ups.

During the first period of practice, we focus on our route running technique, concentration, and catching the ball with our hands — away from your body. Side-by-side, the receivers warm-up. Aligning on the out of bounds line, in our receiver stances, we look down the line of scrimmage toward Coach Miles who is about to snap the ball. He hikes the ball and the receiving corps burst off the line, working on our "get-offs."

Next, we work on our route running technique and our hands. Four bright orange cones are positioned 5 yards apart to form a square. I settle into my stance at the first cone and look down the line at a student manager who is ready to snap the ball. He yells, "Hut!" I sprint 5 yards to the second cone, pitter-patter my feet — which helps me slow down for the break at the top of my route, while retaining as much of my speed as possible — plant my right foot in the ground, and cut to the left. I run straight down the line to the next cone, not drifting off the line created by the two cones.

As I sprint out of the first break, Trent throws a perfect pass hitting me in stride (he's about 5 yards from me). I tuck the ball, then toss it aside before breaking down to make a cut at the next cone. I exit the second break and catch a second pass from the student manager assigned to the wideouts — also a perfect strike. This happens one more time, then I sprint through the finishing cone where it all started.

After a few rounds, which include different patterns around the cones, we line up for our second drill of the period. This drill is meant to work on your hands, your reaction time, and your ability to locate a ball in midair. I step into position. Standing 5 yards away from Coach Miles, with my back facing him — hips slightly dropped, legs bending at the knee, and arms bent, with hands at the ready. I stare into the distance waiting for his call; my focus is so intense I can hear my heart beating in my temples. There it is!

With a football in his right hand, coach yells, "Go!" Slapping the ball with his left hand, he shuffles his feet, preparing himself to throw the football. As he watches me spin through the air with a 180-degree turn, he cocks his arm and gets into throwing position — waiting to see my shoulders turn to him. I quickly twirl in the air, with my eyes and head leading the way. I locate Coach and spot the ball whizzing toward me. My body catches up with my eyes, as my feet hit the ground and I snatch the ball with my hands, then cradle it between my arm and chest.

This process has taken place, without fail, each time we have run this drill ... which is every single day we practice. A drill Trent has led hundreds of times in his coaching career. A simple throw he has easily made a thousand times. But what kind of story would this be if today is like the others?

While my eyes and head are still leading the turn toward Trent, the ball leaves his hand. A bit early, don't you think? I locate Coach, but the ball is nowhere to be found. Where is it? Does he still have it? Did he drop it? WHAM! The scorching football collides with my "equipment," hitting me squarely in the "junk." I fall to the ground in agony, moaning and cursing as I roll about the grass.

I have seen this happen to others many times and had my fair share of unfortunate incidents. Screaming and rolling on the ground are standard reactions. Trent's reaction is not so standard. There is no "sorry" or "my bad" or "oops." Without moving from his pitching mound, 5 yards away, he yells, "Get up, you're fine! It wasn't that hard." After several moments of rolling around in pain, I push myself from the ground, and stagger to my feet — not saying a word to him, I continue with practice.

Fuming the remainder of practice, I do not make eye contact with Trent and only grunt at him in acknowledgment of his instructions. At the end of practice, the team gathers for Coach Willingham's concluding thoughts, then we break the huddle and leave for the locker room. Before I can make my exit, Trent chases me down on field three. "Hey!"

I know he is calling me but continue my exit. "Hey! Matt! What's your problem?!" I turn to face him — exhausted, pouring sweat, and still heated from our incident. "Nothing," then, turn to restart my departure. He sprints to cut me off. I try to walk around him. He shoots a hand to my chest, stopping my attempt at avoidance. We end up chest-to-chest.

"No, no. You've had an attitude all day! Are you still mad I hit you in the nuts?" Confrontationally stepping forward, I say, "F*ck yeah! Five yards away and you hit me in the nuts! You did that sh*t on purpose." He denies the allegations, "F*cking man up! I didn't do it on purpose! Stop being a little B*tch about it!"

As his words flood my ears, a rage from deep within my soul permeates, it takes every ounce of willpower I possess to not break his nose. "Leave me the f*ck alone," I say, before walking around him, bumping shoulders, and trotting to the locker room.

# It's "Turbo" Time

## 33

**November 29, 2003.** A struggling football team, a mere shell of the team we were last season with a 4-6 record, travels to Stanford University. This will be the 35$^{th}$ game of my college career, and I only have two catches for 27 yards (18 yards vs. Rutgers in 2002, 9 yards vs. Purdue this year). Thus far, a career that has not gone to plan, not even close. This year's team and I have a lot in common on this front: our plans have been thrown out of the window.

The team needs some sort of spark, something different. Anything will do. With two games left in the season, I am finally given a real opportunity to make a difference on gameday. I am the fastest guy on the team, I catch everything thrown my way, and I run great routes. Underutilized and buried on the depth chart. But something needs to change, so why not give this type of player a chance? Couldn't hurt.

All week we have been practicing a play designed specifically for you. A play that utilizes your greatest strength. The game kicks off. Moving through the first quarter, our coaching staff analyzes the defense: observing how the defensive coordinator adjusts their personnel based on the players we have on the field (the number of running backs, wideouts, and tight ends), seeing how they adjust to specific formations we line up in, and watching what coverages they use on specific downs and distances. Our offense pokes-and-prods the defense. Searching for weaknesses. Seeking advantage. The coaches sense they have the perfect situation to call your number.

You stand on the sideline, waiting for your play to be called. Two minutes and a few ticks remain in the first quarter. ND is up 7-0. Julius Jones runs the ball to the left boundary, putting the ball on the left hashmark for the next play. Coach calls your name, and shouts, "It's time!" You dash to his side. He barks the play into your ear. For the first time in your career, you sprint onto the field knowing the next play is yours. In the huddle, Brady Quinn quickly and calmly calls the play. He looks at you with intense eyes, saying, "Coming to you." He breaks the huddle, and the team rushes to the line of scrimmage.

As you hurry to the right side of the ball — lining up as the outside receiver, with a tight end inside of you in a three-point stance on the line of scrimmage — your heart is pounding ... endeavoring to break from captivity with an intensity you have never known. In college, you have lined up on the line of scrimmage so many times knowing you may or may not see the ball thrown your way, but this time is different. Unquestionably, the ball is coming your way. You are *the* option on this play.

The drum in your chest amplifies and quickens with every beat. Your impatiently zealous energy can be contained no more — you *need* the ball snapped now. The crowd noise fades. Your focus centers with the steadying of your hands. Brady points to make the mike-linebacker call — telling the offensive line who to block based on where the middle linebacker is located. He points at another defender, yells out a dummy call that means nothing; the defense does not know any better and they make a small adjustment by crowding the line of scrimmage with their linebackers. You continue to scan the defense to ensure the coverage does not change. The defense has two deep safeties, and the cornerbacks are 5 yards off the line of scrimmage. A cover-two defense.

Just before the snap the cornerback takes a few steps toward you, which tips you off they are not in a standard cover-two defense (might be a cover-two-man defense). Brady yells, "Set, Go!" The ball snaps. You burst out of your stance, the cornerback drop steps and runs with you. The CB gives you a free release, which allows you to peek at the strong safety to decipher the new coverage.

The tight end inside runs a 12-yard curl route. The safety on your side of the field rolls down toward the line of scrimmage and locks in on the tight end. At this point, you know the secondary has rolled their coverage from a cover-two into a cover three (both cornerbacks and the free safety are each responsible for covering a deep third of the field).

By the 10-yard mark you start to run by the cornerback. At 12 yards you plant your right foot in the ground, give a head nod faking to the right, and break diagonally left toward the goal post in the middle of the end zone (a "post route"). You have a couple yards on the cornerback. The safety is late rolling from the other side of the field; he isn't going to be deep enough to protect his middle third. The middle is wide-open!

As you make your break at 12 yards, Brady plants his back foot, steps into the throw, and launches the ball. It's just the two of you, a couple kids playing toss under the streetlights — no noise, no defenders, no nothing. You locate the rock blazing through the night sky. You and the ball race north on separate, winding highways toward the same destination ... arriving simultaneously. At the crossroads — the Stanford 25-yard line, 40 yards from the line of scrimmage — time stands still for an instant, beads of sweat suspend in the air. You throw your hands up at the last possible moment. ...

Time stabilizes. Beads release. You pluck the ball from the sky and cradle it into your body with your right arm — the cornerback and free safety collide with one another. The roar of the crowd pours into your ears with each blistering step toward the end zone. Alone and untouched, you cross the goal line — your first career touchdown!

Sixty-five yards, and what becomes a career-long touchdown. Your teammates race to the endzone, swarming you with chest bumps and helmet slaps. An infusion of euphoria, excitement, and adrenaline overwhelm your senses, springing to unfamiliar heights. You jog to the sideline, welcomed by an onslaught of exuberance.

And a 57-7 win to top it off. Can the night get any better for you or the team? Yes! As you approach the buses to leave for the airport, an In-and-Out burger truck is waiting. In no way, shape, or form can this night be any better.

In life, few things are more frustrating than knowing you have the ability to do something but are not afforded the opportunity to prove yourself. You have worked extremely hard at your craft, only to see the chances given to others repeatedly. It's not that other people do not deserve the opportunity, but at some point, being so often passed over can start to send you into a spiral of doubt and resentment.

To this point in my college career, I have felt like a student who studies non-stop for finals but on exam day the teacher doesn't even hand me the test. The level of frustration I've experienced until now is beyond words.

There is no doubt: I could have helped the team more this year. I prove myself every day at practice — a great route followed by a long catch have been mainstays. Jeff Samardzija said, "Shelton can get down the field pretty much better than anyone on the team. And he brings solid hands. I don't think you see Matt dropping too many balls."[34]

My knowledge of the playbook is as good as any receiver on the team, and I can line up at any wideout position for any play called. This is not to say there are not areas of my game that need improvement; I am not the biggest person on the field, so my blocking isn't great, but I am put into the game to block more than I am to run routes. Figure that one out. Why has it taken so long for me to get a shot on gameday? Why did it take so long to utilize my speed? There are any number of answers to these questions. The answer I come back to over-and-over again is one that I am not alone in feeling or seeing.

I am one of Davies' boys. Coach Willingham and his staff didn't recruit me, I am not one of *their* guys. Since I was not recruited by Tyrone, I didn't "fit" their style of play. This is a sentiment felt by numerous non-Willingham recruited players. I spoke with a few of Bob Davies' recruits to get their thoughts on the subject.

Billy Palmer said, "I was recruited by Davie to be a blocking tight end in an option offense. When Willingham stepped in, I was passed over for more athletic tight ends, but I never felt I was being passed over because I was recruited by Davie."

Former wide receiver, Ronnie Rodamer stated, "[Willingham and staff] played their guys and only their guys, whenever possible. Their recruits were given an opportunity before any other players who weren't starters."

Fellow 2001 recruit and offensive lineman Dan Stevenson said, "If the coaching staff had a choice, they would always put one of their guys in, unless a Davie guy was pretty much the only option."

Whether by words or deeds, knowingly or not, this coaching staff continued to communicate, "Wait until we get our guys in the system." This sentiment seeped its way into the thoughts of the university officials, as the following quote affirms: "Regrettably, many of the decision makers within our university tend to dismiss criticisms of the current coaching staff as knee-jerk reactions to painful losses. They chide disgruntled alumni for being impatient and insist that Willingham will win once he 'gets his own players in.'"[35] During a Q&A Tyrone is asked, "Do you feel comfortable you can institute your system and complete your system with the talent that's coming back?" and he replies, "I use a blanket statement there, okay. We have to win."[36] Do you hear any confidence in his answer? Does he even answer the question?

Throughout Willingham's tenure, players feel these words in how they are treated and coached, or not coached, by this staff. In speaking with Ronnie, he states, "Coach Miles was getting so hyped for Rhema [McKnight] and Maurice [Stovall] to join the team, it almost felt like he was throwing it in our faces that these were the next great receivers at ND. Seemed like they were already starters, and they weren't even on campus."

Tyrone, and staff, came to Notre Dame with the mindset that in order to win football games he needs to recruit players who fit his system. The coaching staff does not want to, or perhaps can't, fit their football system around the players they already have on the team. Players recruited by the Willingham staff are, within reason, immediately promoted above Davie recruits. If their recruits screw up, the staff holds their hand and gives them another chance to succeed; if one of Davies' boys stumbles, they are demoted to the back of the line ... again.

I, and other Davies' players, see this clear as day. Marcus Wilson witnessed the favoritism of Willingham recruits during his Junior and Senior years, "The coaching staff clearly favored their guys as much as they could. It felt like they were forcing their recruits to play earlier than they were prepared for. It seemed like there was an urgency to get their guys on the field, so the staff could prove they were great recruiters." We all knew this was happening to us. But we could not focus on this imbalance. Just be prepared and shine when the opportunity presents itself.

I am taken off the shelf and put to good use. I'm finally able to show the Notre Dame family what I can truly do on gameday. Teammates have the same sentiment. Linebacker Mike Goolsby knew what ability lay in wait, ready to make a difference. He said, "Freshman year he was assigned to me as my little brother, so I have a nice little bond with Matt. You've seen him making plays the whole time that he has been here. It's just nice for him to finally get a chance to show everybody what he can do in a big-time game like last week."[37]

Suddenly, I have a new best friend in wide receiver coach Trent Miles. "Oh Matt, I knew you could do it! I knew you'd get a touchdown. We drew it up just for you," Miles says. He begins to treat me like a son. A son who can do no wrong. He starts joking around with me. Hanging out with me like we have been best friends for years. The guy has only shown strong disdain toward me since his arrival. Now, it seems like I am his meal ticket, his pet project that has finally paid off. The meal could have come earlier if only I'd been given the chance.

| 2003 Schedule | | | |
|---|---|---|---|
| Overall 5-7 | PCT 0.417 | Home 3-3/Away 2-4/Neutral 0-0 | |
| Date | Opponent | Location | Result |
| 9/6/2003 | vs. Washington St | Notre Dame, IN | W, 29-26 (OT) |
| 9/13/2003 | at Michigan | Ann Arbor, MI | L, 0-38 |
| 9/20/2003 | vs. Michigan St | Notre Dame, IN | L, 16-22 |
| 9/27/2003 | at Purdue | West Lafayette, IN | L, 10-23 |
| 10/11/2003 | at Pittsburgh | Pittsburgh, PA | W, 20-14 |
| 10/18/2003 | vs. USC | Notre Dame, IN | L, 14-45 |
| 10/25/2003 | at Boston College | Chestnut Hill, MA | L, 25-27 |
| 11/1/2003 | vs. Florida State | Notre Dame, IN | L, 0-37 |
| 11/8/2003 | vs. Navy | Notre Dame, IN | W, 27-24 |
| 11/15/2003 | vs. BYU | Notre Dame, IN | W, 33-14 |
| 11/29/2003 | at Stanford | Palo Alto, CA | W, 57-7 |
| 12/6/2003 | at Syracuse | Syracuse, NY | L, 12-38 |

I have my best season thus far, playing in all 12 games. Primarily participating on special teams, I have 11 kickoff returns for 174 yards. I make, yet again, one tackle — tackling is the worst. Playing in just 21:15 minutes at receiver, with three receptions for 80 yards and a touchdown.

The season ends with a record of 5-7. Half as many wins and twice as many losses as seen in Willingham's first season. ND is tired of losing and this drastic drop in results, from season one to season two, is troublesome.

"Willingham's first two seasons were a study in extremes. The 8-0 start in his inaugural campaign elicited comparisons to Ara Parseghian's magical 9-0 beginning in 1964. Then his 5-7 campaign in Year 2 evoked reminders of Joe Kuharich's second season in 1960 when the Irish finished 2-8. Thus, Year 3 would serve as a 'tiebreaker' and gauge as to what course the program would take under his direction."[38]

*2004, Notre Dame Stadium: Matt Shelton Touchdown vs. Boston College.*

# A Visit from the Future

## 34

**Spring 2004. After an** underwhelming second season, the germination of pessimistic rumblings is matured, whispers in shadow percolate faster and further each day. Murmurs for a head coach change begin to swell, as the world works in its mysterious way. ...

With spring football peeping over the horizon, the team continues the fine tradition of Saturday morning workouts. Saturday sessions are not getting any easier, I still have not come around to the idea of this particular babysitting technique. After an overall poor showing last season, the team encounters an intensified sense of urgency during all offseason training sessions.

As we sleepwalk into our warmup lines, I let out a huge yawn. I lock eyes with Mickey, he shakes his head, and gives me an angered look that says, "You're lucky I don't have a weight." Halfway through the warmup, I hear a commotion to my right. I look up from stretching to find a few unfamiliar faces standing on the track. I take note because we never, and I do mean never, have visitors attend our 6:00 a.m. Saturday workouts. Our normal grueling workout comes to an end, and the team gathers around Coach Willingham for final words before dismissal.

Throughout my Notre Dame career, we have numerous guest speakers who visit practice and speak with the team: Hank Aaron, Joe Montana, Joe Theismann, Rudy (the player, not the actor), Arizona Diamondbacks 2001 World Series Champions (minus Randy Johnson, still stings Randy), Jerry Rice, Tim Brown, Raghib "Rocket" Ismail Jr., Jerome Bettis, and Jon Bon Jovi to name a few. All of these people, plus many more, provide words of encouragement to the team — not Mickey words of "encouragement," until today.

As we gather at mid-field, Tyrone invites the unfamiliar faces to join us. I take a knee, unsurprisingly with sweat dripping from my face, I lean over to our kicker D.J. Fitzpatrick and ask, "Who is this guy?" Neither of us recognize him.

After a purposeful stroll to the huddle, he begins to speak. As mentioned, most speakers offer words of encouragement, but not this guy. He is probably the only person in the history of Notre Dame guest speakers who does not sing the football teams praises, or at least give us some sort of upbeat, positive spin.

His mood and message are that of annoyed criticism, neither constructive nor uplifting — just kind of mad, which takes us all by surprise, as we look around at one another. He really lays into us about our lack of effort on the field, about our sloppy play, etc. He is even calling guys out individually. Attacking the team, hoping to jolt us into a better understanding of who we are, why we are here, and how we can be better.

D.J. said, while walking away from this meeting, he thought, "It would suck to play for that guy."

After the tongue lashing, our guest asks if there are any questions. One of the players, kneeling a few rows from center, asks him if he can see the massive ring on his finger. Our guest removes his ring and tosses it to the player. As the 14-karat, white-gold ring spins through the air, the light bouncing off its 42-diamonds is almost blinding.

This guy is not afraid to let others handle the ring — I don't think I would ever wear it outside of the house. Maybe he is so nonchalant about it because he has a similar one at home. He is a Notre Dame graduate of 1978, soon-to-be 4-time Super Bowl Champion, and current offensive coordinator for the New England Patriots. Charlie Weis.

A real life "Back to the Future," DeLorean, flux-capacitor, vibe thunderclaps through the space-time-continuum. The team is meeting their future head coach, who was invited to speak by our future former head coach. Mind blown.

Be careful what you wish for D.J.

# HOLDING

## 35

At the end of last season, I was presented with a real opportunity to shine and shine I did. With a newfound confidence created by on field success, I have never been more enthusiastic for the offseason. Gameday results have magic within them. This offseason, surprisingly, a new opportunity presents itself. A prospect that will expand my value and my sense of worth as a football player. One that will put me on the field more often and showcase a strength of mine, quick hands.

D.J. Fitzpatrick is in search of a new holder for field goals and point-after-touchdowns. D.J. and I were both recruited by Bob. We have become best friends over the years, so there is another level of trust accompanying the teammate dynamic. He asks if I want to be his holder. I don't have to think about it, "Hell yes!"

Asking is a formality. I embrace helping the team, working with a buddy, and becoming part of the most underrated — but essential — parts of a football team. It's an easy decision for me. D.J. believes I can execute the duties of a holder. He knows I have the hands for the task and trusts I will always get the job done. The coaching staff, on the other hand, still has their doubts.

After a few weeks of finetuning the mechanics for our kicking operation, my audition for holder is here. The first day of spring football practice. I arrive early to practice for the tryout. As D.J. and I jog onto the field I hear the faint yell of Buzz Preston, the Running Backs and Special Teams coach, in the distance. As we get closer his words become clear. "Let's see what you got Shell-Game!" Buzz gave me a nickname! All it took was a 65-yard touchdown for the coaching staff to show some love. As Buzz waits to see if I have what it takes, I crouch into position. No nerves. It is just another day at the office.

The job title is not fancy. Holder. How difficult can it be? It certainly does not look like much on gameday. It is one of those jobs that, if things go according to plan, no one should notice you are even there.

Imagine it's gameday. Put yourself in my shoes, standing in the huddle on the 50-yard line. See the clusters of green shirts scattered throughout the crowd brightening the stadium — you think, "That's a lot of green." Hear the screeching of 80,000 plus devotees. Feel the 10-mph wind across your face on a chilly fall day. Brady calls your number in the huddle. The huddle breaks. You race to the line — know your role and start collecting data: run to the correct side of the field, line up on the numbers, watch your spacing, remember your route, change your route if the defense dictates, where are the safeties, what is your cornerback doing, what coverage do you see, etc. You see a cover-two. Did Brady give you a second play in the huddle?

The ball snaps. You burst off the line, slap the defenders' hands away, and put your head down to drive down field on a deep fade route along the sideline. At full speed, you raise and turn your head to locate the ball — keep your crown steady. There it is! With each stride, the ball bounces up and down in the sky; the wind agitates it side-to-side. You throw your hands up. Snagging the ball at the 5-yard line, and high-step into the end zone to a thunderous cheer from your fans!

Your teammates chase you down and bombard you, almost tackling you to the ground. You make your way through the gauntlet of players slapping you on the helmet in congratulations. Looking for breath after your blazing 45-yard dash. Sweat dripping into your eyes. You locate D.J. standing in the middle of the field. You pound fists, and he gives you a headbutt. Concussion inbound. You attempt to compose yourself for your next job ... your new job.

D.J. finds a nice patch of grass 5 ½-yards behind the long snapper. He stands with his left foot, his plant foot, on the left side of the patch. With the toes of his right foot, he shows you where to place the ball on the patch once it is in your hands. You crouch to the ground, with your left knee at your chest and your right to the side tucked underneath you. You reach your left arm out, going just inside of your left knee, placing your fingertips at the tip of his shoe marking the spot. D.J. takes three steps backward and a couple to his left, getting into position for the snap. You realize your gloves are drenched in sweat. You rub both gloves on your pants, then together, as you quickly try to dry them. Dammit, you lost your mark on the nice patch of grass — all the patches look nice! Where does D.J. want the ball again?

Not fully knowing if you are in the correct spot anymore, you look at D.J. with confidence to see if he is ready. He gives you the nod. The earsplitting cheers turn into an eerie silence you feel on the back of your neck. You can cut the tension with a knife.

You turn your focus to the snapper who is bent over, looking through his legs, awaiting your call. With your left fingertips still marking the "correct" spot, you throw your right arm up to signal the snapper, and concurrently yell, "Hut!" In the blink of an eye the ball zips through the snappers' legs, hurling toward you. At the snap, D.J. starts his approach.

You bring your left hand up to meet your right and catch the ball knee high with both hands. You fight through a bobble!

Muscle memory quickly guides your hands back to the exact spot your left hand was marking. You place one tip of the ball on the ground — still unsure if this is the exact spot D.J. marked — your left index finger presses the top tip of the ball and holds it in position for your approaching kicker; simultaneously, you slightly lean the ball toward yourself and forward, all while using your right hand to spin the ball toward or away from you to ensure the laces are pointing at the goalposts (sometimes the spin is huge, sometimes tiny). D.J. strokes the ball. You lean and encourage the ball to stay down the middle, as it flutters to-and-fro in the wind. It's good! The crowd cheers as one more point is added to the scoreboard.

*2004, ND Stadium: Point After TD with Matt Shelton & D.J. Fitzpatrick.*

The entire operation happens fast, less than 1.35-seconds. After a few more holds Buzz says, "Nice Shell-Game! You've got the job!"

# NOTRE DAME &1 SMARTEN UP

## 36

MAY 5, 2004. DURING recruitment, Bob promised a new world-class training facility would be completed in 2002. A little longer than expected ... groundbreaking commences on the "Gug" (pronounced Goog), the Guglielmino Athletics Complex. On this day Notre Dame Athletics shed their upgrade stagnation, step into the light of the 21st century, and signal a commitment to all things state-of-the-art. This refreshing mentality will attract recruits, please alumni and fans, and kickstart a new era of Notre Dame Football.

The complex sits adjacent to the Loftus Sports Center, which holds the indoor artificial turf practice field and the indoor track. The Gug is a 96,000 sq. ft. facility designed to enhance the student-athlete experience. The first floor has a 25,000 sq. ft. fitness center with cutting-edge equipment, an 8,300 sq. ft. Loftus Sports Medicine and Rehabilitation center, a 50-yard track for speed workouts, a 45x18-yard turf field, and an Equipment room. The Romano Family Locker Room houses 125-lockers, 22-showers, a "mud" room, and a players' lounge with 52-inch TVs and a kitchen. The coach's locker room has 20-lockers and 6-private showers. The Isban Auditorium is 3,800 Sq. Ft. with 150-theater seats, and a

300-foot screen. The second floor is a 7,800 Sq. Ft. area with offices for the football staff and a recruiting lounge to entertain guests.[39]

As the football program gets this new era underway, I too begin anew. I have a brilliant idea. A stroke of genius ... it took long enough. After drinking hundreds of pounds of water over the years, which never stayed on as body weight, I can take no more. I need to "work smarter, not harder."

The first day of summer workouts. Walking into the weight room, I throw my bag to the floor and stare down my old foe ... the water cooler — this "torture device" and I have a lot of history. I bend at the waist, take an honorary sip, and sidestep right onto the scale. Mickey beelines to take note. He clears his throat on approach, "Ahem. Ahem." He looks over my shoulder, does a double take, and goes wild! He throws his clipboard. Runs up and down the weight room shouting, "He made weight! Mickey forces me to stay on the scale while he gathers players and coaches to bear witness to this miracle. Mick's hard work and persistence has paid off.

Smiling ear-to-ear, I jump off the scale. Mickey gives me a chest bump, almost knocking me to the floor. My smile softens into a sly smirk. I triumphantly pick up my workout bag, and head to the restroom before the workout begins. Entering the bathroom, I look around to see if the coast is clear — even crouching to look under the stalls. I am alone. With both hands I reach into my pants, inside my girdle, and pull out two 2 ½-pound weights from my hip pockets and slip them into my bag.

After not being able to "make weight" for years, I eventually smarten up. Refusing to indulge Mickey anymore ... I will never need to drink 6-pounds of water before jumping a rope ever again. Today is a good day!

# TY'S TRY, "TAKE THREE"

## 37

I HAVE FINALLY ARRIVED! After the pains, struggles, and stresses of the last three years, I am no longer at the bottom of the heap. Now, I'm one of the players freshmen look up to when they arrive on campus. I'm always ecstatic for football season to begin, but this year is special. I am a senior!

*2004 Notre Dame
Football Senior Class*

Well, I am a redshirt senior. Seeing as I didn't play my freshman year, I received a redshirt designation. The redshirt concept is that you have five years to play four seasons. So, once I graduate on time, I'll still have one year of football eligibility remaining. This is my year! The 2004 football season, I will finally have a real shot at playing wide receiver full-time.

**September 4, 2004.** The season opens in Provo, Utah against the BYU Cougars. In this game I see an increase in minutes at wide receiver, but don't have any catches. At least the season starts with a change in a positive direction. Nearing the end of the first quarter, I see the first pass of the season thrown my way and it is overthrown, falling incomplete. I jog to the sideline. I do not see the field much during the second quarter, it's a cold enough night that we have hot chocolate at halftime, and I watch the third quarter with the fans.

As though we are reverting to last year, I sit on the bench not involved in the game and forgotten. Do the coaches think I am incapable of helping the team? Did they see anything I did last year, or in the offseason, or during two-a-days? Do they think so little of me? Are they going to use me at the last minute, setting a Bob Davie boy up to fail?

I don't have the answers, but I do have a stiff body; my muscles tighten up from standing on the sideline for most of the game. My body becomes colder and tighter with each passing tick of the clock; with every exhale I see my breath on this brisk evening. Removed from the flow of the game, and frustrated, I do my best to stay focused as the fourth quarter starts.

Without warning or warm-up, I get the call. Trent yells, "Matt! You're in ... going deep." Pumped, excited to get onto the field it only half-registers how stiff I am from being sidelined most of the game.

Brady breaks the huddle. As I run to the line of scrimmage, I continue attempting to warm up my body for the sprint to come. Jumping up and down until I line up. I survey the defense. "Hut, Hut!" I bolt off the line full speed. Around the defender, I race down the field. I look up, find the ball in the air, and "oh hell" Brady has thrown this one far ... like, *really* far. I put my head down and continue barreling down the field. As I look up for the ball again, I realize, I'm not even close. Brady out-throws me by 7 yards. Not his fault. Neither of us takes into consideration that I haven't seen much of the field since the first quarter — my top-end speed is found wanting.

Utilized so little during the game, jumping on the exercise bike to stay warm does not cross my mind after halftime. The coaches do not plan to deploy me or else someone would suggest I hop on the bike to stay warm. Instead, I remain an afterthought and am "thrown to the wolves" when the situation becomes desperate. The Cougars won 20-17. Maybe next week I can help the team, and not simply be a footnote.

**September 11, 2004.** The team returns home for a matchup with the University of Michigan. Last year they beat ND 38-0. So far, this game is more of the same. As the first half ends, Michigan leads 9-0. In the last six quarters against the Wolverines, Notre Dame is scoreless. We can't get anything going on offense and need a spark.

To open the second half the defense gets a much-needed stop on fourth down, giving the football to the offense on our own 39-yard line. Darius Walker rushes for 7 yards, then 3 yards, and we tack on an extra 5 yards from a Michigan defensive offsides penalty. As we stand in our huddle on the Michigan 46-yard line, Brady says, "We're taking a shot." He calls the play and gives me a quick glance. A glance that signals there is a good chance the ball is coming my way.

The crowd is doing everything within their power to help turn the tide — remaining quiet while Brady makes his calls at the line of scrimmage. "Hut, hut!" Brady drops back to pass. I breeze by the defender, who is playing soft coverage off the line, and race toward the south end zone.

Brady sees I have a few steps on the defender — I'm open, he heaves the ball in my direction. Like an eagle tracking its prey, my eyes fixate on the ball. I let off the gas, slowing my forward momentum, recognizing the football is slightly underthrown. I leap into the air. The cornerback turns, jumping into my chest ... I catch the ball on top of his helmet. My feet land in the end zone, as I cradle the ball into my right arm. Touchdown!

*2004, Notre Dame Stadium: Matt Shelton Touchdown vs. Michigan.*

I take a few extra steps through the back of the end zone. Looking into the crowd with a smile, I raise the ball high into the air. With a flick of my right wrist, I toss the football into the Michigan Marching Band, hitting one of them in the head. The band members are visibly shaken by the touchdown and too stunned to react to this taunting. I turn to celebrate with my teammates and eventually push my way through their helmet slaps to locate D.J. for my holder duties.

Momentum officially shifts, but the game is still in favor of "the bad guys" 9-7. But the spark is found! The team secures a 28-20 victory over the #8 ranked Michigan Wolverines. Keeping me involved in the game, as opposed to letting me stiffen on the sideline until the fourth quarter, has paid off.

**September 18, 2004.** The team takes a road trip north to face Michigan State. At the end of the first quarter, we lead 14-7 following a 1-yard touchdown run by Brady Quinn and a 75-yard fumble return for a touchdown by Tommy Zbikowski. It is a close game.

Then, the coaches call my number. Maybe this is where the lesson Brandon Hoyte imprinted onto my neck during our first practice freshman year will pay off... keep your head on a swivel. As I line up as the inside receiver on the left side of the ball, I scan the defense. The defensive back is about 5 yards from me, and a safety is in the middle of the field. The ball snaps, I run directly at the DB, which puts him in a compromising position, because I'm not tipping him off to where I am going. This uneasiness makes him shuffle in his backpedal.

When I get close, I shimmy and cut underneath him to the middle of the field. Continuing to gain ground toward our end zone, I avoid the dropping linebacker (thanks Hoyte, lesson learned), and run at the safety. I slam my foot in the ground 12 yards from the line of scrimmage, give another shake to unbalance the trailing DB, and cut toward the Michigan State sideline to finish my deep crossing route. Brady hits me in stride on the right side of the field, I tuck the ball into my body, and finish through the end zone for a 35-yard touchdown! Extending our lead to 21-7, with 8:52 remaining in the second quarter. In a back-and-forth game, we "get out of Dodge" with a 31-24 victory, and a record of 2-1.

With the most opportunities in my career during one game, I haul in three catches for 123 yards and a touchdown against the Spartans. After the game, my teammates discuss my play:

- *"He's really played off his abilities. He's provided a big spark for our offense that I don't think a lot of people expected com-*

*ing into the season. He's really helping our big-play capabilities."*
— Anthony Fasano, TE

- *"He's got a great knack for getting open and his speed helps him with that. At the same time, he's a smart player and he definitely sees where there's open space and gets to it."* — Brady Quinn, QB

- *"You have to love a kid like Shelton just catching deep balls like that, going up and making that catch against Michigan. I thought that was the play of the game. He deserves it. Matt's been around for a long time."* — Mike Goolsby, LB [40]

The difference-making ability, the value I always knew I could bring to the team, is starting to shine brightly. With opportunity, I have proven on gameday what I have shown in practice for years. And I will continue to help my team in any way possible.

**September 25, 2004.** On this day, two earned honors are bestowed: the first start of my career and team captain. After much adversity — and a lot of hurt and pain along the way — I am overcome with a sense of pride. I am humbled and honored in this moment. Can my day get any better?! Yep! Of course, it can! We still have a game to play, and I am a man on a mission. Not to prove I belong ... I've done that already. Proving I deserve to be a captain and a starter is at the top of my to-do list today.

I have the best game, to date, of my career. In a 38-3 victory against the University of Washington, I lead the team with four receptions for 74 yards, and tie for most touchdowns on the day with two (one of which is on the front cover). The first multi-touchdown game of my college football career. Maybe I was energized by the pregame honors? Maybe these results were going to happen regardless? Maybe I got lucky today? The following quotes feel fitting:

- *"Success occurs when opportunity meets preparation."*
  — Zig Ziglar[41]

- *"Luck is what happens when preparation meets opportunity."*
  — Roman philosopher Seneca[42]

Hidden amongst the masses, buried on the depth chart, fighting to break-through the glass ceiling of being a "Davies' boy," I thrive. No matter the reason for this "breakout" game, I am able to seize the moment. I am ready when called upon. Coming into my own, half of my receptions this season have been touchdowns (4 of 8 catches), with an average of 39.4-yards per touchdown. That's what I'm talking about! I'm on a roll, and the team is on a roll with a three-game winning streak. We have a 3-1 record with some tough opponents remaining. Running-the-table to a BCS Bowl game is the goal.

**November 6, 2004.** A trip home to Tennessee for a game against the Volunteers at Neyland Stadium in Knoxville. With the lights shining brightly upon me, I cannot wait to show the home state what I have grown into. Family and friends from every corner of the state are coming to watch. Though I don't have a catch today, I open the game with a bang.

The stadium is rocking at full capacity with 101,915 fans settling into their seats. This is the loudest stadium I've ever played in. The stadium sprouts from the field straight up into the sky, not outward like most. The stairs on the top level are as steep as the Great Smoky Mountains summit. Traversing these altitudes can be a battle of nerves. Sound reverberates between its towering circular peak. On a foggy day you squint to see the top row from the field. Orange, everything in sight is bright orange.

I take my position near the end zone and await the opening kickoff. This whistle blows. The ball is kicked high into the air. As I track the ball through the fog, I call off my co-returner and cradle the ball into my body. I look up from making the catch to find that my teammates have forgotten to block most of the kickoff team. I take a few steps. ...

CRUNCH! My feet fly into the air. Everything goes dark. I quickly animate from my comatose state and attempt to shake the stars from my eyes. I wobble to my feet and stumble off the field. On the sideline I take a knee to gather myself and find my breath. Coach Miles walks over and says, "You good to go? We need you out there." Barely able to see straight. Breath not found. I answer, "I'm gonna need a play or two."

After the game, under the stadium, I meet with friends and family to say hello. Mom asks, "Are you ok?" Dad laughingly says, "I've never heard 100,000 fans go dead silent so quick. They were loud as hell to start, then a collective 'Ooh' and you could hear a pin drop." Add another concussion to the list of injuries, and a win over the #9 ranked team in the country. ND wins, 17-13.

**November 27, 2004.** Today the regular season comes to an end after a 41-10 loss to USC. Our early season hope of running-the-table is a distant memory. It is almost laughable we once thought it possible to win our remaining games and move onto a BCS game. After dominating Washington, the tides turn as we finish the regular season, losing four of the last seven games: Purdue by 25-points, Boston College by 1-point, Pittsburgh by 2-points, and now USC by 31-points.

With a 6-5 record, there is still a chance we will be invited to a non-BCS bowl game. We leave Los Angeles for ND to begin preparations.

# WILLINGHAM ... THAT'S A WRAP

## 38

**NOVEMBER 30, 2004.** THE 2002 season, the first season under Tyrone Willingham, was stamped as Notre Dame's "Return to Glory" with a t-shirt. Started in 1990, "The Shirt" is an annual student fund-raiser supporting campus clubs, organizations, and activities, along with a charity fund that aids students who need help paying medical expenses. With this shirt, the stadium frequently is overtaken by a "sea of green" ... or blue or gold or any other color they make the shirt.

Whether you are running out of the tunnel, soaking in the sight from your stadium seat, or watching at home on national television, it truly is an awesome sight to behold. The solidarity, the love, the pride you feel to your very core now sits upon your shoulders, and across your chest for all to see. An amazing student-led project rallies the students and fan base, the family, each year. Today the unifying "Return to Glory" shirts rallies the family again, but not as intended.

A mere two days after the shellacking USC put on the team, "The Shirt" is uniting students on a non-gameday. ND students plan an on-campus protest for this evening at the Administration Building where they will throw their "Return to Glory" into a pile, essentially into the trash, demanding Tyrone be fired — the plan is all for naught, as he is fired earlier in the day before their event.

In direct opposition to this sentiment, the night after his firing, there is a protest in support of Coach Willingham. Iris Outlaw, our then-director of Multicultural Student Programs and Services, eloquently states, "Our reaction can serve another purpose: It can encourage Notre Dame to open its arms and truly embrace diversity throughout the institution." Shirts are distributed the following week that read, "It's bigger than football. It's about losing IntegriTY."[43] The firing of Tyrone Willingham is polarizing, with vocal supporters on both sides.

As students prepare for tonight's t-shirt toss, the football team is called to the stadium for a meeting. The players are unsure what this meeting is about. Some think our meeting is to discuss Bowl game options. Others believe the whispers in the shadows — percolating since the end of the 2002 season — will step into the light to be heard and the time of Tyrone will cross into the past.

Sitting in the team meeting room, I am positive we are here only to discuss which bowl game, if any, we will be attending. An agitated buzz hovers within these walls, as players attempt to unravel today's topic of conversation. The doors fly open and in comes the athletic director, Dr. Kevin White. He takes the podium. In this moment, I know I am wrong. Change is here. Our leader is gone; another is on his way. Dr. White informs us the university has "decided to go in a different direction."

In Coach Willingham's final meeting with his team, he chooses to leave us with the immortal words of Dr. Martin Luther King Jr. — words Tyrone shared many times during the past three football seasons, words he used at his first team meeting as the new Notre Dame Football head coach in 2002. Addressing the team for the final time, he says, "If a man is called to be a street sweeper, he should sweep streets even as Michelangelo painted, or Beethoven composed music or Shakespeare wrote poetry. He should sweep streets so well that all the hosts of heaven and earth will pause to say, 'here lived a great street sweeper who did his job well.'"[44]

Tyrone continues by reminding us all that, regardless of what life has in store, we must always strive to be the best we can be. With that, Coach Willingham gracefully exits stage-left, entering the storied history books of the University of Notre Dame as the first Black head football coach.

The team is stunned. Brady Quinn leans over to tell me he is "completely shocked ... had no idea this was coming." This news is received with heavy hearts and stirred minds. No matter what a player thinks about the news, it's difficult to not be impacted, to not feel the "What if" of it all.

What if we practiced a little harder, played a little better, worked-out more intensely, listened more, etc.? What if we simply did more? Our team is in a tough situation, with an uncertain future, and many of us have a sense of déjà vu — the feeling, not the club, get your head out of the gutter. We worry about one another and what the future holds for our team, our family. We think, "How will we get through this change?"

- *"I just have a heavy head, a heavy heart. There's whispers all the time around here about coaching changes. Especially at the time it happened – no one on the team ever thought it would really happen."*
  — Anthony Fasano, TE

- *"It was definitely very emotional, and anger was definitely something that played into it. It was hard, overall, just hard."*
  — Brandon Hoyte, LB

- *"I feel bad for the seniors ... First, they have to go through the [Bob] Davie firing, then [George] O'Leary and now this. Those guys have constantly helped the underclassmen and they've been so selfless, and now they have to go through this again."* — Tommy Zbikowski, DB

- *"We as players don't feel we did enough to help coach out. That's not for me to answer, if he got a fair shot, but there is a sentiment among players that we should have done more, we could have performed at a higher level for coach."* — Ryan Harris, OL

- *"I think it's a shock to everybody. As a player, you think it's our fault. We didn't get the job done. I think Coach Willingham was a great coach, and I enjoyed playing under him."* — Jared Clark, TE [45]

For the first time in Notre Dame history, a head football coach is fired before his original contract expires. At a news conference Kevin White says, "We simply have not made the progress on the field that we need to make. Nor have we been able to create the positive momentum necessary in our efforts to return the Notre Dame program to the elite level of the college football world."[46] Coach Willingham did not produce the results needed, or expected, to remain the head coach at the University of Notre Dame.

Under Tyrone's leadership we had a 21-15 record, his reign began with an 8-0 record that was followed by a 13-15 record. He lost eight games by at least three touchdowns and lost five games by 30 points or more (two of which were shutouts). When he took the reins at ND, we held the all-time winning percentage in college football history with a record of 781-247-42 (.749), ahead of Michigan's 813-265-36 (.746); at the end of the 2004 regular season, we drop to second-place with a record of 802-261-42 (.745) and Michigan jumps into first-place with a record of 842-274-36 (.747).[47]

No matter your view on his firing, it is undeniable that he did not win enough on the field. These numbers, these facts, were factors in him being let go by the university and, likely, there were other various contributing reasons.

Following the 2003 season, many believe the Notre Dame higher-ups asked Tyrone to make changes to his coaching staff, but Willingham refused. Following the 2004 season, it's also widely understood he was again asked to make changes; this time, specifically at the offensive coordinator position in 2004 but he again refused, remaining loyal to his friends, and betting the staff would turn things around.

A 2008 *Bleacher Report* article leans into the offensive coordinator change, stating, "It didn't have to be that way either. If he fired [Bill] Deidrick he could have stayed (something he did anyway when he went to Washington). He didn't and that turned out to be the best thing that has happened to Notre Dame Football in years. It's taken four years to cleanse the stench of losing and divisiveness."[48]

When asked about coaching changes, Tyrone said he "didn't think it was necessary to discuss whether or not he was asked to make any staff changes."[49] Reading between the lines, his answer does allude to him being asked to make changes.

Personally, I believe making coaching changes after either season would have only delayed the inevitable — players would have continued to be uninspired and underutilized. "Tyrone was too loyal to his staff and didn't fire anyone. If he did, then he would have coached a little longer at ND. Honestly, he was a great person — a high integrity guy — just not the coach we needed. The team didn't need life lesson after life lesson ... we chose the hard route in choosing Notre Dame, we were all smart kids who knew the difference between right and wrong, so let's have a focus on football. Coach us up more, be hard-nosed with us on the field, develop us on the field just like Mickey did in the weight room. Not sure if it was bad coaching or just not wanting to develop players, either way we were a talented team who underperformed and that boils down to coaching," said Marcus Wilson in a recent conversation.

I could not agree more with Marcus. I do not think Coach Willingham did much player development, much football coaching. I only remember him teaching me one thing about football, how to hold the ball ... the five points of pressure: fingertips, palm, forearm, bicep, and chest. Along with a reminder to hold the ball "high and tight." He taught us a lot about life and how to be a man but missed the mark on how to be a football player.

Mike Goolsby shares similar thoughts in a 2023 interview, as he recalls our first team meeting with Tyrone. "Whatever he was trying to sell us, I wasn't buying. I can truly remember having that internal dialog with myself. 'This guy is full of sh*t. But I have to go along with it because I haven't started yet, so I have to buy in, as it were. Let's just get to football, not quotes of the day type stuff.'" Mike continues, "I think his intentions were good, but he wasn't a good ball coach. He was a bit of a figurehead, a talking head, and he had some bad assistant coaches. I just call it like I see it, he wasn't a good football coach."[50]

The team craved development. We wanted, and needed, a head coach who could show us how to become better football players, not just better men. At the end of the day, I believe Tyrone stood by his coaches more than his players (more to come on this topic). No matter your feelings about Coach Willingham's firing, he simply didn't win consistently enough at an institution like Notre Dame.

New seasons. New chapters. Change. All can be difficult and scary, but they can also be freeing ... if you allow them to be. Shifting your perspective within a situation can bring to light new opportunities, new hopes, and a brand-new you.

# BAER WITH US COACH #4

## 39

**DECEMBER 1, 2004.** HERE we go again. It is official. No one at the helm. No leader to guide the team. Consistency lost, yet again. With a 6-5 record, the team is invited to participate in the "Insight.com Bowl" on December 28th. But we don't have a head coach. The university advises that the team can still participate in the bowl if we want, and defensive coordinator Kent Baer has agreed to be the interim head coach.

The 2001 recruiting class now has their fourth head coach in as many years, and there are strong odds a fifth is on the way for year number five. But let's focus on the here and now.

Our fate is to be decided by the seniors gathering to discuss Notre Dame's potential participation in a bowl game. We talk amongst ourselves, spit balling and debating, with no end in sight. Those who want to play argue: "We've worked so hard to get here." ... "We deserve it." ... "The seniors who will not be eligible to play next year deserve it." Those against playing in the bowl say: "We barely have a winning record." ... "We have no coach." ... "Let's just regroup and focus on next year." At this point, the seniors are far from a unanimous decision.

With no clear-cut winner, no supermajority, we decide the entire team needs to be a part of this vote and that there will be one stipulation: voting will continue until 75% of the players vote to either attend or not attend the Bowl game. After a passionate, loud, and rowdy team discussion, we vote. Each player writes "yes" or "no" on a piece of paper. Simple, yet effective.

The results are collected and counted. More than 75% of the team submits a "yes" to accept the Bowl game invitation. The overall sentiment is that we need to end the season on a high note for the fans, the university, and ourselves. The assistant coaches vow to stick with the team until after we conclude the season. So, the team is off to Arizona for the Insight.com Bowl with a few objectives: send our seniors out with a win, create a solid foundation for next season, and display who we are to our next head coach ... whomever that might be.

I recently asked Darius Walker to reflect on his first year at Notre Dame, Willingham's last, and this period of uncertainty. "It was important to me to play early in my college career, but I didn't start right away. I didn't travel to BYU for our first game, so I assumed my chance wouldn't come soon." I asked Darius, "Did leaving the university ever cross your mind, due to not starting day one or to Tyrone being fired?" He said, "No. Not even for a minute. I just knew I had to keep working hard and my opportunity would come. It didn't take long, I got playing time in the second game of the season, and slowly increased my playing time every game until I became the starter. Then, Coach Willingham got fired. And I still never thought about leaving. I was absolutely shocked though. I mean, we didn't have a great year, but I thought he would get more time. But me leaving was never an option."

I asked, "Darius, what went through your mind when Tyrone, the coach who recruited you to ND, was fired?" He said, "My first thought was, '*Great*, now I'll need to repeat my freshman year.' What I meant by that was I'll have to learn a new system, then figure out how I fit into that system. I'll also need to learn how to work with a new group of coaches. But still, the thought of leaving never crossed my mind." Darius continued with his thoughts on players leaving in the transfer portal. "But these days, players are transferring left and right on a whim. Difficult times help shape football players. How are these players going to adapt to difficulties if they make it to the NFL? They cannot just transfer because they aren't getting playing time or their coach leaves."

Darius and I share a similar freshman year experience ... losing a coach. Both of us were shocked and in disbelief. The man, the men, who recruited us to the university left us. But we didn't see this as an opening to leave for "greener pastures." We view this as an opportunity to grow. We perceive this change as one that will prepare us for life after college, and after football. Life is not going to be easy, and you must learn to handle adversity. Deal with issues when they arise. Overcome perceived obstacles. Do not take the easy way out by leaving ... roll up your sleeves and find a way to navigate change and setback.

# PART FOUR

## A WEIS GUY & A FAREWELL

# Weis's Will

## 40

THE 2001 RECRUITING CLASS is midway through senior year and we are under the leadership of our fourth head coach, albeit interim, with a fifth in our sights. An unexpected journey. A coaching merry-go-round. Enough head coaches for a pickup game of 5-on-5 basketball.

Bob Davie, the strong and charismatic recruiter, who would lead us through our college years ... fizzled out. The excitement George O'Leary brought to Notre Dame was quickly replaced by a stain of regret. The emergence of Tyrone Willingham brought hope of a "Return to Glory," which dwindled each year. Kent Baer is our steadfast stopgap. With Willingham's firing hope is once again tapped. For quite some time, the ND fanbase's sense of hope and excitement have hibernated ... waiting to be awakened. A campus, a community, an entire family spanning the globe awaits the announcement of a singular person who will once again wake the echoes.

**December 12, 2004.** Twelve days after releasing Tyrone Willingham from his coaching contract, and buying out the remaining two years, Notre Dame announces our new leader. Campus jumps to attention. Hope and excitement lie in wait no more.

University President-elect Father John Jenkins says:

"At the University of Notre Dame, the success in our football program consists of three things: Acting with integrity,
giving our students a superb education, and excelling on the
field. Meeting all these goals is a tremendous challenge. But
I believe we have found a person in Charlie Weis who can
lead us to such multifaceted success. Charlie is a Notre Dame
graduate, an offensive coordinator of the New England Patriots and holder of three Super Bowl rings; a man of tremendous character and a man who understands and embraces the
highest ideals of Notre Dame. Charlie was clearly the most
impressive candidate we interviewed, and I could not be hap-
pier that he will be the new football coach at the University
of Notre Dame."[51]

This announcement ushers in a bright future. Resurrects hope. Fades
the tarnish of recent failed and ineffective hires. A crowning that restores
brilliance to the Golden Dome. The final player, completing our "starting
five" of ND head football coaches from 2001-2005, has been picked.

Coach Weis possesses three Super Bowl Championships, eventually
a fourth, and an undeniable track record of NFL success. This offensive
juggernaut, this savant, ends the 2001 recruiting classes' coaching carousel
and the search for Notre Dame Football's next savior.

What stories will Charlie add to my journey? How will his chapter
on the team compare to his other four "teammates?" What will his legacy
become, and how will it be viewed?

The football team gathers in the stadium for another team meeting ...
a lot of those these days. Coach Charlie Weis is introduced to the team for

the first time. Well, the first time as the head coach — he was our "A Visit from the Future" speaker earlier this year, and the future is now.

Coach Weis begins speaking and chills race through my body. The way he speaks makes me sit at attention and cling to his every word. He commands our respect, speaking very directly and to the point, not beating around the bush. "You are what you are folks, right now you're a 6-5 football team," Weis said. "And guess what? That's just not good enough. That's not good enough for you, and it's certainly not going to be good enough for me. So, if you think they hired me to go .500, you've got the wrong guy." Charlie continues to inform us that we are going to be a "nasty" football team. We love what we hear from this guy! It is a new, forgotten intensity that was stripped away systematically over the years.

Football is a "nasty" sport and the type of attitude he brings to the table, as our leader, will seep into the core of our teams' hive-mind, our collective-consciousness. A mindset that will make opponents fear this team. "I come here with a plan, and the plan is [that] the first thing you've got to do is you've got to take care of the guys you already have here," Weis says. "Everyone wants to hear about recruits, but they forget about the players that are already here."[52]

He gets it! There is no time to waste! Charlie plans to mold his football scheme, his offensive and defensive concepts, to the players he already has — instead of using the old regime's mentality of needing to find recruits who fit their system. A refreshing take from the viewpoint of a player who has been "kicked down the road" year-after-year with his leaders whispering, "wait until we get our guys."

# NFL SUPPORT?

## 41

THERE IS NO DOUBT I will return to Notre Dame for a fifth year of college football. Not only because I am ecstatic about my new head coach, but because he can prepare me for an NFL future. He can mold me into a great college football player and propel me into the NFL. Not only does he come with unrivaled offensive prowess and multiple NFL Super Bowl wins, but he also brings NFL contacts. A rolodex of connections. When the time comes for me to move on to the NFL, Charlie will truly be able to help with the process.

He can call anyone in the league, and his call will be answered. His resume commands it, and his new stable of players mandate they listen. "It impresses me. It gives me a sense of confidence in him because he knows what it takes to get there," Brady Quinn says. "He's coaching guys, he's had success and he's winning Super Bowl[s]. It's only going to help us, to give us more confidence and inevitably buy into his program and his system."[53]

The hope I have that Charlie will help me reach the next level reminds me of how Tyrone "helped" an NFL hopeful; Justin Tuck is trying to decide if he should declare for the NFL and looks to Coach Willingham for clarity.

In Justin's junior year, 2003, he breaks Notre Dame's single-season sack record with 13.5-sacks, which he still holds when this book is published. This accomplishment is followed by an impressive senior campaign where he breaks the record for career sacks at ND, with 24.5-sacks — a record that stood for 18 years prior. Notre Dame has seen good players, great players, and phenomenal players ... Justin is in the phenomenal category. That may even be an understatement ... that's just how good of a player he was at ND.

I mention a small sampling of Justin's resume to illustrate he is not simply a senior who thinks he is good enough to reach the NFL. He is an elite no-doubt-about-it player who does not need help with his draft stock. Like any employee looking for a promotion, Justin schedules a meeting with the boss, CEO Tyrone, to discuss the future.

Justin asks Tyrone if he will reach out to his friends in the NFL to see what they are saying and hearing about him. Justin is contemplating leaving for the NFL, not returning to Notre Dame for his fifth year, and wants to make an informed decision. Coach Willingham tells him, "I will not exploit my friendships in the NFL to help you." In full disclosure, during my interview to confirm these words, Tuck doesn't remember them, but multiple players do — a few even recite the quote before I finish asking if they recall this meeting and what was said.

Wow! Really? What is your job as a head coach? What is your job as a CEO? Is it to keep your employees down or help them improve? Will finding ways for an employee to succeed be for the betterment of the company or hurt the company? I believe your most important job as a head coach, at any level, is to help your players when asked ... and when not asked. It is to make sure your players graduate, become better human beings, become better football players, and to help them reach their highest potential — in this case, reach the NFL.

When college players rise into the NFL ranks, I would contend, a head coach only benefits — it increases their value as a head coach in the eyes of any onlooker (even if you have been recently fired, it will help you at your next gig). Recruits will see players from the team you coached playing in the NFL, where they would like to be one day, and view you as someone who can help them achieve their goal. And aren't friendships created to help one another, to extend a helping hand, to be there for one another?

Tuck isn't asking Coach Willingham to lie to his friends or anyone in the NFL. He isn't even asking Tyrone to advocate for him. He is asking him to pick up the phone and have a conversation with a friend. He is simply asking for clarity. What does the NFL think about Justin Tuck the football player?

Tyrone stands by his coaches, potentially getting himself fired by not making changes to his staff, but he was unwilling to stand by his player by simply picking up the phone.

# A Bowl "Gift"

## 42

AFTER OUR MEETING WITH Coach Weis, we still have a bowl game to win and an opportunity to prove who we are as players, and a team, to the incoming regime. The regular season ends with a lot of turmoil, but the team remains focused. We have great practices, as we prepare for the Bowl game. With a new head coach leading the pack, our energy level is through the roof. The guys are excited to play in a Bowl game — a team vote now might produce all yeses. There is a buzz about the team as we take flight to Arizona and continue preparation for the game against Oregon State. In a Q&A interim head coach Kent Baer is asked:

*Question: "What is the mood of the team? Trying to get everybody united?" Answer: "You know, the three practices we've had have been good, real good. I thought there was a lot of enthusiasm. I think they're really intent on getting into this game plan. I'm enthused about it, two finals, it's tough that way a little bit, because there's a lot of guys that have to miss because of study groups, preparing for finals, that sort of thing. We're just*

*going to try to work around it all. We'll have a handful of guys*
*missing here and there, but for the most part, pretty good."[54]*

This enthusiastic mood wanes as the team touches down in Arizona. As we settle into our hotel and begin practices in Phoenix, the team is a shell of its former self. The balloon that was an excited, reenergized team in South Bend just a few days ago appears to have a slow leak. The puncture — a long season, the firing of our head coach, the turmoil to Bowl or not to Bowl, and the hiring of our new head coach — has taken a toll on this drained and deflating team, as we near gameday and the end of the 2004 campaign. We are becoming increasingly lethargic; our decision to participate in a Bowl feels somewhat masochistic.

The Holiday Season is upon us. Many players wish they were with their families instead of practicing. Wishing they were sitting around the tree on Christmas Day waiting to open their presents at home. This year's present is not a shiny new coach under the tree ... we opened that gift a few weeks ago. On this Christmas Day, the team and I receive a gift we cannot return.

Practice! A beautiful, sunny Christmas Day with practice in full pads. The perfect thing to get us in the spirit of this most Holy Day. Sure, we cannot return this gift, but this is not the gift I want to return.

The team is not happy about practicing today and we let the coaching staff know. As practice opens, stretching as a team, there are many voices longing to be heard. There are loud moans and groans, and catchy phrases like: "Not smart to practice on Christmas," "Somebody is gonna be struck down for this sh*t," "Come on, it's a Holy Day," and "Aren't we a Catholic university?" I begin calmly speaking to Coach Miles in an attempt to convince him we should not be practicing. I say, "God's Team shouldn't be practicing on Christmas ... and you know it." These words are met with laughter and a smile. Jokes aside, I have a bad feeling in my gut. Something really does feel off about today. Though I cannot put my finger on it.

It is the halfway point of practice. The horn sounds. We sprint to our groups for the special teams period. Up first, kickoff return. The scout kickoff team lines up to kick the ball. I line up with my feet on the goal line and await the kick. The whistle blows, D.J. kicks the ball high into the air and down the middle of the field. I call off the other kick returner, as he nearly crashes into me. I cradle the ball into my body, tucking it into my right arm, put my head down, and sprint full speed ahead. Immediately locating my blockers and looking for the hole they are working to create.

As I am doing my thing, the kickoff team is flying down the field looking to impede my progress. I spot the opening! Full speed, nearing the hole, I notice someone has not done their job — just like the Tennessee game earlier in the year. A player on the kickoff team has thrown his blocker off him and blazes toward me. I violently plant my right foot into the ground to cut left. ... SNAP!

Jerome Collins crashes into me and drives me to the ground. Screaming, rolling around on the ground, writhing in pain ... again. Cursing up a storm ... again. I do not need anyone to tell me what I already know. The trainers do their job rushing to my aid to evaluate the situation. Upon their arrival, I have already internalized the pain and break the news: "Torn ACL, let's get some ice on it."

The team crowds around hoping for the best. The coaches check to see if I am okay, then proceed to berate Jerome. "Why would you hit him hard like that at practice?" "How can you be so stupid?" "What the f*ck were you thinking?" Composing myself, I yell, "Hey! He didn't do this. Leave him alone."

From everyone else's vantage point this is without a doubt Jerome's fault. They see me sprinting into the hole and him laying me out. They see a bang-bang play and believe his hit causes the injury. From my vantage point, terrible blocking is the real issue — he is surprised how quickly he gets around his blocker and by the time he locates me again we are on top of one another. Just as my right knee snaps, Jerome's eyes are bigger than a "deer in headlights." He sees me going down and does everything in his power to take his foot off the gas. To swerve and not make things worse.

The reality is that it would have been better for him to hit me before I attempted making a cut. The cut is the cause. Football is a collision sport and I wish Jerome would have put me on my butt before I tried to make a cut — or that the blocker did a better job.

SNAP! ACL tear number two. Another knee injury occurs without a collision to blame. Aren't I a lucky guy? Again, rolling around on the grass and screaming bloody murder. The pain is excruciating, but the rolling and yelling do help, as again there are no tears rolling down my cheeks. The training staff helps me to my feet. I gingerly walk to the cart, hop in, and my day is officially over. Well, I did want the day off, but not this badly.

Spiritless. Sagging across the trainer's training table. I watch doctors examine another damaged knee. The doctor pats my thigh and says, "Yep, it's a torn ACL. Sorry Matt, but you'll be back in no time. You've been through this and know what it takes." For the second time in four years, I sit on the training table pondering my future. Will I ever be able to play again ... after a second ACL? If I can, will I regain all my capabilities ... or will I lose a step, again? What does my future hold? Are my NFL dreams dashed?

As these troubles dance in thought, I feel them leach across my face. Sadness. Despair. Self-pity. Doubt. Inching through every muscle. My spirits are dismantled until one-by-one and two-by-two teammates come to check on their fallen comrade. D.J. Fitzpatrick and Dan Stevenson, two of my best friends on the team, are the first to walk through the door.

Worry and sadness paint their faces, as they hesitantly approach. I throw on a brave smile with a subdued chuckle — hopeful this mask of concealment is strong enough to contain my feelings from boiling over into existence. With each step in my direction, the frail tattered cloak barely holding me together melts from my face. My disguise of strength disappears. Their worry, their love, their care is too much for me to handle. The boiling cauldron of worrying thoughts overwhelms. Fear of the known journey ahead materializes. Tears rain from my eyes. My chin quivers uncontrollably. But in them, my dismantled spirit begins to rebuild — there are times we need to completely breakdown, so we can make room to heal.

Teammate after teammate visit, revealing an underlying truth about a football team ... we are a compassionate, united family. When one hurts, on some level, we all hurt. By the end of their visits, my feelings are returned to the cauldron of my mind to be held captive once more. Masked again and recomposed, a sense of determination brews from their encouragement and support.

Yes, you've had a setback. Yes, you have been knocked to the ground. Now it is time to get up. Rise, reframe the moment. You have been here before. Find strength in the known aspects of the uncertain journey that looms. Remove self-pity. Surrender to sorrow no more. Stabilize your shaken foundation — regain your composure. Build from knowledge gained during past injuries and obstacles. An awful monster from yesteryear has reared its ugly head; you have conquered this beast before. You can do it again. Start by believing in yourself ... you've got this!

"You have the ability, simply remember your courage."

# RECORD HUNT

## 43

THE COACHING STAFF PRESENTS me with two options: stay or go home. Be a cheerleader for the team or fly home to be with my family. Injured, I refuse to go home. I will not leave this family for another. There is plenty I can do to support my brothers. Over the next three days I do not miss a meeting (nor am I late) and I help as much as possible at practices. Pompoms in hand, I am ready to cheer and willing to do anything asked of me.

Two days before the game I receive more disappointing news. An extraordinarily rare opportunity is at my fingertips: a 25-year-old school record that has withstood the test of time — Tony Hunter has held this record since 1979. So close to gracing the pages of immortality ... etching my name into the sacred University of Notre Dame Football record books. One play! One catch away! Needing 20 catches to be eligible to hold this record, I stand at 19. Even worse, the catch only needs to be -7 yards or better to break the record for most yards per catch in a season. One event. One missed block. One setback. One injury has ripped this potential feat from my grasp ... or has it?

When this knowledge curls into my ears I erupt into hysterical urgency. Pleading with doctors, trainers, and coaches. "Please check again!" "Just clear me for one play!" "Let me break the record!" "Are we sure it's even torn?" I say anything and do whatever it takes to persuade permission for a single play. After a considerable number of consultations, he makes a decision. With a grin on his face the doctor says, "Matt, you really can't hurt your knee much more than you already have. You can play." Yes! First hurdle cleared! My commotion is beginning to payoff.

Next on the list, convince interim head coach Kent Baer to give me one play on gameday. For all the buildup in my mind, this obstacle ends up being an easy one. Coach Baer and all the assistant coaches are ecstatic this opportunity is at hand. Kent says, "Of course! You just need to talk Coach Weis into it, and you'll break that record."

Sounds easy enough. I just need to track down my brand-new head coach who is on the hunt for a Super Bowl Championship — whom I have never spoken with, who may or may not know my name — and somehow convince him to allow risk of further injury in the chase of immortality ... record holder. If I walk away unscathed, no harm, no foul, and an achievement I never imagined possible will be mine. But if I further injure myself, Coach Weis will potentially have one less weapon in his arsenal as a first-year head coach. Cautiously optimistic, positive thinking to the max, I hope Charlie will give me the go-ahead. So, I shoot my shot.

Jim Russ, the head athletic trainer, and I take a seat in the hotel ballroom being used as our team meeting room. Jim previously spoke with Charlie about my injury, and he was not happy to hear the news. My name already holds a sour taste. Jim pulls his cellphone from his pocket and calls Coach Weis. On the phone, Jim reminds Charlie of my injury and informs him of the new situation. "Matt needs one catch to become the record holder for most yards per catch in a season. There's not too much risk involved. He really cannot hurt his knee more than he already has," Jim says. After this explanation Jim hands me the phone.

Thank the Lord that Jim spoke with Charlie before me. By this point I am a nervous wreck. Palms sweating. My left knee rapidly bouncing up and down. I put the phone to my ear and muster two mid-puberty-like, shaky words, "Hey Coach." "Matt, I do not approve of you taking this risk." My heart stops. My head drops when this news is breathed into existence. My cautious optimism dwindles to the depths of disappointment. I will not be etching my name in the Notre Dame record books.

Weis continues, "With that being said." Wait a second ... you're telling me there's a chance! The creases of my lips start to dance. "I understand what it means to be a record holder at the University of Notre Dame. I get why you want to do this, so as long as you take every precaution possible to ensure your safety on the field, you can give it a go." Coach of the year! Holy cow! My persistence is rewarded. Inexplicably, I have my chance to join the Notre Dame record books!

**December 28, 2004.** Gameday, the Insight.com Bowl kicks off tonight. After meetings and meals, the team caravan arrives at the stadium. It is a perfect day for football, with an idyllic Arizona evening at the Bank One Ballpark. The retractable roof is open. As a capacity crowd of 45,917 fans trickle into the stadium, Jim wraps my knee in the clubhouse. The elastic bandage is so tight my toes are tingling ... circulation is at risk. Jim slips a fabric knee brace over his wrap-job to further stabilize the knee. A second brace, made of graphite, is slipped over the wrap and the fabric brace. Total knee support at its finest! Once Jim is satisfied that the knee is as safe and secure as possible, I jog onto the field for testing.

Running straight ahead, no problem, no pain. Cutting in any direction is a different story. Cutting causes a lot of pain. Pain creates doubt and uncertainty I can perform today. Continuing to push my limits, I persist. I fight through the hurt. Out of the corner of my eye I see Jim walk onto the field and in my direction. I put a smile on my face, overlooking my doubts, as he asks, "How do you feel?" No matter what I am feeling, whether I am fine or not, there is only one answer ... "Good to go, Jim!"

Shortly before the game, sitting in the locker room, I have a brainstorming session with my new best friend. Coach Miles tells me the coaches have decided on the safest play for me. He says, "Matt, how do you feel about a shovel pass?"

I have never executed a shovel pass in my football career. To my knowledge, our linemen have never blocked for a shovel pass (years later Bobby Morton, an offensive guard, confirmed this to be the case ... even stating he tried to talk the coaches out of calling this play) — it's fair to say I am a little hesitant about the play call. But what's the worst that can happen?

We discuss a few other options, they do not feel any more comfortable, so I say, "Sounds good, shovel pass works." In saying these words, I am assuming there will at least be a specific blocking scheme for this play.

As the first quarter ends, light rain drizzles through the roof opening. The second quarter comes and goes with the closing of the roof. The third quarter takes an eternity. The fourth quarter arrives; you've waited almost the entire game for coach to yell your name. Near the end of the fourth, you get the call. Yes, you are stiff from standing around all game, but at least you get a heads up this time. You quickly warm up on the sideline.

Sprinting onto the field, you try hiding behind a tight end entering the game with you. Brady calls a shovel pass and breaks the huddle. You line up in the backfield for the first time in your college career ... the game looks vastly different from back here. Still attempting to hide from the defense, you bend over at the waist to conceal your number until the ball is snapped. You're not as stealthy as you think — the defense easily spots the new guy in the backfield. They call out your number and shift their defensive alignment to account for your presence on the field. Adrenaline courses through your body, the pain and throbbing in your knee melts away.

Brady begins his cadence, "Down ... Red 13, Red 13, Set-Hut!" The ball hits Brady's hands and you run in unison to the left. You move underneath him toward the line of scrimmage. He shovels the ball to you with his right hand. Spinning end-over-end, you watch the ball all the way into your hands — do *not* drop this, you may not get another chance. Secured with both hands, you start to tuck the ball into your body, and turn your eyes to the defense. KABOOM!

A collective groan erupts from the crowd ... again. Before taking a full step with the ball, you are destroyed. The defensive end runs around our left tackle, hits you low and holds your left leg. You continue fighting for every inch. As he pulls your right leg into his clutches, an unblocked outside linebacker — with an 8-yard head start — lands a jaw-dropping, vicious hit. Everything goes dark.

Your body is literally bent in two, sideways and backward. Your helmet hits the ground before any other part of your body. You have been hit a thousand times during your football career, but never had a collision of this magnitude. Without the wrap and two knee braces, there is a chance the linebacker would have severed your leg, at the knee, from your body. After blacking out for a split second, you flail to your feet with stars in your eyes — grappling to find balance — and push your feet back into your shoes, then lurch to the sideline. One catch for -3 yards! The record is all yours!

Shuffling to the sideline, catching yourself from a fall at each step, you notice something is wrong. In a dizzy panic you take inventory, you discover both knees are fine — thank the Lord. There is nothing new to report from the waist down. Sure, you blacked out for a minute, but that happens fairly often and is not the "something" of concern. Uh-oh, you can't feel your left arm! No pain ... just no feeling.

As you cross the sideline threshold, you are swamped by an on-slaught of congratulatory chest bumps and helmet slaps (those are probably helping the concussion). Smiles can be seen from end to end on the sideline, as the team recognizes your accomplishment and tough-ness. Coach Miles is there, "I told you we would get you that catch!"

You push your way to the bench, Jim rushes to meet you, "Are you okay?" "Never better Jim ... but I can't feel my arm." From the shoulder to the tips of your fingers you are completely numb. For the next 20 minutes you cannot feel or move your arm. Swaying side-to-side or twisting are the only ways it moves. You think, "Well, this can't be good."

After seeing the monstrous hit on the field and noticing that you can't move your arm, D.J. asks, "Was it worth it?" With a huge smile, you nod, and say, "Hell yeah!" Just as you start to really freak out, your fingers come to life — twitching with reanimation — a tingling sensation gradually rolls skyward, feeling returns to your arm.

| 2004 Schedule | | | |
|---|---|---|---|
| Overall 6-6 | PCT 0.500 | Home 3-3/Away 2-2/Neutral 1-1 | |
| Date | Opponent | Location | Result |
| 9/4/2004 | at BYU | Provo, UT | L, 17-20 |
| 9/11/2004 | vs. Michigan | Notre Dame, IN | W, 28-20 |
| 9/18/2004 | at Michigan State | East Lansing, MI | W, 31-24 |
| 9/25/2004 | vs. Washington | Notre Dame, IN | W, 38-3 |
| 10/2/2004 | vs. Purdue | Notre Dame, IN | L, 16-41 |
| 10/9/2004 | vs. Stanford | Notre Dame, IN | W, 23-15 |
| 10/16/2004 | vs. Navy | East Rutherford, NJ | W, 27-9 |
| 10/23/2004 | vs. Boston College | Notre Dame, IN | L, 23-24 |
| 11/6/2004 | at Tennessee | Knoxville, TN | W, 17-13 |
| 11/13/2004 | vs. Pittsburgh | Notre Dame, IN | L, 38-41 |
| 11/27/2004 | at USC | Los Angeles, CA | L, 10-41 |
| 12/28/2004 | vs. OR State (Insight Bowl) | Phoenix, AZ | L, 21-38 |

The 2004 season, once full of optimism and excitement, ends in disappointment with a 38-21 loss to Oregon State (Coach Baer is 0-1 as interim head coach at ND) and a changing of the guard, as we welcomed another new head coach. When looking at the two seasons of change in my college career, 2001 and 2004, I quickly notice a few of their similarities.

Both seasons begin with one head coach at the helm and end with three ... of sorts: Davie, O'Leary, Willingham (2001) and Willingham, Baer, Weis (2004). Both start with through the roof excitement — yes, every season starts that way — and rumbling of change, then end with six loses and a head coach being changed ... and changed again. At the end of both seasons I doubt my future: did I make the correct choice in choosing ND, and will I ever see the field (2001); will I ever again be the player I had just become, and will I even be able to play football again (2004).

It is okay to question your future, to have doubts; these aren't inherently bad things, as both have the ability to push you in the "right" direction if you let them. When you ask questions, listen to the answers ... open your mind to the possibilities. When you have doubts, search for understanding ... try not to freeze or overthink the path forward.

I am setting a huge goal — get 100% healthy and return to being the player I became this year. To get there, I choose to focus on the next step, not the end goal; within my steps, the goal moves closer. "Take it one day at a time." Cliche? Yes. But things turn into cliches because they make sense, they work. Now, I will go under the knife. Next, I will relearn how to lift my leg and walk, Then, I will continue to push myself at every turn. I have the ability and I know where my courage is.

Senior season is in the books ... literally! With a Notre Dame record in hand, I look at all I've accomplished during this break-out year.

*"Played in all 12 games, starting three contests (Washington, Purdue and USC) ... set the single-season mark for yards per catch, averaging 25.75 yards per reception ... made 20 catches for 515 yards and a team-high six touchdown receptions ... returned from a knee injury to catch his 20th pass of the season, to qualify for the season-best record, against Oregon State in the Insight Bowl ... was the team's most valuable deep threat ... finished second on the team with 515 receiving yards ... had the second-most touchdowns on the squad ... caught a 46-yard touchdown pass in the Michigan game, Notre Dame's first score on the way to a 28-20 upset of the seventh-ranked Wolverines ... had three receptions for a team-high 123 yards versus Michigan State ... hauled in a 53-yard touchdown pass against the Spartans ... in his first collegiate start, he caught two touchdown passes versus Washington ... one went for 27 yards and the other was a 24-yarder ... caught four total passes for 74 yards against the Huskies ... had three receptions for 61 yards versus Purdue ... grabbed two passes for a team-high 40 yards in the Navy game ... longest catch against the Midshipmen went for 30 yards ... grabbed a 33-yard touchdown pass against Boston College ... hauled in three passes for a career-high 128 yards against Pittsburgh, including a 36-yard touchdown and a 46-yard reception ... had two catches for 13 yards in the USC game ... made 48 special teams appearances and logged 159:51 of playing time at receiver.*"[55]

# REPEAT & RINSE

## 44

EARLY JANUARY 2005. SURGERY at ND or surgery at home? Memphis it is! The Notre Dame trainers and doctors are not happy about this decision. They want their people to work on me, not some other doctor.

Well, that some other doctor, Dr. Randall Holcomb, performed my first ACL surgery in high school ... so, this is not a decision to use some random, unknown surgeon. He is a person I trust. A doctor they should trust, my left knee has been remarkable through college — aside from the inevitable, perpetual, and unavoidable patellar tendonitis (the middle third of my patellar tendon was removed to become my new ACL). I have great confidence he will provide me with another successful surgery.

Before surgery, Coach Weis calls, taking time from chasing another Super Bowl ring, to see how I am feeling. I have only heard him speak two times and had one phone call with him. Even though our contact has been limited, he feels it is important to check on my wellbeing.

Post-surgery, Dr. Holcomb stops by for a chat, "Surgery went really well. But wow, the difference between your high school knee and this one is night and day. The high school knee was immaculate. This knee looks like a 70-year-olds knee. Bone-on-bone, with no cartilage. Odds are you'll have at least one total knee before you're forty."

Wrong ... the time of Doc's prediction, not the eventuality. A few days after surgery Weis calls again to ask how recovery is going. I like this coach! We discuss my future at ND, and he reassuringly confirms he wants me back for my fifth year when he begins his first year as a head coach.

Certainly, there are people who doubt a successful, and timely, return is possible. Doubting my ability to help the team this season. After all, this is my second ACL surgery. Admittedly, with only seven months until two-a-days start, returning to full health will be difficult. I cannot afford any bumps on the road to recovery. My leg needs to heal perfectly and quickly. I must learn to walk again. I must strengthen my leg again. I must get back to being a deep-route specialist. Returning will not be easy.

As I work my way back to full health, I'll need to pay close attention to a handful of body related things: issues stemming from the recent surgery, tendonitis in my left leg, and constant shooting pains in my lower back.

While managing these, I will somehow need to return to football shape ... in both strength and endurance. I was fortunate and strong enough once, can I do it again? Although, I did lose a step in my 40-yard dash time, going from 4.23-seconds to 4.27-seconds. If I lose another step, will a return be viewed as successful? Will I hold any value as a player if I cannot run a 4.2-something? If a step is lost, a successful return is that much more difficult ... speed is kind of my thing.

A familiar journey — a known journey — I do not wish upon my worst enemy, but here I am. I have a lot of work to do. Little do I know just how difficult the journey will become.

# CHARLIE'S CHANGES

## 45

WHILE I REACQUAINT MYSELF with post-surgery obstacles, Charlie has challenges of his own. He is working two jobs. Not just any two jobs, but two highly stressful, high-profile jobs: offensive coordinator for the New England Patriots and head coach for the University of Notre Dame. Multitasking skills are fully engaged as he chases another Super Bowl win, evaluates and recruits high school football players, and works to keep his college football team from falling apart in his absence — all while constructing a coaching staff.

**January 4, 2005.** Charlie announces his coaching staff. David Cutcliffe — assistant head coach on the offense and quarterbacks. Former ND player, Michael Haywood — offensive coordinator and running backs. Rob Ianello — wide receivers and recruiting coordinator. John Latina — offensive line. Bill Lewis — assistant head coach on defense and defensive backs. Rick Minter — defensive coordinator and linebackers. Jerome "Jappy" Oliver — defensive line. Bernie Parmalee — tight ends. Brian Polian — assistant defensive backs and special teams.

This staff is stocked with talent and experience. All together they have 77 postseason bowl appearances, 45 top-25 finishes in the final Associated

Press rankings, 42 bowl victories, 29 seasons of experience as offensive or defensive coordinators, 21 postseason bowl appearances, and 12 seasons as National Football League assistant coaches.

Unfortunately, Cutcliffe's time at ND is cut short when heart complications arise, forcing him to take time off from coaching. This position is filled by former NFL European League head coach, Peter Voss.

When I compare Weis's staff to Willingham's staff, there are a hundred differences. Two stick out in my mind: ability over friendship, and effort.

Ability over friendship. Charlie puts together an experienced supporting cast for his first coaching job in college football. Charlie surrounds himself with assistant coaches, both established and up-and-comers, who he feels have the ability to take his job one day. The best he can find. Tyrone surrounded himself with friends. Most of the "guys club" from Stanford joined him at ND.

Effort, or lack thereof. I previously depicted this when discussing player development — both on the field and in the meeting room. A 2008 article suggests another area was found wanting: "In Willingham's second season at Notre Dame he recruited one of the worst overall ND classes in decades. In this third season, he was doing it again, only this time it looked even worse. ... What made all of this maddening to ND fans was that Willingham wasn't even trying, he simply expected recruits to come to him. Recruiting analyst Tom Lemming labeled Willingham and his staff outright lazy. Willingham would wait and wait to evaluate and offer kids while other coaches mounted full court presses."

I highlight this to accentuate efforts on the recruiting trail, not to suggest his recruits were "bad" just because a recruiting service ranking was low. In fact, many of their recruits were talented players, and some still hold Notre Dame records. In 2003, Tyrone and staff inked the #32 ranked class in the country (according to *Rivals*[56]). In 2004 Allan Wallace, editor at

*SuperPrep Magazine*, called the class, "Highly unusual. I've never seen a Notre Dame class ranked anywhere close to that poorly. ... I think that had some reason to do with why he was let go. Since when does Notre Dame, a program with the greatest tradition in college football, end up battling it out for a mid-range class?"[57]

I asked Coach Bill Reagan, what differences between the coaching staffs did you see during your time at ND? "Plenty of differences, but one that really stuck out to me was their mentality in the office. Davie's group ... bunch of grinders. Walk down the office hallway, any day, and the assistant coaches were all working hard. Everyone feared Davie; we had a saying, 'Don't bring the big dog off the porch.' Nobody wanted Bob on their butt. Willingham's staff, the opposite. Walk down their hallway: feet were on desks, TVs were on, not many guys were on the phone. Nobody really feared Tyrone and it showed in their work."

Bill, any notable differences between Tyrone and George, even though his time at ND was short? "O'Leary was all business. He was very serious. ... He came in with a plan: retain three ND assistants, bring three from [Georgia] Tech, and find three new guys. Tyrone put on a little bit more of a front, behind the scenes he was not as stoic and stern as people thought he was. His plan was different, he invited the entire Stanford staff. Both ways work, and both speak to how a coach will operate his program."

On signing day in February, Charlie inks the #40 recruiting class in the country (per *Rivals*). Few thought he could salvage a top-fifty re-cruiting class while coaching full-time in the NFL. Weis signs 15 recruits, the smallest haul in the history of Notre Dame recruiting at this time. So, in one-and-a-halfmonths at the helm, Charlie puts together a stellar staff, rallies the troops hauling in 15 recruits, and wins a Super Bowl Championship — that is a lot of effort. Not a bad start to the year or a new job.

Yet again, things are completely different when the team returns from Christmas break. The players are greeted by a confident, nasty, and prepared coaching staff who are ready to kick our butts into shape. Our constant, the Torture Technician of all Torture Technicians, Mickey Marotti will beat us into shape no more — he joins Urban Meyer at the University of Florida. A towering building-like man, Ruben Mendoza, replaces him. Now the team must learn a new coaching staff and a new strength staff. So many new people working in the Notre Dame Football offices ... again.

*Early 2000's: Sign Displayed in the Locker Room.*

# MISERY & A FLUSH

## 46

EVERYTHING IS ROLLING ALONG perfectly for the team and the university. The new head coach has settled in nicely. The new coaching staff is hitting the ground running with recruiting and getting to know their new team. The new strength coach has arrived. And spring football is on deck. Personally, I am working my tail off to get healthy for the season. I cannot work out with the team, so I basically live in the training room with Jim and his team of trainers.

My progress post-ACL surgery seems slower this time around. I begin feeling frustrated by my perceived lack of improvement; I do my best not to ruminate on this thought, as the doctors and trainers are okay with my progression. I do not believe anything is wrong or different than before — just slower.

I "remember" having sharp shooting pains in my leg. I "remember" not being able to sit still for more than two minutes without pain. I "remember" not being overly hungry. I "remember" losing weight last time, but 25-pounds in a week seems excessive. I "remember" running a fever. I "remember" my knee feeling hot to the touch. But how do I know? Are these struggles new or are they the same? Are they real or figments of my imagination? Am I making connections where there are none to be made? With these connections, am I burying my head in the sand?

**January 21, 2004.** Friday evening in South Bend, Indiana. I have a hot date with my beautiful girlfriend of two years, Lindsey Walz. She has absolutely been dying to see *Phantom of the Opera* in theatres. Being the amazing boyfriend I am, we head to the movies for a "night out on the town." We arrive at the theatre with time to spare.

As the opening trailers and credits roll, I can't sit still, shifting back-and-forth from one butt cheek to the other. Constantly adjusting my recovering, traumatized knee and struggling to find a comfortable position. I think to myself, "Deal with it. I'm ok. Only need to make it a few hours." Lindsey continues checking in with me, "Are you okay? Do you need anything?" Of course, I say, "I'm fine."

A few minutes into the movie I can handle the anguish no longer and excuse myself from the theatre with a quick "I'll be right back." For the next 20 minutes I sit outside the theatre with tears in my eyes. Unable to sit still, I rock forward and backward. Huffing and puffing. The smell of buttery popcorn wafting in the lobby nearly makes me vomit. The pain builds, and tears swell with each adjustment.

Sensing something is wrong, Lindsey leaves the movie to investigate my disappearance. She doesn't see me in the hallway. She tries calling my cellphone, then walks out to the concession area. As she turns the corner, she looks to her right to find me sitting alone on a bench rocking back and forth. I'm startled, as she takes a seat beside me. She clasps her hand on top of mine. Doing all I can to hold back tears and hide my trembling chin, with a stammer I ask, "How's the movie?"

She laughs it off and again asks, "Are you okay?" Obviously, I am doing great, so I tell her, "I'm fine, go back and finish the movie. I'm just going to sit here a bit longer." Without much pushback, she convinces me to leave the theatre. As we sit in her bright yellow punch-bug, she starts the car and asks, "Why didn't you just ask if we could leave?" With big, puppy dog eyes I say, "Because I know how badly you wanted to see this movie." Brownie points!

Lindsey's parents don't live too far from campus, so we trek to their place for a homecooked meal and support. While on the road, I call Jim Russ to ask if he will increase my pain pill dosage and have them ready for pick up first thing tomorrow morning. He asks if I have enough to get through to Monday, and I do. He says, "Ok, good. Let's wait until Monday and if we think you need a stronger prescription we'll speak with the doctor before doing anything."

My shifting from cheek to cheek continues in the car. There is still no comfortable position to be found. After a painful ride, which takes much longer than I remember it taking the last 50 trips, we arrive at Lindsey's parents' home. Instead of having me sleep in the basement, I am put upstairs near her parents' bedroom just in case.

The following day a few family friends gather at the Walz's home for a late lunch. Having taken a couple of pain pills to help me sleep through the discomfort, I miss the start of lunch. Some food is sent up to me. I only have the energy and hunger to eat two bites of a baby carrot. All I want to do is sleep. I do not want food. I do not want to move. I certainly do not want to visit with anyone downstairs.

Later that evening, Lindsey takes my temperature. It is 103.5 degrees. She takes note of how pale my face looks. She runs downstairs to get her mother. Mrs. Patti Walz tries convincing me to go to the emergency room, but I resist. I insist everything is fine, telling her, "I went through this last time I had ACL surgery. Everything is the exact same." After a few minutes of discussing my wellbeing, both ladies leave. Victory! Now, let me get back to that good, can't feel my body, pain pill popping sleep.

As I tuck myself into bed and bury my head in the sand, the bedroom door bursts open. Mr. Tom Walz slides into the room. He shouts, "You look like sh*t! You're going to the emergency room right now!" The stern look, piercing glare, red-face, and steam emanating from his ears tell me there is only one correct answer. "Yes, sir."

Reluctantly, I check into the emergency room and wait with Lindsey to be taken to a room. By the time I am taken to a room my temperature jumps to 104.5, my knee is now bright red, very swollen, and extremely hot to the touch. The doctor runs a few tests to assess the severity of the situation. Come on ... not another giant needle in the knee! He reaches for a needle the length and circumference of a straw meant for a coffee cup — maybe it's the fever talking, but it doesn't seem the size of a Big Gulp straw this time. Lindsey looks away just as the needle pierces my skin.

He jabs the needle into my throbbing knee all the way to the hilt. My entire body violently jumps, almost hurling me from bed, as I practically rip the metal railing off the hospital bed. Lindsey gasps and glances to see if I am still on the bed or if I jumped through the ceiling. As the doctor draws the fluid out, filling the syringe barrel, I try to relax my body and allow my muscles to cease firing. Yet again, the doctor leaves the needle in my knee while squirting the fluid into a testing container. I am grateful he doesn't remove the needle. I don't want to be jabbed again but hold the stupid thing steady!

The doctor returns to our room with the test results. To our surprise the doctor says, "I am not impressed with your knee. There is nothing seriously wrong with it at this time. You can go." The doctor leaves the room. With this good news in hand, we prepare to leave the hospital. I sit up, smile, and inch off the bed ... until I hear a knock at the door.

A second doctor enters the room. A shift change. The new doctor is starting his early morning rounds to evaluate patients who are now in his care. He is responsible for the entire ER, so he is double-checking everyone before releasing them. He says, "I'm going to take a real quick look just to make sure everything is okay before you leave." Just when I thought I was out, he pulls me back in!

"But the other doctor told me I'm good to go, so we're leaving," I state with confidence. He puts his hand out, signaling me to sit back down. He reiterates, "I'm in charge now. We're taking another look. If I like what I see, I'll release you." I slump down and back onto the exam table. The doctor touches my knee. Gives me a glare. Looks at the chart, then flips to the second page. He gives me another glare ... one of perplexing concern. He touches my knee again. Then, with a troubling look, moves his attention back to the chart.

He shakes his head and rubs his chin, as his wheel spins. "Your knee looks horrible. Your test results are off the charts bad. You're having surgery immediately." In shock, I say, "What was that? No. No. That's a ... that can't be right. The other doctor said I'm fine and can go home." He simply says, "He was mistaken. You're having surgery as soon as possible."

Are you kidding me?! How can a doctor be so incompetent? Doctor number one almost allows me to leave the hospital with a "staph infection, which is caused by staphylococcus bacteria. This germ is commonly found in the nose or on the skin of healthy individuals ... But staph infections can turn deadly if the bacteria invade deeper into your body, entering your bloodstream, joints, bones, lungs, or heart. A growing number of otherwise healthy people are developing life-threatening staph infections."[58] Doctor number two enters the scene and in less than two minutes tells me I am having surgery ASAP.

WOW! Apparently, bad doctors slip through the cracks. And a miracle is performed with a timely shift change.

The hospital rings the on-call orthopedic surgeon for a visit. Fortunately for me the doctor on-call is a Notre Dame doctor, Dr. Mike Yergler. Dr. Mike walks into the room, checks the chart at the end of my bed to see what exactly the issue is, and decide how to proceed. While looking at the chart, he slowly walks to my bedside. "Holy sh*t Matt! Nobody told me it was you!"

Mike assures me I will be okay, as the nurses prepare me for surgery. Mike leaves the room, and the anesthesia eventually puts me to sleep. Before surgery, Mike speaks with numerous colleagues to ensure the best course of action is taken. If there is any chance of me playing football this year, he must save the new ACL residing within my knee. If he cannot, then at some point we will need to have a second ACL surgery, which means my football season is over before the spring starts.

An hour later, after Dr. Mike has multiple conversations, we begin surgery to flush out the infection, which has overtaken my right knee. During surgery — understanding how important it is to me and the football team — Dr. Mike stands over me on the operating table for hours, blasting every nook and cranny to clean the infection site. He flushes 12-bags of fluid (36,000 mL) through my knee; comparatively, per Pat Reagan and a Dallas operating room, a knee scope at a surgery center uses 1-2 bags and a hospital uses 3-5 bags — each bag contains 3,000 mL. With an abundance of caution and diligence, Mike does everything in his power to give me a chance of playing during the upcoming 2005 season.

After surgery Dr. Mike visits to see how I am doing and let me know how the surgery went. These are the first words out of his mouth ... "If you waited another day to come into the ER you would've lost your leg, or you would have died." My jaw drops and eyes widen. I reply, "Wait a minute. What do you mean I would've died if one more day passed?" He continues, "Yeah, one more day and you may have died, you're extremely lucky we caught this because it's a silent killer, of sorts."

Throughout this ordeal, since the original surgery in Memphis, I do not tell my parents any of the negative events happening to me. Nothing about pain. Nothing about not eating. Nothing about weight loss. Nothing about a fever or a hot knee. Mom and Dad are a ten-hour drive from ND, and I don't want to worry them ... plus, all of this was normal — in my mind. In the early morning of surgery, Mrs. Walz calls my mother to break the not-so-good news about her son, and that evening Mom is by my side in the hospital room. It is amazing to have Mom with me. She helps pick up the pieces of a terrified son who was cluelessly knocking at death's door.

The doctors need to monitor my condition, so I get an all-inclusive and all-expenses-paid insurance trip — whether I want it or not — to stay at the hospital for five more days. During my stay, I am on a morphine pump and pain pill combo to manage the non-stop agony. I am pumped full of vancomycin, which is the strongest and one of the most-toxic antibiotics on the market. We hit the Staph infection with everything we've got.

On the day I am released from the hospital doctors inserted a Peripherally Inserted Central Catheter line (a "PICC" line). The PICC line is a slender, small, but long, flexible tube the nurse inserts into my basilic vein, which is the large vein you see in your arm where your elbow bends. The nurse numbs an area on the interior side of my right bicep. She makes a tiny incision, inserting a cannula, then advances the line through to the larger veins and stops with the tip in my chest, just short of my heart. This procedure allows the PICC line to obtain intravenous access, which will more quickly disperse the vancomycin antibiotic throughout my entire body to neutralize any remaining bacteria.

The PICC line remains in-place for the following six weeks. Fortunately, we make arrangements with the University Health Services center on campus for me to visit twice a day, two hours each, to receive antibiotic treatment. During each visit, a softball size plastic bag of vancomycin is attached to the PICC line. The antibiotic slowly trickles into my body, directly into my heart, and circulates throughout my entire body. Additionally, I take antibiotic pills twice per day for four months.

My body is being flooded with so many antibiotics there is no doubt I would survive a nuclear fallout with the cockroaches, at least for a few years. I cannot miss a single day of treatment. My spring break trip to Cancun is cancelled, and I feel as though I am the only student soul on campus, as all my friends are gone. I can barely walk, I have a tube sticking out of my arm, and I am attempting to navigate a snowy campus at least twice a day on my own. A spring break to remember!

As I am sure you can imagine, a PICC line is neither comfortable nor convenient. Rubber bands and garbage bags are back to being ridiculous mainstays in my life. To shower, I throw a garbage bag over my right leg and use rubber bands stretched to the max in an attempt to keep water from saturating the surgical wounds. The fresh wrinkle of this recent surgery is adding a bag and bands to my dominant right arm ... love that.

After securing bags to the appendages on my right side, I hobble to the community shower like a cyborg trashman going in for a polish. I turn on the shower and step in for a halfhearted endeavor to get clean. On the bright side though, once the leg wounds heal, I only need to shower with one trash bag to protect the PICC line — the insertion spot is an open wound that cannot heal until the line is removed in six weeks or so.

# A Close Call

47

Still not fully realizing how fortunate I am to be alive, a friend handed me the February 2005 *Sports Illustrated*. The article, titled "A Menace In The Locker Room," speaks about methicillin-resistant staphylococcus aureus or MRSA as an emerging epidemic.

"Ricky Lannetti, a senior wide receiver for Lycoming College in Williamsport, PA., wasn't so lucky. He discovered what appeared to be a pimple on his buttocks as he was getting dressed for practice one afternoon in December 2003. He called his mother complaining of nausea on a Tuesday, and by Saturday he was dead. ... It only takes the smallest opening in the skin for MRSA to infiltrate the bloodstream. ... Unless you've washed your hands in the last few minutes, they probably have bacteria on them at this moment. ... MRSA is on the rise ... particularly in segments of society in which large numbers of people are in close proximity, such as prison populations, the military and athletic teams."[59]

As I read the article a sense of shock and awe overtakes me. An uneasy quietness takes hold of my mind. The awareness of how close to death I truly was jolts me to my core. Fortunate, lucky, or a gift from above? I believe all three. Fortunate to have a loving girlfriend, with caring parents, who all force me to visit the hospital. Lucky a shift change occurs just before I walk out of the emergency room. A gift from above in the form of Dr. Mike Yergler being on call and him knowing how important saving my ACL graft will be for my career. Others have not been so lucky, and I thank the Lord for the gift of good fortune.

With all the knowledge and experience my doctors have accumulated in their lives, they still cannot tell me if my ACL, or my leg, will survive the infection. They can only tell me to "wait and see what happens." Not the most comforting words, but better news than many people receive who have found themselves in a similar position.

Post-surgery there are two big concerns — we did not eliminate all the infection, or the staph infection irreparably interfered with the healing process; both of which would require a third surgery to replace the staph-ridden ACL. My ND career and my hopes of making it to the NFL may be over. Here I sit, antibiotics coursing into every crevasse of my body — my mind scrolls through thoughts of mortality, as death was at my door, and somehow, narrowly escaping my maker's call to come home. Doubts creep deeper and deeper into my mind. I ponder my future ... once more.

"Everything happens for a reason." I genuinely believe in this concept. There will inevitably be both good and bad events in your life — learn to appreciate both. The yin and yang of it all ... it is all connected. Make the choice to open your mind to this belief, this concept, and you will find understanding within the threads of connectivity.

Without good, how would you know when something is bad? Without bad, how would you recognize or appreciate when something is good? Where is the good in a broken back? Where is the good in a torn ACL, then a second? Where is the good in a staph infection that nearly took your life? Many people would see these experiences as bad signs and decide to give up on their dreams — thinking, "The deck is stacked against me."

I chose, in each moment of bad, to find the silver-lining. To find the light. Though I may not see or fully comprehend its purpose at the time, there is a reason for these events. I choose not to dwell on the bad but instead seek out the good. Maybe the back injury did make me faster — like my high school friends jested. Maybe the first ACL guided me to Notre Dame — to etch my name in the record books and forge lifelong bonds with these teammates specifically. Maybe the second ACL and staph infection are guiding me to something amazing in the future — I created the foundation of this book during treatments at Health Services. Decide to find the good when life presents you with something bad.

Truly, a close call. Is this "something bad" a warning sign? Would it be wise to put an end to my career now? Would it be naive to press my luck? Perhaps, a bit of both?

Whatever the case may be, I decide to move forward with a refocused and persistent drive that emanates from the depths of my soul. I will not give up. Slipping through the grim reaper's clutches, I accelerate onward with reckless abandon into an unknown future.

Is getting up after being knocked down an addiction? I seemingly revel in the idea of pushing myself from the mat and overcoming the obstacles in my way. Hitting rock bottom and climbing my way back through the unfamiliar becomes my anthem. Please tell me, "You can't make it back," "It's going to be a long road," or "You will never be the same." And I will thank you for the motivation and fuel. I will prove you wrong. I am an athlete. Athletes do not know how to give up or stay down. Wisely or foolishly, I press on.

# Spring Back

## 48

**March 29, 2005.** This spring, football practices are quite different from years past. New coaches? Needing to learn a new playbook? Nope to both ... been there done that — all too familiar with the obstacles a head coaching change brings. The difference this spring is that I am unable to practice as I recover from two major knee surgeries.

I hate sitting on the sidelines. I have worked my entire career to get off the sidelines and onto the field. I finally accomplished this last season in a big way, but injury presents me with a huge complication in my progression as a football player. Practice is spent rehabbing, lifting weights, and riding a stationary bike for the entire two-hour practice instead of working on my craft with teammates. I would rather be on the field with family and not riding a bike with our new Torture Technician and Jim Russ leading me through a workout.

But here we are. There is no way for me to spin this in my mind. This sucks. I am finding it difficult to locate the good or a silver-lining. Where is the good? Will there be any good to come from this?

The first day of practice begins Tuesday afternoon under a clear, beautiful blue sky. Emerging from the frigid depths of winter, this mid-60-degree day feels more like 80. The team takes the field for warm-ups, and I take my place on the sideline. The stationary bike calls my name; I dare not disregard it. Jumping on the bike, I am envious of my teammate's ability to practice on this perfect day. As I rehab, I get my first taste of Charlie's on-the-field coaching.

Soon after I begin pedaling, the sun hits me across the face, and I start sweating. Naturally, I roll up my sleeves to cool down. Also, my pasty white arms can use a little sun after the long winter ... a tan would be nice. Maybe Bob Davie was on to something: "It's a *damn* country club," at least for me today. Shortly after my sleeves are rolled as high as possible onto my shoulders, I see a student manager racing in my direction. He stops on a dime 5 yards away from me and says, "I've got a message from Coach Weis."

I slow my pedaling with excited anticipation. Maybe he wants me to stop and join him on the field to hear play calls. Nope. "This isn't a *f*cking* country club! Roll your damn sleeves down or get the *f*ck* out." Ha! I knew this place wasn't a *damn* country club... can't fool me, Bob.

I look over to Charlie, he throws his hands up with a glare that says, "What's it gonna be?" Like a chastised teenager, I drop my head with a pout, lower my shoulders, and roll my sleeves down — then pick up the pace on the bike.

I eventually find the good in this situation ... there is no pressure to learn the new playbook. I do not need to "learn on the fly." I can take my time. I can learn the plays and concepts more thoroughly without the pressures of preforming on the field. I am unable to show the new coaching staff my on-field abilities, so I need to show them what I can do in the meeting room.

A new, different notion presents itself and I make learning plays my number one focus this spring — aside from rehab. This is the "good" buried underneath the "bad." It takes a little time to find, but here it is. And with this revelation comes a welcome attitude adjustment ... a healthier mindset has found a home. I stop dwelling on what I cannot do and start focusing on what I can. I recognize this is not much, but nobody says a silver-lining needs to be some big grandiose thing or notion.

Another positive mental adjustment is found in a somewhat unfamiliar concept — one missing from previous beginnings with new position coaches. Rob Ianello, the wide receiver coach, is providing support from the start. He is taking time to coach me, teach me, all the while knowing I may never play football again. Knowing he might be wasting his time on a player who may never play for him.

This is my third position coach; he is the first one to give me the time of day when he first arrives. Yes, I am an experienced senior this time around. Yes, there is an outside chance I will play this season. But there are no guarantees ... I am not out from underneath the sinister shadow of infection.

For the entirety of my college career, I have imagined what it would be like for a coach to take me seriously as a football player. To afford me an opportunity. To see value in what I bring to the table. This coach does not put me in a box and toss me on the shelf that is the sideline because I am coming off an injury or because I am someone else's recruit. Here I am, dreams coming true, and I cannot step foot on the field. I have two jobs this summer: get healthy and learn the playbook.

# A College Grad's Realization

## 49

May 15, 2005. After four years of continual change, my consistent hard work in the classroom pays off. I am a graduate of the University of Notre Dame.

Earning a Business Administration degree, majoring in Marketing and Sociology. This is a huge moment in my life. Graduating from Notre Dame, while playing football, and enduring the unprecedented change of four head coaches — currently on my fifth — has been far from easy. Every day, since August 2001, has been a physical and intellectual grind I have needed to conquer.

With graduation, the mentally challenging aspect of college disappears and the physical challenges I face become my singular focal point.

Becoming healthy is the only thing that matters in life ... it is my life. I set a huge goal for myself, a promise to prevail. My physical ailments will not keep me down and I will play in Notre Dame Stadium again on Saturday afternoons.

The doctors are still uncertain if my body will ultimately reject the new ACL. There is no way of knowing. They do not know if I will need another surgery ... though they believe the infection is gone. They cannot provide me with anything concrete ... though they think the ACL graft will be unaffected by this ordeal. "Time will tell," the doctors continue to say. I will either make it to the season or my ACL will simply "pop."

But in my heart, I know exactly how this will end. Optimism pilots my thoughts as I enter summer with the formidable assignment of getting healthy and back into football shape. I move forward with hope. Every day is a test of my will. There are days when I want to give up. I want to stop. I want to let the pain win. I want to take the easy route. On many days, these ideas seem the most sensible course of action. There is so much pain, physical and mental, following the two recent surgeries.

In addition to these new pains, I am still managing pain in my other reconstructed knee and my lower back. Throughout my career, and to this day, I've had more back pain than my knees combined. Sitting, walking, standing, or sleeping, my knees and back are always aching. As I try to enjoy this final summer at ND, I constantly remind myself that these feelings to quit, to give up, are sentiments I have overcome before, and this time will be no different.

I thought my last summer as a Notre Dame Football player would be full of excitement and anticipation. I should be excited. I should be happy; I am almost done with college. I should be ecstatic; I am on the verge of entering the next season of my life. If all goes according to plan, I will have a shot at making it to the NFL. How could I not be happy?

I am neither happy nor sad. A bittersweet sensation, last felt in high school, returns. This chapter in my life, Notre Dame, is ending. I know time is going to fly from this moment forward. Soon I will be moving on from this place, a place that has become home. Soon I will run out of the tunnel in front of 80,000 screaming fans for the last time. I will put the gold helmet on for the last time. I need to savor every moment in my last season as a Notre Dame Football player and enjoy this final year with my teammates.

Once I leave, I will never be able to view the University of Notre Dame from the same perspective. A Notre Dame Football player no more. Instead, I will be an alumnus who played football and not a player at ND.

*2004 Pep Rally at the Joyce Center: Shirley Shelton, Matt Shelton, & Ed Shelton.*

# CORSO VS. THE TEAM

## 50

SUMMER HAS COME AND gone in the blink of an eye. Two-a-days are back for the final time while wearing blue and gold. After only four months of real rehab, when experts say eight months of rehab is paramount for a successful recovery, I prepare to practice with my team for the first time since Christmas Day.

I ease into two-a-days, practicing full speed sparingly and taking breaks when needed. The trainers and doctors want to see how the knee responds to the intensity that accompanies live practices. I need to get my reps in during practice while being mindful, I am not 100% healthy. At this point in time, there is no reason to put my health at risk.

On the first day, after practice number one, I tell our head trainer I am in too much pain to participate in today's second practice. Surprisingly, Jim Russ tells me I need to clear it with Coach Weis. In years past when a player was hurt, or sick, Jim had the power to excuse the player from practice without consulting any coaches. Charlie has a different approach to how this dynamic is supposed to work.

Any player who believes he should not partake in practice has to speak directly to Coach Weis. The player must tell Charlie about the ailment and why he needs to sit out for the day. This method of reporting injuries keeps Charlie well-informed on the health of his team. It is also an effective way to sniff out guys who are just looking for a day off.

Hesitantly, I approach Coach Weis. With dread and a hint of indignity written upon my face — because I am a tough football player — I tell Charlie, "My knee is killing me. I'm in too much pain to practice this afternoon." He looks at me with those intense, scary head coach eyes and says, "Okay." That's it? Wait, wait, wait. That is all it takes? I wound myself up for no reason. He continues, "Come see me anytime the pain is too much, and you need the day. You got it, no questions asked."

I appreciate his words, but rarely approach him for this matter. I suck up the pain and fight through every grueling step I can possibly tolerate. The last thing I want to do is put doubt of my ability or my health into the minds of my new coaches.

Two-a-day practices are complete, game week is starting, and it's time to prepare for an away game in Pittsburgh. As I take a seat in the auditorium at the "Gug" Center, a realization brings a smile to my face ... a goal reached. After tearing my ACL on Christmas I set a huge goal — get 100% healthy and return to being the player I became last year. The pragmatic cliche of "take it one day at a time" is proven effective.

Climbing from my Christmas fall became an unexpected battle of life and death. There have been many moments over the past eight months — within each and every day — where I felt sorry for myself, cried, and wanted to give up; I would have too, if it were not for a "next step" mentality. To look up from the ground in these moments, at my mountain of a goal, I would have thought it impossible to reach this summit ... yet, here I sit. At the top, 100% healthy and pretty darn close to being the player I was last year.

After the team's poor showing last season, and a coaching change, few people in the football world think we have a chance at a winning season. The team and Charlie know better than to listen to the "talking heads."

At the first team meeting of the week, Charlie shows an ESPN clip of Lee Corso sharing his thoughts on the Irish. Corso says, "The Irish have zero talent, they're average, and they will start the season off 0-6."

The auditorium erupts. This clip of Lee disrespecting our team ignites a fire. The team hasn't shown this many "give a f*cks" since Tyrone's first season. The noise is thunderous; boos shake the Gug. Anger boils over as the clip ends. The team is visibly upset by this disrespect.

At our second team meeting this week, Charlie shows Lee Corso's clip one more time. Just in case we missed it the first time ... the team's anger is equally high. Every practice this week is high-energy. A hunger grows within the team, and it will only be satisfied by a win against the Panthers.

*2004, Notre Dame Stadium: Matt Shelton Touchdown vs. Pittsburgh.*

# GAME WEEK + "THE BUS"

## 51

GAME WEEKS ARE A change for the better in the lives of football players. The team settles into the normalcy of a classroom and football schedule. The constant day-in-and-day-out beatings of two-a-days are over. We hit one another more infrequently, reducing the risk of injury.

Monday becomes our day off from practice. Tuesdays and Wednesdays are the toughest practices of the week with full pads, as we run full speed hitting and tackling, plus conditioning afterward. Thursday practices are accompanied by those thin foam shoulder pads and the pace of practice is slowed; we focus on the details of our game plan and working on what adjustments are needed depending on what the opponent shows us at the line of scrimmage. Fridays are just helmets, no pads whatsoever, as we run through every detail of the game plan to finalize the finer points of our strategy.

**September 2, 2005.** Fridays are also travel days. Today we travel to Pittsburgh for a match up against the Panthers. Throughout my time at Notre Dame, game weeks have been pretty much the same. The way we travel, the treatment we receive, the entire process has been similar over the years. If a game is more than a three-hour drive, the team charters an airplane. The buses usually leave for the airport around 2:00 p.m. or 3:00 p.m. We exit the bus and proceed to a hanger located beside the South Bend Regional Airport. The team goes through security, metal detectors, dogs, and all. We walk directly onto the tarmac to board the plane.

On the plane we are greeted by smiling flight attendants. Seating is first come, first serve, except for the emergency exit rows, which the linemen have already battled it out for, so they have extra leg room. Each seat is loaded with chips, fruit, candy, and drinks that are ready to provide you with the energy needed for a direct flight to anywhere. Before takeoff, the flight attendants ask if we need anything. I always ask for more candy … stop judging, please and thank you.

Per usual, the middle seat of three is empty to ensure every player has enough room. The plane takes off and the movie begins. Sometimes there is a meal, other times there is more snacking, but the attendants do not miss an opportunity to give us more food in the air. After landing, we skip the potential debacles of the terminal — so as not be slowed for any conceivable reason — and step off the plane onto the tarmac to board the chartered buses that await. The "animals" are loaded, along with their luggage, and the buses leave for the opponents' stadium.

This week it is Heinz Field. Escorted by police cars and motorcycles, our buses never stop at red lights, as the cops block every intersection to clear a path. We are on a schedule people! (We even had a corvette police car stop highway traffic for the team buses … Florida is great.) We make it to our pit-stop, and it is time for a team walk-through on the stadium field.

During this time, we review the gameday script and add a twelfth man on offense and defense to obscure the play concept from our opponent … who is without a doubt filming from above (every team participates in "Spygate"). After an hour of running around on the field, we are taken by our police escort to the hotel for some rest, bible study if you like, dinner, and meetings. Got to tell you, this is the way to travel.

Friday evening, in our Pittsburgh hotel, we have a short team meeting to review the game plan and talk with our coaches before heading to bed. Just before we break the team meeting, Coach Weis says we have one last thing to talk about. He says two words, "The Bus." Notre Dame great and NFL hall of fame hopeful Jerome Bettis (inducted in 2015) walks through the double doors. Coach Weis is bringing out the big guns to provide more motivation.

Jerome has the team's full attention. "Football is not an individual sport, but few look at the game as a game filled with individual battles." He continues, "To be a great team, each and every member must win their own individual battles. By winning these battles you will help the team and, if each one of us wins our battle every time the whistle blows, we cannot be beaten. When one person loses his battle, the team is put in jeopardy of losing that play and maybe even the game, depending on how big that particular loss is in the grand scheme of things. Every person on the team has to trust that their teammates are going to win their individual battles for the good of the team."

I have heard Jerome speak several times in the past, but never quite like this. He speaks with such passion and fire; it feels like he is suiting up with the team tomorrow. I can hear in his voice that he feels Coach Weis is doing everything the right way, and Charlie will bring Notre Dame back into the glory days. Pumped up and ready to play tonight, the meeting breaks.

After a Friday night team meeting, for the last four years, there are nighttime snacks waiting for the team. The snacks are always great. Buffalo wings, fries, fruits, power bars, drinks, milkshakes, desserts, and more are lined up buffet style for players to take with them to bed. I mean, you can't have a player starve the night before a game, plus energy reserves are needed for the grueling competition to come. A few extra calories will only help the collective cause. I grab some wings, a double order of fries, a banana, a milkshake, and a Gatorade before heading to my room.

As I crawl into bed and turn on the TV, I hear a knock at the door and the zip of a key card. The door flies open. Two coaches burst into my room yelling, "Bed check! Bed check!" The night before a game, along with the late-night snack, we enjoy a team-wide curfew. It is not lights out and go to bed. Just a check to confirm everyone is in their assigned room and no one is in your room who should not be, i.e., friends, family members, or girlfriends. The coaches leave and I turn my attention back to the TV, before falling asleep with a gorged belly.

**September 3, 2005.** Gameday is upon us! For evening games, without fail there is an optional breakfast early in the morning. I grab yogurt and an apple, then it is back to my room to watch College GameDay before meetings start. After our first meeting of the day there is more down time before the game. I return to my room, turn on the best football game I can find, review the playbook, make a phone call or two, then take a nap. The alarm sounds, relaxation is over, and it is time to get ready for football!

Taking my travel bag with me, I jump in the elevator and head to the pre-game meal. As usual, I scarf down pasta, with red sauce, and grab a banana for the road before sitting down for another team meeting. We review the game plan again and discuss the first 10-15 scripted plays on offense: these are a combination of plays we think will give us the best start to the game, plus help to setup other plays we will call later in the game, and plays that will force the defense into showing how they will defend against specific situations and different formations. After the meeting we have a team mass, then leave for Heinz Field.

Police escorts clear a path the entire way and guarantee there are no delays. As the bus pulls into the stadium area, we are greeted by rowdy tailgating fans who love to say hello with double barrel middle finger waves of welcome. We exit the bus to "boos" and "hisses," with sprinklings of cheer. I check out the locker room and put the bottom half of my uniform on before jogging to the field.

Before every game, while fans are tailgating, players are exploring field conditions and changing cleats if needed. Some players choose not to go onto the field and keep a low profile waiting in the locker room for warm-ups. After catching a few balls and chatting with teammates, I jog back to the locker room for the other half of my uniform. As fans begin to fill the stadium, the team runs onto the field for warm-ups, twelve-man offensive and defensive plays are run, and special teams that end with a punt before the entire team sprints into the locker room to put game faces on. I sit, calmly waiting for the signal that it is time to go.

As I sit in my locker, Coach Weis walks over for a brief conversation. He tells me he is going to hold me back from playing until he sees how the game unfolds. If we are dominating the game, then I may not play today. If possible, he wants to give me more time to heal and not risk injury or setback during the game. I have never received this level of communication from my college coaches.

He doesn't want me to wonder why I am not playing or if I am in the "doghouse." He opts to keep me "in the know" by walking me through his thought process. Charlie wants us to be on the same page. I wonder if this level of transparency comes from his NFL experience or is this just the type of person he is. In any case, I am fully prepared for any decision Charlie makes.

We get the signal, and the team takes the field for the first game of the 2005 season — running onto the field to a ballad of "boos" is intoxicating, it's food for the soul. Midway through the second period we are winning 28-10. With the game going according to plan, Coach Weis informs me I will not be playing today: "No need to risk putting you on the field too early today, Matt." Disheartened, but in agreeance, I say, "That works for me Coach." Phenomenal communication before and during the game. A refreshing start to the season.

And a great start for the team, as we prove the media wrong with a dominant win over Pittsburgh 41-14. We are not starting 0-6 this year Lee Corso! After the game, in the locker room, Coach Weis gives Father Jenkins and Dr. White game balls for bringing him to Notre Dame.

After showering, dressing, and saying goodbye to my family waiting outside, I walk to the bus, and the team is off to South Bend — plane rides home are always better after a win, you're allowed to talk. The team never stays overnight after a game. We always go home because there is work to do on Sunday before the school week starts. There are several times we do not arrive on campus until sunrise.

On Sunday morning, we have treatment for any injured or sore players. Then, we have a team workout and conditioning session to remove the lactic acid build-up from our systems — helping to reduce the amount of time a player is sore from the game.

Sunday evening, we have another team meeting. Coach Weis gives the team his thoughts on the Pitt game, then we break and meet with our position coaches to watch last night's game. As soon as we are done reviewing and discussing every play of the game, we begin studying film on our upcoming opponent to jump-start preparation for the week.

Now the week starts all over again, with Monday being a day off, aside from treatment in the training room, if needed. For five years, this has been the basic outline of a game week.

# TEAM BANNED

## 52

**SEPTEMBER 18, 2005.** I move off-campus this year to live with D.J. and his cousin C.J. I am fast asleep in my bed, after a loss against Michigan State by a field goal in overtime. The front door slams open, shaking the wall below, and startling me awake. Footstep after footstep squeak on the floor. Commotion drifts up the stairs into my room, as the front door slams shut. My hopes of falling back asleep are lost.

I throw my door open, with sand in my eyes, and stagger downstairs. Halfway down I yell, "What the hell is going on?" I am greeted by six large football players in the foyer, blabbering like Gossip Girls whose adrenaline causes their words to be incomprehensible. Back and forth they go. I shout again, "Yo! What the hell are y'all talking about?"

Here is their story, as I heard it. To commiserate over losing to Michigan State, a few of the guys hit a local bar, Rum Runners. Toward the end of the night, the bell for last call rings. Ryan walks to the bar for one more. Another patron bumps into this mountain of a man. Words are exchanged in a heated conversation. A crowd helps usher them outside into the parking lot. Ryan's teammates are scattered throughout the bar; they don't see the beginnings of this quarrel. Last call has been initiated, so they think the move outside is simply a part of closing time.

Outside, Ryan has his hands full. Two guys jump him. Swinging, kicking, and clawing, they do everything in their power to wrestle the giant to the ground. Ryan stands at 6'5" and weighs over 300-pounds. He is easily handling these guys. Huddled around a pickup truck, a couple drunkards watch their buddies being manhandled by a single person and they can take no more. Two more guys jump in to help beat the beast into submission. One of Ryan's teammates, Neil, pushes his way through the onlookers to see what the commotion is. He explodes into battle.

Neil rips off his shirt and vigorously barks, "Who wants the hammer?!" One opponent leaves his partners to answer. SMASH! One punch and the contender crashes to the ground. Neil growls for another, "Who wants the hammer?!" Another opponent answers the call. Neil one-punch drops him too. Ryan is still "cleaning house." The four other ND players trickle out of the bar to see the crowd encircling their teammates; they shoulder their way through to the center just in time to see all four opponents scrambling to their feet and fleeing the scene.

Later the next week, Coach Weis calls a meeting at his office. One player takes a seat. Another player takes a seat. Then another and another. The players look around and realize everyone at the weekend fight is sitting in Charlie's waiting room — multiple hands rise to meet foreheads in an "Oh, no" moment. The phone rings, and the secretary lets them in to see Coach.

"Alright guys let's watch a little film," coach says. He hits play. "Nice right hook Ryan. Neil, great upper cut." He continues to watch the "game film" with his players. He eventually turns off the film from the bar parking lot. Coach yells and curses at each player, spitting on them with his New Jersey wise-guy accent, asking how they can be so stupid. Then, says, "Because you guys are so stupid, the entire team is banned from the bars."

Little does Charlie know the parties and celebrations will go on. And thrive! For the rest of the year, after every home game, the team and our friends party at our house. Good thing C.J. is a party animal!

We have hundreds of people at our quaint three-bed, two-and-a-half-bath home. We have bonfires in the backyard, hit golf balls across the highway, have people perform feats of strength for a beer from the fully stocked fridge, and 300-pounders in the middle of playing "Edward Forty Hands" greet cops at the door every Saturday night. The cops always say, "Guys, just turn the music down." With the music down, the parties wrap up well into the next morning.

*Players Earn this Title for Success on the Field and in the Classroom.*

# Reunion & Honor in Washington

## 53

**September 24, 2005.** Emotions run high this week. The anticipation in the air is unlike any the team has felt before: a potentially awkward reunion, and an honored dedication that is as distinct as it is solemn.

We travel west to face the University of Washington Huskies and our former head coach, Tyrone Willingham. Before the game pleasantries are exchanged with handshakes and smiles. No awkwardness to speak of, just strange to see people who were a part of the family now on the outside looking in. The team stays focused, not succumbing to the distraction of seeing our former coaches (a handful of assistants joined Tyrone at Washington) on the other side of the field.

Coach Weis and Coach Willingham meet before the game to discuss the "circus" that is this game. After the game, Weis says, "I think we were both glad to get to kickoff and get it over with, because no matter how hard you try, you know what it's going to be about ... I think that we got to share a little chuckle together because we were both thinking the same thing."[60] In addition to the high emotion of playing against the former staff, we are fueled by a young man's battle and request. The team is awaiting the most meaningful play of our careers.

The first play of the game is dedicated to Montana Mazurkiewicz, a ten-year-old boy suffering from an inoperable brain tumor. Coach Weis met with Montana earlier in the week, on Wednesday, attempting to lift the boys' spirits as he is in the midst of losing his battle.

"I was able to get a couple smiles out of him," Weis said. "His mom got to take a couple pictures. She said it was the first time he really smiled in about three months." "To watch a kid that's 10 years old only get a smile to his face because of his passion and love for Notre Dame Football, that's really a good moral to tell your own players ... It's not just the university they're representing, it's all the people who support that university."[61] Before leaving the boy on Wednesday evening, Coach Weis asked, "Is there anything I can do for you?" Montana simply said, "A pass to the right side of the field to open the game Saturday."

Late Thursday evening Charlie receives terrible news. Montana lost his battle with cancer, just one day after Coach lifted his spirits. Charlie reminds the grieving family, "This game is for Montana, and the play still stands." The Irish offense takes the field with heavy hearts. We understand the gravity of the upcoming play.

Brady Quinn's feet are in the Notre Dame end zone, but Coach Weis will not change the play call for any reason. Conventional wisdom says to run the ball in this situation ... it is the safe course of action. Try to get a yard or two. Create some space for your offense to work. Get your quarterback's feet out of his own end zone, so he can feel more comfortable throwing the ball. A turnover this close to the end zone or a safety will be a horrible, maybe insurmountable, start for the team. But football is just a game. That is the reality. And honoring the request of a dying young man, who recently passed, is worth any amount of risk the team takes on the field.

Brady calls the play, "Sprint 339 Naked," and the huddle breaks with a clap. The offense sprints to the line. Brady surveys the defense, making a few dummy calls. At the snap of the ball, Brady fakes the handoff to his left and rolls to the right side of the field. The defense bites, and crashes toward the left side of the offense.

At the same time, Anthony Fasano blocks down on the defensive end, pushing him toward the middle of the field, and releases to "the flat" on the right side, heading toward the sideline. Anthony is wide open. Brady, 9 yards deep in his own end zone, throws a perfect strike to Fasano at the 4-yard line. Anthony barrels down the sideline looking to gain every possible inch during this emotionally charged play. A defender darts at his legs, attempting to make the tackle. Then, as if Montana himself is lifting Anthony into the air, he leaps. He hurdles the defender for an extra 3 yards, and a first down!

After the game Coach Weis simply says, "I hope he's smiling in heaven right now." A promise kept, a reunion in the books, and a 36-17 win over the Huskies. After the game, the team paid their respects to our former coaches. Many of us seek out the men who guided us over the last three years to say hello. "I expected that to happen, I expected them to at least say they knew me, so that's what happened," Willingham said.[62]

# A Pep Rally & A Push

## 54

OCTOBER 14, 2005. THE Notre Dame Pep Rally. Friday night before every home game, Notre Dame holds a pep rally in the 11,418 seat Joyce Center basketball arena. The pep rally is the personification of the Notre Dame spirit.

At my first pep rally, the team entered the arena to a serenade by the Notre Dame Victory March and the roar of cheering fans. In that moment I felt the full force of the tradition, history, passion, and excellence that is Notre Dame. Waves of emotion ripple throughout the entirety of my body. It was a truly magical spectacle to behold. I never thought the experience of my first pep rally would be topped by another, but I am wrong.

Tickets for tonight's rally are in such a high demand, the university decides to move it to Notre Dame Stadium. The team gathers in the tunnel and prepares to take the field under the stadium lights. The thunderous roar of fans creates a thrilling wave of excitement that closely resembles gameday. A sensation of chill bumps undulates from within.

In suits and dress shoes, the team rushes onto the field in front of 45,000 fans, the noise level truly rivals that of a Saturday. Fans greet the 4-1 Irish hoping to carry us onward to victory. Players, coaches, and guest speakers take to the microphone, each inflaming the fans' expectations for what tomorrow will bring. Fireworks explode into the night sky.

*2005, Pep Rally at Notre Dame Stadium: The Fireworks Show.*

The pageantry that is the pep rally culminates with the playing of our alma mater. Forty-five thousand fans interlock arms over shoulders to create an impenetrable weave of unity, as they begin swaying side-to-side with the music in a euphoric display of affection as part of the Notre Dame family. A truly awesome sight to behold before we face one of our rivals.

**October 15, 2005.** The team is fully prepared for today's fight. The #9 Fighting Irish are ready to do battle against the #1 team in the land, the University of Southern California Trojans. After warm-ups we return to the locker room, as we do each game, but this time a gift awaits.

As I walk up the stairs a rumble grows from within the locker room. I clear the top step and am engulfed by a sea of green. Each locker dawns a dark-forest-green jersey with gold-coated numbers — check out the back cover of the book. The locker room is going crazy!

"Henry [Scroope, our ND equipment manager] and I talked in the summer, and I told him to have a set [of green jerseys] made. I thought maybe if we made it to a bowl game, it would be a nice way to fire the kids up. This game was like a bowl game. If you could have seen how fired up when they went back in the locker room and saw them. They worked so hard preparing for this game. I thought that I'd give them something back."[63] Rocking our new jerseys, the team rushes the field. The atmosphere is electric! The fans belt out a roaring scream, the likes of which I have never heard before in this stadium. Chicago probably hears a distant crackle that is mistaken for the faint sounds of thunder.

We battle back-and-forth the entire game. An instant classic in the making. With 2:04 remaining in the game, Notre Dame takes a 31-28 lead on a 5-yard Brady Quinn scramble to the right side of the field for a touchdown. The game is now in the hands of our defense. The defense looks remarkable, as they feed off the energy from the crowd, whose howls grow louder with each stop. They force the Trojans into a fourth-and-9 scenario at the USC 26-yard line. Then, tragedy strikes our defense in the form of a perfect throw.

Matt Leinart zips the ball to Dwayne Jarrett for a gain of 61 yards. On the next play, Leinart scrambles from inside the 5-yard line and launches himself toward the end zone in the hope of winning the game with a touchdown. He is met by a ferocious hit from linebacker Corey Mays who stops him just short of the goal line and sends the ball flying backward out of bounds. The clock ticks down to 0:00. I rush the field with my entire team. Jumping, running in excitement. I begin yelling at the losers and throwing up double barrel middle finger waves of goodbye. We just beat the #1 team in the country ... or did we?

Officials huddle in discussion ... I watch, and think, "This isn't good." The officials decide to put the ball inside the 1-yard line with 0:07 on the clock. I return to the sideline cautiously optimistic, as we await the next play. Leinart snaps the ball, runs a quarterback sneak, and is stuffed at the line of scrimmage. He barely moves an inch until Reggie Bush slams into Leinart's back, *illegally* propelling his quarterback into the end zone, and securing a USC victory. My head sinks. I am sick to my stomach. Triumph once at my fingertips is ripped away.

In this era of football, the NCAA just began testing instant replay. The visiting team makes the decision whether to use the replay system or not. Before the game Pete Carroll chooses not to help test this new concept, which ultimately helps his team. Replay would have changed Pete's play call and the outcome of the game.

Sunday arrives. Somber and visibly upset, I watch the fourth-and-9 play for 61 yards and the "Bush Push" a hundred times. Ambrose Wooden plays great defense against Jarrett. His hand even grazes the ball before it is caught. It's as though the "Matrix" glitches at the exact moment Ambrose swipes for the ball. Bad luck is on our side during this play.

The "Bush Push" wouldn't have happened if Pete decided to use instant replay. The Pac-10 officials would have seen the ball go out of bounds at the 3-yard line and not the 1-yard line. Likely, Leinart would have spiked the ball opting for a field goal to force overtime, and never attempted a quarterback sneak. Who knows what the results would have been? I like to believe we would have won the game, ended the season 10-1, and punched our ticket to the national championship game.

We do eventually, and technically, win the game due to illegal practices at USC during this timeframe. Though, a victory a few years down the road is a hollow one that means nothing. But I have always wondered what may have been, if only Pete had selected to further the evolution of the game by allowing instant replay on this day. Way to hold football back, Pete!

# The ND Farewell

## 55

November 19, 2005. We make it. Here we stand. Underneath the stadium, in the locker room, sitting in our lockers before the last home game of our college football careers. The seniors prepare. We lace up our cleats, put on our pads, and adorn the Notre Dame jersey for the swan song that is this day. Four seasons ago the Notre Dame family welcomed us into their home with an explosion of cheer ... today we will say our goodbyes.

Staying focused, while engraining every sensory experience of this last dance, is a difficult pirouette to perform. The countdown begins. The concluding moments of an era are underway. Wearing *the* gold helmet, I run out of the tunnel for the final time — goosebumps rise for the occasion.

The game passes as quickly as it starts. The final whistle blows in one of the most physically and emotionally draining games of my career. I drop to a knee in exhaustion and overwhelming emotions on this chilly winter day. Looking at the ground I see my hurried breath. A brisk wind nips at every uncovered piece of skin. I think to myself, "This is a moment." I try to take it all in. The smell of home soil and grass, mixed with the aroma of popcorn twirling about in the crisp air. The echoing, persisting rumble of an amazing crowd. The sight of my brothers celebrating.

I am swarmed by teammates, as I stand to join in the festivities. The senior class gathers in the north end zone for one final salute to the home crowd. Calves still cramping from the game, I hobble to join my classmates for a memorializing lap around the stadium to say thank you to the fans. The feelings I have in this moment, with my brothers, are ones I will revisit until my time runs out in this life.

Notre Dame wins 34-10 over Syracuse, I have three catches for 62 yards, and my final home game becomes an unforgettable memory. This is a day I wish I could relive over-and-over, not because of individual success, but because of the aforementioned feelings and the goosebumps ... oh, those goosebumps — they were different today.

My fifth year has been a great one so far. We finish the year at 9-2, losing to Michigan State and USC at home. The #5 ranked Irish are invited to the BCS Fiesta Bowl in Tempe, Arizona to face the #4 ranked Ohio State Buckeyes, who are also 9-2. I feel great about the bowl game this year, mostly because I will be at home on Christmas Day instead of taking my chances on the practice field. The only gifts I receive for this Christmas are real presents under the tree. No injuries. No new coaches. We have a good team that is poised to win Notre Dame's first Bowl since the 1994 Cotton Bowl against Texas A&M.

The final whistle of my college career rings within the stadium. I pull my golden helmet off for the last time. The inevitable ending of a college athlete, inching closer since I first stepped foot on campus, is at hand. Standing on the field I am overtake with sadness. The game ends, my college football career ends, and my life as a Notre Dame Football player ends. One whistle marks them all.

Entering the locker room, a sea of emotion envelops every corner. Fellow seniors are crying. Some sit in solitude trying to compose themselves. Others hug out their sorrows. Smiles weakly attempt to mask the realities of the moment. Underclassmen want to help but have no idea how best to console. Tears spring to my eyes, trickling down my face, as I am punched in the jaw again by reality — this is the last time I will share a locker room with this brotherhood. We will never play football together again wearing Notre Dame Blue and Gold.

The seniors' last game in a Notre Dame uniform is a tough one. I can honestly say the team and I gave it our all, but we are bested by a better football team — the Buckeyes win 34-20.

| 2005 Schedule | | | |
|---|---|---|---|
| Overall 9-3 | PCT 0.750 | Home 4-2/Away 5-0/Neutral 0-1 | |
| Date | Opponent | Location | Result |
| 9/3/2005 | at Pittsburgh | Pittsburgh, PA | W, 42-21 |
| 9/10/2005 | at Michigan | Ann Arbor, MI | W, 17-10 |
| 9/17/2005 | vs. Michigan State | Notre Dame, IN | L, 41-44 (OT) |
| 9/24/2005 | at Washington | Seattle, WA | W, 36-17 |
| 10/1/2005 | at Purdue | West Lafayette, IN | W, 49-28 |
| 10/15/2005 | vs. USC | Notre Dame, IN | L, 31-34 |
| 10/22/2005 | vs. BYU | Notre Dame, IN | W, 49-23 |
| 11/5/2005 | vs. Tennessee | Notre Dame, IN | W, 41-21 |
| 11/12/2005 | vs. Navy | Notre Dame, IN | W, 42-21 |
| 11/19/2005 | vs. Syracuse | Notre Dame, IN | W, 34-10 |
| 11/26/2005 | at Stanford | Palo Alto, CA | W, 38-31 |
| 1/2/2006 | vs. Ohio State (Fiesta Bowl) | Tempe, AZ | L, 20-34 |

The season was not what I hoped it would be, but I had a solid campaign, and the team had an amazing year. I end my ND career on a high note with five catches for 52 yards against the Buckeyes. Not bad for a guy who tore his ACL a little over one-year ago on Christmas Day. Not bad considering I had a staph infection and scarcely avoid losing my leg or dying only 10 months earlier. Not bad considering my rehab was cut in half due to the infection. And a 9-3 record is not bad for a team who was supposed to start the season 0-6. And not bad for a first-year head coach who doesn't have "his guys" in the system yet; instead, winning with "19-seniors and fifth years who started or took a large share of the reps: BOB DAVIE'S guys."[64]

I worked hard during the offseason and the fruits of my labors paid off:

*"back into the rotation ... ranks sixth in Notre Dame history for average yards per reception in a career (18.9 ypc) ... has averaged 40.6 yards per touchdown catch in his career (seven for 284 yards) ... has played in 11 games this season, starting twice (BYU and Syracuse) ... has 23 catches for 277 yards (12-yard average) this season ... made two catches for 31 yards against Stanford, including a 25-yarder on a key third down play in the fourth quarter ... caught three passes for 62 yards (20.7-yard average) in the win over Syracuse, including a 32-yard catch ... had one reception for six yards in the win over Navy ... made one catch for six yards versus Tennessee ... started against BYU as the Irish opened in a five-receiver set ... made one catch for eight yards against the Cougars ... made one catch for five yards against USC ... had a career-best seven receptions for 68 yards against Purdue ... had six catches for 87 yards (14.5-yard average) against Michigan State, including a 33-yard reception ... had one reception for four yards against Michigan ... has logged 102:05 of playing time with five special teams appearances."[65]*

*2006, Fiesta Bowl: Matt Shelton Catch vs. Ohio State.*

As sad as I am with the passing of my Notre Dame Football career, I am more heartbroken about parting ways with my teammates. My teammates made football fun. I played harder and strived to be better for them. Teammates are the real loss for me on this day. The friendships, the bonds, the trust created by being part of Notre Dame history together will forever keep these men in my heart. I would drop anything and everything to help one of my brothers, if they only ask ... I know they would do the same. Notre Dame Football is not just about football, it is Family.

# PART FIVE

## "ACHILLES" & THE NFL

believe

# NFL SUPPORT!

## 56

UNFATHOMABLY, AFTER TWO ACL surgeries, a broken back, and a staph infection, there is still a realistic opportunity for my boyhood dream of reaching the NFL to become reality. There is a chance to reach the pinnacle of my chosen profession at 23 years old.

On my journey there have been an obscene number of ups-and-downs, twists-and-turns, beginning before freshman year of high school. But here I am. A new opportunity awaits. I stand at the precipice looking into the shadowy void of a mysterious future. There will undoubtably be rough waters ahead and obstacles to navigate. But I am ready. I am prepared. I am confident. I will succeed. I will persevere through anything thrown my way. Plus, I have an "ace in the hole" to help guide me ... Charlie Weis.

After the bowl game I return to campus with a shifted focus. I do not work hard for my teammates or university anymore. I work hard for myself alone, hopeful of finding a new team and a new locker room to call family. I work to become the best NFL prospect I can be and in my corner is an NFL heavy-hitter, with four Super Bowl championships.

There is no better "cut man" to fight with me and work on my behalf. Charlie rubs elbows with the "who's who" of the NFL. He exudes confidence in his abilities to help his players reach the next level. He is willing to use any tactic and anyone at his disposal to support my efforts. NFL scouts know him and trust his ability to evaluate football players. If Charlie vouches for me, there is a 100% chance I will have a shot at the next level.

Before diving into my experience, I would like to offer some counterbalance: Justin Tuck. A year prior, Justin met with Coach Weis to discuss staying at ND or leaving for the NFL.

Charlie, an offensive guru, tries selling the idea he will groom Justin like he did Tom Brady. Look, if Charlie is meeting with Brady Quinn, or any offensive player, this angle succeeds effortlessly. But a defensive player, sworn enemies of all quarterbacks and offensive players? Sell Tuck on how you will make him, develop him, into a better NFL prospect. On how returning for one more year will help the team, his brothers, his family. Do not try selling him on how great you made a quarterback. Why make a sales pitch about your offensive prowess to a defensive star?

Feels more like an ego move about grooming Tom, rather than a smart business move. Speak with Justin about how you are going to groom him to be the next Richard Seymour (Pats DE from 2001-2008, who was inducted into the 2022 NFL Hall of Fame). "Read the room" and tweak your pitch.

As Tuck tells me this story, my jaw drops with the realization of just how close we were to having Justin back for the 2005 season. And just how close we were to winning a National Championship ... there is no doubt in my mind, or Justin's, that if he returned for his fifth year we would have another trophy in the locker room. So, Tuck does not find much guidance from Charlie, but I sure do.

Coach Weis becomes a completely different person around me — calm and relaxed, always smiling. These characteristics were not mainstays last season, so to witness them every time we speak is unsettlingly refreshing.

His focus shifts too — from teaching and motivating to counseling and guiding. Charlie and I schedule a meeting to discuss my future.

As I wait outside Charlie's door, I am optimistic and excited for the conversation to come. Percolating thoughts of the future are welcomed this time around. I am not nervous about a new head coach, new coaching staff, new teammates, or a new city — I do not care who or where, as long as there is a next. Successfully navigating so much change over the years has become a part of my silver-lining attitude. The difficulties of my past have led to a comfortability with anything thrown my way. I am the calm within the storm.

The phone rings, Charlie's assistant gets the call to let me in. As I walk into his office, he stands from his desk to say hello. We shake hands and take a seat at a small conference table overlooking the practice fields to the south. Coach tells me he will do whatever it takes to ensure I get a shot in the NFL. I do my best to stay grounded and keep cool ... tough for a smiley person. He reminds me about his friendships with most of the NFL coaches, and scouts, and tells me they will listen to him for a couple reasons.

"First, my name is Charlie Weis, four-time Super Bowl Champion. Second, Brady Quinn has one more year and everyone in the league wants to be on my good side when the draft comes around next year."

Then he tells me what people think and say about me: "The NFL guys say you're a solid player, very fast, you run good routes, and you're a smart football player." These words bring a smirk and laugh from me, followed by, "That's great Coach, good to hear." "You don't f*cking believe me, do you?" Charlie continues, "I'll pick up the phone right now and call any head coach in the NFL and they'll tell you the same thing." I adjust in myself in the chair, smile, and say, "No Coach, I believe you." Before I even get the words out of my mouth he reaches for the phone. As he pushes the speaker phone button he says, "I'll f*cking prove it to you, these guys will answer my call cause of what I got in the stables."

Coach Weis calls an NFL head coach and leaves the speaker phone on. Ring, ring, ring ... "Hello." Charlie does not tell him I am in the room listening and says, "What do you think about Matt Shelton?" As though rehearsed, he says, "He's a solid player, really fast, runs good routes, and he's a smart football player." Wow! Mind blown. I can barely contain myself. I want to jump off the walls with excitement. Coach Weis says his goodbyes, then looks at me and says, "I f*cking told you, didn't I?"

Smiling with an ear-to-ear grin that can be seen for miles, I tell coach, "I never doubted you and thanks for doing that for me." I don't think my smile can be any bigger. Then, repeating the protocol above, Charlie calls two more NFL head coaches, and they pretty much say the same things about me. I am smiling so much my cheeks hurt. My head has never been this big. Put me outside, attach a basket to my feet, and this bright red hot air balloon can fly anywhere.

With more confidence than I have ever had in my life, I prepare to showcase my abilities for NFL organization at the combine. I begin working closely with the Notre Dame strength coaches. I take control of my training schedule for the first time in my life. I decide what is important, what I should focus on, on my remaining path to the next level.

Switching things up a little bit, I concentrate on gaining strength, gaining size, and increasing my speed, with a focus on combine testing drills: the 40-yard dash, 3-cone drill, 20-yard shuttle, 60-yard shuttle, bench press, vertical, broad jump, and position specific drills. Conditioning is out the window. This type of training is an absolute blast! Training hard, testing, and competing against the clock, attempting to beat my personal best make workouts exciting. Unfortunately, I do not receive an invite to the NFL combine in Indianapolis, so I must wait for the on campus pro-day to showcase what I can do.

The day arrives and I am officially ready to show what I've got. Astonishingly, I weigh-in at 180-pounds and don't have two 2 ½-pound weights in my hip pockets. Removing conditioning from my workouts and continuing to eat the way I had for the last four years (five meals, five protein shakes, and snacks throughout the day) finally pays off. Since my first day on campus, five football seasons ago, Mickey's one goal has been for me to make this weight. If he were here today, he would have punched a weight tree or thrown an honorary weight at my face, no question about it.

I bench press 225-pounds 16 times, crush all the agility drills, and run a 4.32-second forty, which ties for third fastest at the Indianapolis NFL combine. With this number on the board, we see exactly how surgeries affect my 40-yard dash speed — 4.23 is the best before surgeries, 4.27 is the best after ACL number one, and 4.32 is the best after ACL number two; a step or two lost, yes, but still impressive ... in some ways, maybe more so.

I have a great day, and I am eager for what is to come. When all the testing is complete, comparing my numbers to the NFL combines numbers, I am among the top five in this year's draft class of wide receivers for the 40-yard dash, 3-cone, both shuttles, and bench press. Jumping has not been a strong suit since my first ACL, so broad and vertical jump numbers are lacking.

Leading up to the draft, the New England Patriots, the Chicago Bears, and the Indianapolis Colts have a lot of interest in drafting me. Coach Weis tells me he is hearing good things from his friends in the NFL. My hopes are extremely high. Per usual though, I am cautiously optimistic, as I try to contain my excitement — nothing in life is guaranteed.

I have done everything within my power to showcase my talent to NFL teams. My play on the field shows them I can get the job done. Holding the record for most yards per catch speaks to my speed and catching ability. Pro-day couldn't have gone any better. My individual workout with the Patriots and Colts, where I run routes and catch footballs for them at Notre Dame, goes perfectly — I am a route running technician with no drops.

Though I carry a history of injury with me, I also carry a history of resilience, toughness, and strength to overcome any obstacle. No matter what the result of the upcoming draft is, I am proud of what I have accomplished and how I've handled myself along this journey.

Draft day! My answer to who will draft the little guy is on its way. Not unexpectedly, the first day of the draft passes without my name being called. With the arrival of the second day come butterflies fluttering around in my stomach. The nervous energy is apparent to everyone around me. Opting not to sit around watching the draft this day, D.J., C .J., Dan, and I hit the golf links. We decide waiting will be torturous; let's take our minds off the unfolding events, which are out of our control.

On the tee box of the eighteenth hole my phone rings. A call from an unknown number. I nervously answer the phone, "Hello, this is Matt." It's the Colts! My cautious optimism turns into enthusiastic reality. Then, he tells me, "We've run out of draft picks; we almost drafted you in the sixth-round but went a different direction — we don't have a seventh-round pick this year or it would be you."

The reality seeps into my mind, as my hopes of being drafted are all but over. There are picks remaining in the seventh-round, but my odds are slim when you look at the needs of the remaining teams and their low interest in me. As I sink the last putt on the eighteenth, so too do my hopes of being drafted. The 2006 NFL draft has announced the last name and

Matt Shelton is absent from the announcement. I am not Mr. Irrelevant but feel very irrelevant in this moment.

Undrafted, I am in the driver's seat of my future. I have a choice between the interested teams: Bears, Colts, and Patriots. I get to choose which situation I believe is the best fit for me. Each team offers a signing bonus and with it an opportunity to make the team, just as any player drafted. Just because you are drafted doesn't mean you will make the team, though the odds are increased. I will have a chance to prove myself like any drafted player must do. The question at my feet is, does money up front outweigh a better fit — a better opportunity to make the team?

I schedule a meeting with Coach Weis to discuss my future again. His input will weigh heavily on my decision. Charlie laid it all out on the table for me. "The Colts are offering more money. The Patriots offer a brighter future. You already know 99% of the New England offense, giving you a better chance of making the team. There is no decision here. Your goal is making the team. Then, the money comes." After the meeting, I return to my place for deliberation.

My mind swirls as I wrestle with this decision. After much contemplation, I find clarity. Coach is correct. The path to earning a spot on the roster is clearest in New England. Patriots, here I come!

# THE "HEEL" WINS

## 57

WHEN I ARRIVE IN New England, I am immediately the second most knowledgeable wide receiver in the room. Even wide receiver coach Brian Daboll, now head coach of the New York Giants, stops meetings to ask me how Charlie would handle certain situations versus specific defensive formations. He eventually removes Charlie from the equation, asking, "Matt, what would you do here?" before asking anyone else in the room.

These early conversations with Daboll confirm I made the correct decision in choosing the Patriots over the other interested teams. Plus, I cannot wait to catch a ball from Tom Brady ... Tom, freaking, Brady!

On my first day of practice with Tom in the building, I walk to the line of scrimmage and settle into my wideout stance. I look to my left, and I swear Tom is walking in slow motion with wind in his hair (even though he has a helmet on), and crouches to take the center's snap. He looks me dead in my eyes, stands up, and waives me off. I rise from my stance, look at Coach Daboll, and he waives me over to stand by his side.

I give him a what the hell was that look. "Tom doesn't want to waste a rep on a player who might not make the team. Once you make the team, he'll cross you up all day," Daboll says. This feels like an insult. But with time to reflect, the logic is there, and I simply need to prove myself to earn Tom's respect and passes. Nothing changes for me ... the goal is still the same.

Matt Cassell, the backup QB out of USC (of course!), becomes my new best friend. We quickly find chemistry — completion after completion, we are on fire — and work closely together throughout camp.

As camp progresses, it becomes clear my likelihood of making the team is extremely high. My odds increase every day. With this eventuality, Tom crosses me up with his passes, i.e., he throws the ball with such velocity the end-seams of the football leave a cross on your chest because you don't have time to catch the ball away from your body with your hands.

I bust my butt daily, on and off the field, to earn a roster spot. Camp is going great until my injury-prone body is stricken once more. I burst off the line of scrimmage on a "Deep Go" route. I glide by the defender. Tracking the ball, I realize it's thrown really far, so I try to find another gear to chase it down. RIP! My groin tears. It's better than a SNAP ... I hope. I limp off the field to locate the training staff for a conversation.

Afterward, I work tirelessly to get healthy again; I am not there yet and need more time to fully heal. The trainers will not allow me to run straight ahead full speed, as they do not want me to "open it up" and risk tearing my groin further to the point of needing surgery. After rehab and time off though, they do allow me to participate in agility drills and take part in team testing day. They will not permit me to run the 40-yard dash, but I do break the Patriots records — at that time — for the 3-cone drill and the x-drill ... all with a torn groin. Not a bad day's work.

During rehab I make great strides, but 100% health still eludes me. I practice anyway. The doctors clear me to play again. I am almost back to full speed and fighting defensive backs every day. I reaggravate the groin but fight through the pain. Limping in-between plays, I show my grit and determination. I'm having a solid practice and need to keep it up. There is a lot on the line, and missing more time could prove disastrous.

During the first half of practice, sprinting down the field I make a quick cut and show the quarterback my numbers. The ball is already hurling toward me. It's high! Leaping into the air with my underwhelming vertical, I snatch the football from the cornerbacks' hands.

As I land, my feet simultaneously hit the ground sending shockwaves through my legs and up my spine. Pain receptors are firing on all cylinders. My knees are on fire; they feel like someone is stabbing both patellar tendons with millions of tiny spikes freshly forged in fire. I crash to the ground but hold onto the football ... that a boy! I climb to my feet and gingerly walk to the huddle. My knees will not bend, they are stiff as a board. Each attempt to bend them causes immense pain.

Time, continual overload, and surgeries have caught up to me. Moreover, in each knee, I have two-thirds of a patellar tendon fighting to do the work of a full tendon. Because of the doctor's surgical technique, the middle third of each tendon was removed and are now my ACL's. Perfect. A reaggravated groin and two fresh knee injuries. After a few weeks of not seeing improvement in my health, the Patriots need to make a decision.

Ultimately, the team decides to place me on Injury Reserve. Head Coach Bill Belichick tells me I would have made the team if I did not get hurt, so they want to put me on IR to get healthy for next year. Here we are again. Yet another time in my football career where I am injured and need to fight my way back to being healthy.

While on Injured Reserve I am not allowed, by the NFL, to participate in practices. The NFL has "inspectors" whose sole purpose is to make sure teams are following the rules. The inspectors show up randomly at different team facilities to see if anyone is breaking the rules. In my mind this is great, considering the situation I find myself in. I will have multiple months to get healthy and ready for camp next year, with no pressure to practice before I am 100%. The Pats have other ideas.

After a few weeks of rehab, my health isn't getting much better. My knees and groin are still causing a great deal of pain. Coaches begin asking me when I will be ready to practice. What? I thought, by rule, I cannot practice this year. At this time, the Patriots expect their players on Injury Reserve to help the team at practice when they are healthy enough. I can still barely bend my knees when riding a stationary bike, and they want me to practice full speed every day?

I am unable to sneakily help them at practice, so toward the end of the year Scott Pioli, the Vice President of Player Personnel, calls me into the office. I take a seat at his desk, and he presents me with unwelcome news. Scott informs me I am being released by the Patriots.

He proceeds to tell me I am not healing fast enough, and the organization believes I will never play football again due to my health issues; guaranteed if I were able to illegally help during practice, in any capacity, they would have kept me on the team — no matter how I was progressing. I am especially surprised because I thought while on Injured Reserve an injured player cannot be released.

My shoulders drop, I sink into the chair heartbroken by his words. Attempting to soften the blow, he adds, "I never call a player into my office to let him go." Usually, a player is told he is released by a note at his locker and a packed bag. Since I am Charlie's guy this is a different situation. "Out of respect for Charlie, I wanted to give you the news face-to-face," Scott says. Visibly shook I simply say, "Oh. Okay. Well, thank you for the opportunity, and I'm gonna prove you wrong ... I'll be back."

News in hand, I walk out of Gillette Stadium for the last time. Proud of what I have done and determined to get healthy for a return to the NFL next year. I set my sights on proving the Patriots wrong. I will be back!

Orlando here I come! I move in with D.J. Fitzpatrick, as we both start a comeback for next season. He and I play a ton of golf and train five days a week. My groin feels fine, and my knees are as good as they can be at this point in my career. I push myself and test my health by constantly running, lifting, and participating in other sporting activities. I know I can make an impact on an NFL team in the upcoming season. I may not be a team's number one wideout, but there is no doubt I can be a slot receiver on any team in the NFL. After all, the Patriots saw the potential in me, envisioning me to be Wes Welker before he was "Wes Welker." Expectations are high with the return of my health.

While using a pickup game of basketball with friends as training ... SLIP! Driving the lane, I stop on a dime to pull up for a jump shot and my shoe keeps sliding forward atop bits of gravel. While sliding, I catch myself just before falling to the ground. Shockwaves again ripple through my body.

I reinjure my groin and both patellar tendons are on fire once more. The tiny fire daggers at the Patriots practice are returned. The pain is on the exact same level. I can't bend my knees. The "Do not proceed" and "Stop" signs are shouting. My body is telling me something yet again. In this moment, I learn months and months of rehab were simply a Band-Aid that can easily be ripped off by an innocent slip on a few pebbles. A slip, like hundreds of slips I've had before, sets me back months.

More time and more rehab are now needed. After a few weeks of rest and contemplation, I start rehab again. The exercises seem more difficult this time around. Each movement causes more pain. Each pain creates doubt ... doubts I have never experienced during my previous climbs after being knocked to the ground.

I wonder, "Why does each day feel more difficult than the last? Is the pain too much? Has there been *any* improvement?" I have never paid attention to the negative thoughts that unavoidably creep into one's mind during times of struggle. I have never paid attention to these calls from my body asking me to throw in the towel. Always being able to ignore them or push them from my mind.

But these thoughts persist. Accumulating like ants stumbling into a dollop of honey. One walks into a sticky, sweet swirl, and cannot seem to wiggle its way out. A second accidentally puts a foot inside and is quickly overtaken by the rolling spread of negativity. And another. And another, until the entire colony turns the once glistening gold blob of honey into a black sea of sorrow.

This battle feels different than the rest. I cannot shake these doubts. I cannot rub the pain away like I have done countless times before. The pain is too much. Too many injuries have compounded within a body that feels past its prime at the ripe old age of 24.

Reluctantly, I heed the call and obey the signs. Stopping. Going no further. I unravel my fingers and drop the towel. As it hits the ground my future again becomes uncertain ... the only certainty is I will never again play the sport I love. Never again will I have this type of family: a locker room full of like-minded competitors, brothers, who rally together for weekly fall battles. I will never again be part of anything remotely comparable.

Today is the day. The totality of this journey that has haunted me for years, nipping at my heels, finally consumes me. Its chase surpasses my injury-riddled body's capability to return. I can evade its grasp no longer.

# PART SIX

## THIS JOURNEY'S END

# Aftermath-N-Thoughts

## 58

This game, football, has hurt me more times than I can count, and yet it has given me so much joy. One might think after numerous injuries, countless sacrifices, and tremendous pains, the finality of my football career would bring a feeling of peace. You would be wrong.

Football has been my life since seventh grade, my passion, my one drive and focus. Sports in general, especially football, have been the reason I get out of bed in the morning for as long as I can remember. It has defined me. It has brought me comfort. It has provided me with so many extended family members. Football is who I am. The only thing I have ever truly and deeply known.

Throwing in the towel, giving up, has never crossed my mind. I have always believed there are no obstacles I cannot overcome on my path to greatness as a National Football League player. The realization there are mountains I cannot climb is a difficult pill to swallow.

To know I was good enough to have a career at the top level in the game I love, and have it ripped away due to health issues, is painful. It is a thought that will linger in my mind the rest of my life ... "what if?"

What if I did not break my back before high school? What if I did not tear an ACL during senior year of high school? What if we did not practice on Christmas Day in 2004? What if I never contracted a staph infection? What if I had surgery with the team doctors in South Bend, would the infection have found me? What if we did not take the bandages off my knee earlier than my Tennessee doctor advised, would I have still gotten staph?

I would rather the Patriots tell me I am not good enough to play in the NFL. I can live with that understanding. But health causes my journey to end. I have the talent to perform on Sunday, but I cannot stay healthy. My body failed me. And this is the only reason I could go no further. That is a tough one for me.

I have the ability. I have the willingness, passion, and desire to work on this craft of football that I love so much. I am officially assigned, evermore, to the PUP list (physically unable to perform). As I hang the cleats up, I retire a part of who I am. A part of me fades, disappearing into the chasms of yesteryear. Another casualty of the violent game that is football. The game I love leaves me with memories, scars, and daily pain of a failing body. A journey I would gladly begin again.

As I reflect on my time at Notre Dame, I realize just how chaotic and painful my time truly was. From the years 2001 to 2005, the university, the fans, teammates, and myself, alike, had many ups and many downs. From Bob the entertainer, to George the time guru, to Tyrone the philosophical sitter, to Kent the caretaker, to Charlie the bold, we bore witness to an unprecedented era of change.

These four massive alterations alone are near insurmountable. Now add to the mix a handful of personal obstacles to navigate. Persevering through two major knee injuries, injuries that have ended countless sports careers. Battling a life-threatening infection. Managing residual pain from a broken back. Finding balance after multiple concussions. And handling unrelenting academic pressure. This equation equals a very unexpected journey. These obstacles molded me into the man I am today. A man with a unique ability to adapt and an unwavering fortitude. At one of the most prestigious universities in the world I, along with the recruiting class of 2001, endured an unprecedented amount of change, as did the entire Notre Dame family.

The University of Notre Dame has had a few missteps over the years as they searched for "the one." "The one" head football coach who would return the university to glory and to college football greatness. University officials were steadfast in their searches. The ever-changing landscape of college football pressured them into believing they needed this return to happen quickly. In haste, officials may have chosen incorrectly ... a couple of times.

Five head coaches, in the span of five years, is not what one expects during a collegiate career. When I left the university, I thought the football team was in great hands with Charlie Weis. I believed Charlie would thrive. I felt his "nastiness," his passion for the game, his love for his players, his confidence, and his will to win would propel the team back into the national championship conversation for years to come. Unfortunately, this would not be the case. The university continues its search after Charlie's chance.

**November 30, 2009.** Trying to overcome missteps of another coaching change, after five seasons and a 35-27 record, Coach Charlie Weis was released from his contract by his alma mater. Charlie may not have been the second coming of Jesus Christ, as some had hoped, but he did get Notre Dame Football back on track. Coach Weis recruited top-notch talent to the university and left the "stables" full for the arrival of "the one."

**December 10, 2009.** Notre Dame has a new head coach for the sixth time in nine years, Coach Brain Kelly. Coach Kelly led the 2012 Notre

Dame Football team to a regular season mark of 12-0 and the first National Championship berth since the storied 1988 season. Again, I see Notre Dame in good hands: Brian serves 12 years at the helm, amassing a record of 113-40.

**December 3, 2021.** Notre Dame hires Marcus Freeman as the new head coach and again I believe Notre Dame Football is in good hands.

What I have come to realize over the years is Notre Dame will always be in good hands, and undoubtably have plenty more missteps. I believe there will always be men and women at the wheel with unwavering character who are willing to fight for, and uphold, the legacy and standards that are the University of Notre Dame.

Even with the "best of the best" running the institution, we are only human, and this world is ever-changing. Leaders will make errors. People under their purview will make mistakes. You and I will have our own blunders. Change is coming, it is always coming. We cannot predict the future. We can only hope there are systems in place to navigate the progress to come and have faith that we as individuals and our leaders are strong enough to endure and overcome. We can only hope the university, any university, is learning and growing from its mistakes. I have faith this is indeed the case.

Maybe my "realization" is simply that: one of faith. I have faith that, no matter who leads the football team, or who runs the university as president, Notre Dame will always be in good hands, as will the Notre Dame Family.

# Epilogue

Since the last time I sprinted onto the field in front of 80,000-plus screaming fans. Or the last time I laughed with a locker room full of family. Or the last time I stepped foot on campus with an unshakable understanding of who I am ... a lot of "life" has happened.

I was married, then divorced. My once open, unguarded heart itself encircled by the tallest of walls and encased by a seemingly impenetrable coat of armor. I thought my life was going to have the white picket fence the books painted into my dreams. I thought I would have children waking me at an ungodly hour on Christmas morning to open presents Santa left under the tree. I thought that after my dreams of football were ripped away, I would find my new life-long passion. "Man Plans, and God Laughs."

I have been lost. I have been found. Then lost and found again. Life has not gone according to plan, at least to my plan, and I am okay with this understanding. If life went according to my plan, I would have missed out on so many wonderful experiences and amazing people. I have found friends who have become family and will continue to grow my family, as I seek out good, trustworthy people. Somehow, I have found my locker room again. I have found a life full of love, laughter, compassion, joy, and growth. Life continues to throw curveballs at me, at us, and we are there for one another to navigate any obstacle that comes our way.

While living in Los Angeles, I found an "honorary sister" who went to USC, and we bicker every football season; I walked her mother down the aisle when she married a man who has become a brother. I've danced the night away at silent discos on the beach. Had midnight swims in the Pacific Ocean. And played beach volleyball with Leonardo DiCaprio.

I have been to countless Hollywood parties and premieres — *Star Wars: The Force Awakens* was my first. I've partied with George Lopez at his place multiple times — from what I remember, the conversations were some of the most interesting and entertaining of my life.

I had dinner with Tommy Lasorda. I've won softball championships with a Los Angeles Dodger Justin Turner coaching the team. I raced a 3 ½-pound Teacup Yorkie, named Dodger, down the ice at Staples Center during intermission at a Kings game, thanks to Tyler Toffoli.

I have spent numerous holidays with Notre Dame classmates and teammates whose families have taken me in, allowing me to become a part of their family. Life has had so many amazing things in store for me since my college days when I "knew" what my future would hold.

Like my football career, I've had many ups and many downs. The relationships forged at Notre Dame, and on the unexpected path afterward, have sustained and supported me at every turn. I have surrounded myself with friends who are family; they have been there for me and will continue to be there for me the rest of my life — as I will be there for them. Would I have found these lasting connections if life had gone more smoothly, or as I planned? What if after being knocked down, I kept my head in the sand instead of getting up? What if my mindset did not allow me to find the small glimmer of light when surrounded by darkness?

I don't have any of these answers, nor do I need them. I know who I am, and I am not defined by my path. I am an imperfect person striving to simply be better than I was the day before. I am a person who is cautiously optimistic in every situation; I am a work in progress and hope I always will be — I never want to stop growing.

I hope in joining me on the journey that is "Rising thru <u>every</u> Fall" a smile was brought to your face. And hopefully you took a little time to recall and honor the defining chapters of your own journey. As you put this book on your shelf, I hope you keep a few thoughts with you.

First, SNAPS happen. Pain, change, and doubt happen. Bad things happen in life. Allow those events to shape you ... not define you. Allow your reactions to define you. Do not dwell on being knocked down. Revel in how you have risen through the negativity, the adversity. Do not focus on the crashing. Focus on the rising above it all and persevering through an event that could have kept you from your dreams. Falling is inevitable; surprise people by rising.

Second, no matter what you are going through in life, there is always light within the darkness — seek it out and fan the flame.

Third, talk to your "locker room" when times are tough; you are never alone, no matter what has happened. You have people who are willing to help and support you during difficult times, if only they knew you needed them ... reach out, take the first step along a new path.

Lastly, **"You have the ability, simply remember your courage!"**

# THE END OF THIS JOURNEY.
## — MAY YOU TOO CONTINUE TO RISE. —

# Two Favors & A QR Code

1 - Should you find any typos, your keen eye for detail and your help are greatly appreciated. Let me know via email at RisingThruEveryFall@ gmail.com, please address to "Typo Support."

2 - Thank you for reading! If you enjoyed the journey, please suggest the book to your friends and family — and leave a review online wherever you purchased your copy; I'm hoping the QR Code below will make this easy for you. Reviews are hugely important; I appreciate your support and look forward to hearing what you have to say!

Scan the QR Code below to check out a few links: Bruton's Books, Book Review Sites, Social Media Accounts, and The Book's Website!

# Acknowledgments

## Thank You

"It takes a village." The accomplishments of my athletic career and the writing of this book were not forged alone. Family, friends, teammates, coaches, physical therapists, doctors, trainers, and managers were all profoundly involved. You are all appreciated.

First and foremost, a huge thank you to my family. In each decision, each stumble, each complication, and each success you have been by my side. Your love and support can never be repaid or reciprocated enough. Mom, a special thank you for your support in the creation of this book.

The Walz family. You saved my life; I am eternally grateful to Patti, Tom, and Lindsey. Words will never express how thankful I am you are a part of my life.

Thank you, Taylor Lanier. Your editing experience, knowledge, and guidance truly rounded the rough edges; you helped breathe life and clarity into so many aspects of the book. Thanks, cuz!

Thanks to Diane Belanger. I am not sure what I enjoyed more, working with you on the book or walking you down the aisle at Cat and Tyler's wedding. In either case, your insight and encouragement to finish this book were invaluable.

Dr. David Bruton, Jr., and family, I am honored you joined me on this book journey; your foreword, your heartfelt words, truly honors and embraces the books message. I am grateful our paths intertwined at ND. I wish you all, and Bruton's Books, continued blessings and success.

Lisa Kelly and Rocket Ismail, thank you both for joining me as a part of this journey. I truly appreciate your kind words, your support, and your friendship. I wish you both nothing but success in your own journeys.

Michelle Szorak, you went above and beyond at every turn: from finding the perfect pictures to bringing the vision of my cover to life ... you were a joy to work with, thank you! And, a special thanks to your father, Mike Bennett, for his beautiful photography.

Frank Bocchino, your thoughts on story structure and cover design were a huge help in guiding me to a better path for this book. Thank you.

To my Doctors, Physical Therapists, and Trainers, my body hurts every day and I shudder to imagine the pain I would be in today without your hard work so many years ago. Thank you all. And a special thank you to Dr. Mike Yergler for your diligence and helping to save my life.

To my coaches. From Middle School to High School to College to the NFL, I thank you for all the "good" and "bad." Both helped support and push me to become a better player, a better person, even if I did not see it at the time. I hope you are all well.

To my teammates, from the backyard to the NFL, thank you for the memories. As much as I miss football, some days, it does not compare to how much I miss our bond and clowning around in the locker room. I appreciate you all. You are all a part of my locker room, reach out anytime for anything; I will do what I can.

# ENDNOTES

1. Scooby Axson, "Who has the fastest 40-yard dash in NFL combine history? These are the top times.," *USA TODAY*, February/March 2024, https://www.usatoday.com/story/sports/nfl/2024/02/23/top-10-best-40-times-nfl-combine-history/72711528007/.

2. University Press Release, *Notre Dame Athletics*, http://www.und.com/sports/m-footbl/spec-rel/082301aaa.html.

3. Vinny Cerrato, "Davie dismissal right move for Notre Dame," *ESPN*, December 2, 2001, http://a.espncdn.com/ncf/columns/misc/1288853.html.

4. John Heisler using 'Beano' Cook quote, "Sunday Brunch: Playing Quarterback at Notre Dame," *Notre Dame Athletics*, September 30,2017, https://fightingirish.com/sunday-brunch-playing-quarterback-at-notre-dame/.

5. University Press Release, *Notre Dame Athletics*, http://www.und.com/sports/m-footbl/spec-rel/010102aab.html.

6. Avani Patel and Tribune staff reporter, "Davie hopes he will give offense a jolt," *Chicago Tribune*, October 3, 2001, http://articles.chicagotribune.com/2001-10-03/sports/0110030342_1_coach-holtz-notre-dame-stadium-carlyle-holiday.

7. Avani Patel and Tribune staff reporter, "Davie hopes he will give offense a jolt," *Chicago Tribune*, October 3, 2001, http://articles.chicagotribune.com/2001-10-03/sports/0110030342_1_coach-holtz-notre-dame-stadium-carlyle-holiday.

8. *Sports Reference*, https://www.sports-reference.com/cfb/years/2001-team-offense.html.

9. *Sports Reference*, https://www.sports-reference.com/cfb/years/2001-team-offense.html.

10. *Sports Reference*, https://www.sports-reference.com/cfb/years/2001-team-defense.html.

11. *Sports Reference*, https://www.sports-reference.com/cfb/years/2001-team-defense.html.

12. *Fighting Irish,* https://und.com/wp-content/uploads/2022/10/NDFB_2001_Final_Stats.pdf.

13. Todd Helmick, *Nationslchamps.net*, http://www.nationalchamps.net/NCAA/statistics200 2/miamiFL.htm.

14. University Press Release, *Notre Dame Athletics*, https://und.com/wp-content/uploads/202 2/10/NDFB_2001_Final_Stats.pdf.

15. *University of Notre Dame – The Observer*, December 12, 2001, http://www3.nd.edu/~obs erver/12032001/News/3.html.

16. Joe Drape, "College Football: The No. 1 Ranking A Distant Memory, The Irish Fire Davie," *New York Times*, December 3, 2001, http://www.nytimes.com/2001/12/03/sports/college -football-the-no-1-ranking-a-distant-memory-the-irish-fire-davie.html?ref=bobdavie.

17. University Press Release, "George O'Leary Named Head Football Coach," *Notre Dame Athletics*, December 9, 2001, https://und.com/george-o-leary-named-head-football-coach/.

18. Adrian Wojnarowski, "O'Leary brings some baggage to South Bend," *ESPN*, December 12, 2001, https://www.espn.com/columns/wojnarowski_adrian/1294704.html.

19. John W. Fountain with Edward Wong, "Notre Dame Coach Resigns After 5 Days and a Few Lies," *New York Times*, December 15,2001, https://www.nytimes.com/2001/12/15/sports /notre-dame-coach-resigns-after-5-days-and-a-few-lies.html.

20. University Press Release, *Notre Dame Athletics*, http://www.und.com/sports/m-footbl/spe c-rel/010102aab.html.

21. University Press Release, "Tyrone Willingham Named Notre Dame Football Coach," *Notre Dame Athletics*, December 31, 2001, https://und.com/tyrone-willingham-named-notre-da me-football-coach/.

22. Associated Press, "Willingham accepts 6-year deal to coach Irish," *ESPN*, December 31, 2001, https://www.espn.com/ncf/news/2001/1231/1303561.html#:~:text=Willingham%20replac es%20former%20Georgia%20Tech,embarrassing%20moments%20in%20school%20history.

23. University Press Release, *Notre Dame Athletics*, http://und.collegesports.com/sports/m-foo tbl/spec-rel/123101aaa.html.

24. University Press Release, *Notre Dame Athletics*, http://www.und.com/sports/m-footbl/spe c-rel/040402aab.html.

25. University Press Release, *Notre Dame Athletics*, http://www.und.com/sports/m-footbl/spe c-rel/010102aab.html.

26. University Press Release, *Notre Dame Athletics,* http://www.und.com/sports/m-footbl/spe c-rel/010102aab.html.

27. *Sports Reference,* https://www.sports-reference.com/cfb/years/2002-team-defense.html.

28. *Sports Reference,* https://www.sports-reference.com/cfb/years/2002-polls.html.

29. *Sports Reference,* https://www.sports-reference.com/cfb/years/2002-team-offense.html.

30. *Sports Reference,* https://www.sports-reference.com/cfb/years/2002-team-offense.html.

31. *Sports Reference,* https://www.sports-reference.com/cfb/years/2002-team-defense.html.

32. *Sports Reference,* https://www.sports-reference.com/cfb/years/2002-team-defense.html.

33. Tim Booth, "Willingham's fall drastic since first year at Notre Dame," *Holland Sentinel,* October 25, 2008, https://www.hollandsentinel.com/story/sports/2008/10/25/willingham-s -fall-drastic-since/45242046007/

34. Jeff Carroll, "No Hard Feelings Toward Volunteers," *South Bend Tribune,* November 5, 2005, https://www.southbendtribune.com/.

35. University Press Release, *Notre Dame Athletics,* https://ndsmcobserver.com/2004/10/repla cing-willingham-eventually/.

36. John Heisler – University Press Release Q&A, *Notre Dame Athletics,* https://und.com/foo tball-signing-day-press-conference-transcript/.

37. University Press Release, *Notre Dame Athletics,* September 20, 2004, https://und.com/foo tball-player-quotes-washington-game-week/.

38. Lou Somogyi, "Year 3 Countdown: Ty Willingham," *Irish Illustrated,* July 1, 2012, https://247sports.com/college/notre-dame/Article/Notre-Dames-crucial-Year-3-cou ntdown-Ty-Willingham-79300/.

39. https://fightingirish.com/facilities-gugathleticscenter-html/

40. University Press Release, *Notre Dame Athletics,* September 20, 2004, https://und.com/foo tball-player-quotes-washington-game-week/.

41. Zig Ziglar, *Goodreads,* https://www.goodreads.com/quotes/536931-success-occurs-when-o pportunity-meets-preparation.

42. Melanie Pinola, *Lifehacker*, July 19,2013, https://lifehacker.com/luck-is-what-happens-wh en-preparation-meets-opportunit-821189862.

43. Meghan Gowan, "A Program's IntegriTY," *Scholastic Notre Dame's Student Magazine*, January 2005, https://archives.nd.edu/Football/Football-2004s.pdf.

44. Julie Hail Flory, "Spotlight: Going for the Green (The Shirt raises record $235,000)," *University of Notre Dame*, February 29, 2004, https://news.nd.edu/news/spotlight-going-for-t he-green-the-shirt-raises-record-235000/.

45. University Press Release, "Majority of Players Remain in Silent Shock After Firing," *University of Notre Dame - The Observer*, December 2004, https://ndsmcobserver.com/2004/12/ majority-of-players-remain-in-silent-shock-after-firing/.

46. University Press Release, "Majority of Players Remain in Silent Shock After Firing," *University of Notre Dame - The Observer*, December 2004, https://ndsmcobserver.com/2004/12/ willingham-fired/.

47. Board Ops, "The Ty Willingham fact sheet," *NDNation Inc.*, November 9, 2005, https://n dnation.com/boards/showpost.php?b=faq;pid=20;d=thi

48. CFS360.com, "Willingham's Scorched Earth, Aftermath of Bad Recruiting Classes for UW," *Bleacher Report*, October 5, 2008, https://bleacherreport.com/articles/65809-willinghams -scorched-earth-aftermath-of-bad-recruiting-classes-for-uw.

49. Matt Lozar, "Willingham addresses firing with class," *University of Notre Dame - The Observer*, December 2, 2004, https://archives.nd.edu/observer/2004-12-02_v39_062.pdf.

50. Sean Moriarity and Benjamin Wolters, "Notre Dame's Mike Goolsby on Tyrone Willingham," *The Two Irish Brothers Show*, December 26, 2023, https://www.youtube.com/watch?v=Wo LIHVHbHfw.

51. University Press Release, *Notre Dame Athletics*, http://www.und.com/sports/m-footbl/spe c-rel/121304aaa.html.

52. Avani Patel and Tribune staff reporter, "Weis fulfills a dream," *Chicago Tribune*, December 14, 2004, https://www.chicagotribune.com/news/ct-xpm-2004-12-14-0412140251-story.html.

53. Unidentified, "A Weis guy: Irish's Quinn responds to new coach," *Toledo Blade*, December 6, 2005, https://www.toledoblade.com/opinion/2005/12/06/A-Weis-guy-Irish-s-Quinn-re sponds-to-new-coach/stories/200512060053.

54. Doug Walker, "Interim Head Football Coach Kent Baer Holds Press Conference," *Notre Dame Athletics*, December 10, 2004, https://und.com/interim-head-football-coach-kent-baer-holds-press-conference/.

55. University Press Release, *Notre Dame Athletics*, http://www.und.com/sports/m-footbl/mtt/shelton_matt00.html.

56. https://n.rivals.com/team_rankings/2004/all-teams/football/recruiting

57. Bud Withers, "Recruit? Willingham put to the test," *The Seattle Times*, December 16, 2004, https://www.seattletimes.com/sports/recruit-willingham-put-to-the-test/

58. Mayo Clinic Staff, "Staph infections," *Mayo Clinic*, May 25, 2022, https://www.mayoclinic.org/diseases-conditions/staph-infections/symptoms-causes/syc-20356221.

59. Phil Taylor, "A Menace in the Locker Room," *Sports Illustrated Vault*, February 28, 2005, https://vault.si.com/vault/2005/02/28/a-menace-in-the-locker-room.

60. Mike Allende and Herald Writer, "Willingham, Weis share a laugh." *The Daily Herald and Herald Net*, September 24, 2005, https://www.heraldnet.com/sports/willingham-weis-share-a-laugh/.

61. The Denver Post Staff, "Weis makes the call that matters," *The Denver Post*, September 25, 2005, https://www.denverpost.com/2005/09/25/weis-makes-the-call-that-matters/.

62. Los Angeles Times Staff Writer, "Irish Leave Ty in a Knot," *Los Angeles Time*, September 25, 2005, https://www.latimes.com/archives/la-xpm-2005-sep-25-sp-irish25-story.html.

63. Nick Ironside, "'Instant classic!': The Bush Push game retold 10 years later," *Irish Illustrated*, October 12, 2015, https://247sports.com/college/notre-dame/Article/Instant-classic-The-Bush-Push-game-retold-10-years-later-40175862/.

64. Jim S., "Winning with Tyrone Willingham's Guys at Notre Dame," *Bleacher Report*, August 18, 2008, https://bleacherreport.com/articles/48718-winning-with-tyrone-willinghams-guys-at-notre-dame.

65. University Press Release, *Notre Dame Athletics*, http://www.und.com/sports/m-footbl/mtt/shelton_matt00.html.

Made in the USA
Columbia, SC
29 September 2024

43271059R00190